A Lester Young Reader

Edited by Lewis Porter

A
Lester
Young
Reader

Smithsonian Institution Press

Washington and London

Editor: Aaron Appelstein
Production Editor: Duke Johns
Designer: Alan Carter

Library of Congress Cataloging-in-Publication Data

A Lester Young reader / edited by Lewis Porter.
p. cm.
Includes index.
ISBN 56098-064-8. — ISBN 56098-065-6
(pbk.)
1. Young, Lester, 1909–1959. I. Porter, Lewis.
ML419.Y7L47 1991
788.7'165'092—dc20
[B]   90-24922

British Library Cataloguing-in-Publication Data is
available

Manufactured in the United States of America
98 97 96 95 94 93   5 4 3

♾ The paper used in this publication meets the
minimum requirements of the American National
Standard for Permanence of Paper for Printed
Library Materials Z39.48-1984

Contents

Preface   ix

Part One: The Man   1

Young Lester Young   4
  Phil Schaap

The Young Family Band   16
  Lee Young with Patricia Willard

Lester Young   25
  John Hammond

Lester's Style: The Lee and Lester Young Band   32
  Lee Young with Patricia Willard

The Lee and Lester Young Band   40
  Jimmy Rowles with Lewis Porter

I'll Take Flip Any Time!   44
  Mike Nevard

Lester Young   47
  Nat Hentoff

Pres   74
  Whitney Balliett

Lester Leaps In   82
   Dan Morgenstern

The Last, Sad Days of Lester Willis Young   89
   Robert Reisner

Presidents Ain't What They Used to Be   93
   Graham Colombé

The House in the Heart   99
   Bobby Scott

Pres: Lester Young   119
   Ralph Gleason

The Last Years of Lester Young   122
   Frank Büchmann-Møller

Part Two: Young in His Own Words   127

"You Got to Be Original, Man"   131
   Allan Morrison

Pres Talks about Himself, Copycats   136
   Pat Harris

Here's Pres!   140
   Leonard Feather

The Blindfold Test: Pres Digs Every Kind of Music   148
   Leonard Feather

He Holds His Office Graciously   152
   Derek Young

Lester Young   154
   Bill Coss

Pres   157
   Nat Hentoff

Interview with Lester Young   165
   Chris Albertson

Interview with Lester Young   173
  François Postif

Part Three: The Music   193

Lester Young: Style beyond Swing   197
  Martin Williams

East of the Sun: The Changes of Lester Young   203
  Loren Schoenberg

Review of *Prez: Lester Young Solos* by Bernard Cash   208
  Dave Gelly

Why So Sad, Pres?   211
  Louis Gottlieb

Lester Young's "Shoe Shine Boy"   224
  Lawrence Gushee

Pres and Hawk: Saxophone Fountainheads   255
  Don Heckman

Trumbauer, Parker, and Young   264
  Bernard Cash

The President   277
  Whitney Balliett

Lester's Blues   281
  Barry Ulanov

Lester Young: The Postwar Years   285
  Erik Wiedemann

Time and the Tenor: Lester Young in the Fifties   292
  Graham Colombé

Reconsiderations   301
  H. A. Woodfin

Prez in Europe   305
  Dan Morgenstern

Appendix 1: Miscellaneous Short Recordings of Young's
Voice   311

Appendix 2: Where to Find Unusual Published Photographs
of Lester Young   313

Index   315

Preface

Lester Young (1909–59) remains one of the most important figures in twentieth-century American music. The life and music of the "Pres" are legendary. But for years it looked as if Young would be another neglected legend. Within two years of his death, two books on Young's life appeared—one in German by Werner Burkhardt and Joachim Gerth (*Lester Young—Ein Porträt* [Wetzlar: Pegasus-Verlag, 1959]) and one in Italian by Vittorio Franchini (*Lester Young* [Milan: Ricordi, 1961]). Both were short tributes of under one hundred pages. But there was no book in English for many years. The first in English was a softcover publication by the Norwegian researcher Jan Evensmo (*The Tenor Saxophone and Clarinet of Lester Young, 1936–1949*, 2d ed. [Oslo: Jan Evensmo, 1983]), an annotated guide to Young's recordings of the years given, with much original research.

Beginning in 1984, Young has been the subject of several studies. That year Dave Gelly's biography (*Lester Young* [Tunbridge Wells: Spellmount Ltd.]) appeared in England (now readily available in the United States [New York: Hippocrene Books, 1984]). It was followed in 1985 by my own book, *Lester Young* (Boston: Twayne Publishers), which studies Young's music and contains the most thorough listing of his recordings up to that time. (Gelly's well-written effort includes some very thoughtful observations on Young's music as well, in nontechnical terms.) A 1987 biography by Luc Dellanoy (*Lester Young—Profession: Président* [Paris: Editions Denoël]) is most notable for its details about Young's visits to Paris, as told through interviews with musicians. And historian Douglas Daniels has a book in progress, tentatively entitled *Blue Lester: The Life and Times of*

Lester Young, which is eagerly awaited by Young's devotees because it will contain the first thorough research on Young's family tree and will place Young's life story in its historical context.

In 1988 Minneapolis filmmaker Bruce Fredricksen released a ninety-minute documentary, *Song of the Spirit: The Story of Lester Young,* which chronicles Young's life through interviews with his family, musician friends, and jazz historians. It incorporates most of the footage that exists of Young, and an excellent print of the classic short film *Jammin' the Blues* (1944) is appended to the tape, introduced by Harry Edison, who performs in it. (The tape is available in VHS, Beta, or 3/4 inch format, from Song of the Spirit, P. O. Box 444, Willernie, Minnesota 55090.)

Finally, two volumes by Danish researcher Frank Büchmann-Møller were published in spring of 1990 by Greenwood Press, in English. The first volume (*You Just Fight for Your Life: The Story of Lester Young*) is by far the longest and most accurate biography of Young ever. It includes many new interviews with Young's friends and colleagues. It also clarifies the chronology of Young's career, presenting for the first time a complete description of his every movement from his birth in 1909 to his death in 1959. The second volume (*You Got to Be Original, Man! The Music of Lester Young*), available separately, is a complete guide to Young's recorded legacy, a "solography" (as Evensmo describes this type of work) that includes a description and critical review of Young's solos on every issued record and on every scrap of private and unissued material. It includes recordings discovered since my book was published and gives newly researched personnel lists for all sessions. This volume includes music notation for about eighty of Young's solos and excerpts of as many more.

Since my book appeared, I have continued to collect biographical and discographical information on Young, as well as photographs. I have noticed with regret that many of the best articles on Young's life and music are becoming increasingly hard to find and that some fine new ones are being published in obscure places. As researchers are becoming interested in Young, it becomes more and more important that they have easy access to the relevant literature. In addition, the fan will derive immense pleasure from reading these articles, most of which are nontechnical and provide insights into the man and his music. *A Lester Young Reader* was conceived as a forum for these valuable source materials.

This *Reader* is in effect a symposium on Young, the man and his music. There are three parts—biographical articles, interviews, and discussions of the music—as well as a selection of rare and unpublished photographs. In my selections for each part, I have not attempted to bolster any particular argument. Rather, I have included as many publications as possible, with an eye out for those that are historically important, those that have had wide influence, and those that I have found most stimulating, whether or not I agreed with them. In particular, in my previous book I defended Young's later recordings at some length. But I have plenty of respect for the point of view that holds that his early works are by far the best, and I have included several thoughtful articles that take that stand.

Some of the contents will be new even to scholars. The interviews with Lee Young and Jimmy Rowles and the analysis by Bernard Cash have never been published. The Wiedemann article has never been seen in English. Perhaps most exciting, the two legendary taped interviews of Lester Young are presented in new, authoritative transcriptions, approved by the original interviewers.

The present volume is not only a reader; by virtue of my commentary between articles, it is a sort of annotated guide to the literature on Young. I sometimes provide short quotations from other articles that are worthwhile but not included here. In some cases I provide a few citations for further reading.

Wherever possible, the authors have seen and approved any editing of their work. I have edited all historical information to conform with recent research, by adding bracketed comments. In every instance where Young's first recording date is given as October 9, 1936, I have changed "October" to "[November]," since it is now well established that it was November 9 (see my previous book, and Frank Büchmann-Møller's books). All words and dates in square brackets are my additions; full sentences are followed by "Ed." I have updated all LP references in the articles by simply changing label names and numbers, without comment. It was also necessary to abridge some of the articles—as noted in their respective introductions—in order to avoid redundancy, particularly where one quotes from another. I did not abridge Young's interviews, even though they are sometimes redundant, because his words have historical value in their own right.

Obvious typographical and grammatical errors have been corrected silently, and all articles have been edited for stylistic consistency with respect to spelling, capitalization, punctuation, number and date style, treatment of titles, footnote and list formats, and so on. The "flavor" of each author's writing style has not been touched, except perhaps in the two articles by Danish authors, Büchmann-Møller and Wiedemann, which have been edited for idiomatic English usage. In some articles with

music examples (Part Three), references to and placement of examples
have been modified to improve the integration of music and text and to
accommodate layout. Each author is responsible for the accuracy of his
musical examples, but in a few cases I could not resist correcting obvious
errors of transcription.

The idea of compiling an anthology dedicated to Young was originally suggested to me in a note from Bob Perlongo, author of a Young
memorial piece. About the same time, by total coincidence, Martin Williams suggested the idea to me. It seemed that fate had spoken, so naturally I accepted the invitation, and I began work on the book during a
Faculty Academic Study Leave from Rutgers University. Williams has, of
course, a vast experience in publishing on jazz, and his guidance during
the compilation of this reader was invaluable. During the editing process I
found Duke Johns of the Smithsonian Institution Press and copy editor
Aaron Appelstein to be thoroughly professional, meticulous, and person-
able.

I owe thanks to each of the authors, publishers, photographers, and
photograph collectors for allowing me to use their works. A few individuals went beyond the call of duty. Dan Morgenstern, director of the
Institute of Jazz Studies at Rutgers University, whose office is right down
the hall from mine, graciously allowed himself to be trapped into several
long sessions of trivial pursuit, mostly along the lines of, "Whatever
happened to ———— ?" Dave Gelly, François Postif, and Frank Büchmann-
Møller, my fellow Pres authors from England, France, and Denmark,
each came to the rescue with energy and enthusiasm when I needed help
in contacting authors from their respective countries. They even went to
the trouble of contacting authors for me.

Harry Swisher, founder of the Lester Young Society, came through
on short notice with wonderful photographs from his large archive. Fellow musician and researcher Loren Schoenberg agreed to advise me
about photographs. He took the time to look over all of the prints I
acquired, to help me remember which had been published and where,
and to give his personal opinions about which would be most worth
publishing. John McDonough helped me with several queries. The tire-
less Phil Schaap and I have been keeping each other updated on "Pres
news" for some years, and his tips have often proved to be of value.
Finally, my wife, Gail, has, as always, provided many useful suggestions
and much-needed support.

Today there are still fanatic "Presophiles" all over the world and
even a Lester Young Society in Virginia. The Mississippi Jazz and Heri-

tage Foundation in Jackson held the first annual Lester Young Memorial Jazz Festival in 1990. Young's most devoted fans are probably those who were lucky enough to have seen him in performance, but there is a new audience who know Young through recent record reissues. Perhaps some became interested in Young through the 1986 French film *Round Midnight* (directed by Bertrand Tavernier and starring saxophonist Dexter Gordon), which was largely based on Young's life and dedicated to him and Bud Powell at the end of the credits. I hope that this volume brings pleasure to fans, old and young alike, and serves as a resource for scholars.

Part One
The Man

We begin with Young's biography—not only the names and dates, but the personality as well. There is some unavoidable duplication among the articles in this section. Almost every one originally included a statement about Young's greatness and covered some of the same biographical ground. In my editing I have reduced these repetitions to a minimum. But a certain amount of overlap is healthy. There are many ways to tell the same story (even when Young himself is telling it, as we will see in Part Two). Each author chooses to focus on different moments, and each one supports his choices with original interviews of Young's colleagues.

The authors bring their own experiences to bear on the telling of Young's life, and white writers may have had a very different and more limited relationship with Young than did musicians, regardless of race, and family members. For example, John Hammond notes with regret that Young was "either unwilling or unable to communicate" with him, but pianist Bobby Scott, also white, remembers long conversations with Young filled with personal revelations. Black musicians quoted in Graham Colombé's contribution also remember Young fondly. So the reader will do well to keep in mind throughout this volume that the authors' voices do come through (although I hope less prominently in Part Two, which concentrates on Young's own words).

Phil Schaap

Young Lester Young

We open with details of Young's early years. This article reconstructs
Young's family history and his own story through 1927. As with most
African-American artists of his generation, Young's childhood survives
only in interviews with him, his family, and his friends. Piecing all this
together and trying to establish dates is a daunting task—as I know well,
having done this type of work to write about Young's early years in my
previous book.

Since my book appeared, Douglas Daniels and Frank Büchmann-
Møller have uncovered a small but significant number of newspaper ads,
landowner's deeds, census reports, and other datable items that can be
cross-checked against the oral histories. In addition, oral histories can be
cross-checked against each other and against other known dates. More
oral histories have come to light, and some that already existed have been
more fully examined. The most important of the latter is an interview
with Leonard Phillips, conducted in 1983, which is part of the Oral
History archives at the Institute of Jazz Studies, Rutgers University. The
idea of interviewing Leonard Phillips was an inspired one. A little-known
trumpeter, he had uncannily lucid memories about the many better-
known people with whom he played. Phil Schaap has provided a great
service by putting much of this information into a readable narrative and
adding a great deal of his own research. (The Phillips interview is quoted
at length in Frank Büchmann-Møller's Young biography.)

Originally published in the WKCR-FM program guide, vol. 4, no. 3 (November 1987). Copyright © 1987 by
Phil Schaap. Reprinted, with slight revisions, by permission.

Phil Schaap—jazz historian, radio commentator, record producer—is a constant presence on the New York jazz scene. Schaap speaks almost daily on Columbia University's radio station, WKCR-FM, airing interviews and new musical finds from record company vaults and from the collections of musicians and older fans. He is constantly talking to musicians who knew Young, in an attempt to learn more about his life and music. Many of the unattributed comments in the present article come from his own research—including the references to Eric Banks, Eddie Barefield, Paul Quinichette, Lee Young, Shelby Ballott, Dr. Shaw, and the Turrentine family, as well as Irma Young's birthdate.

Schaap is also an audio engineer on the cutting edge of the restoration of old recordings for conversion to CD format. (His efforts earned him an audiophile award from Wayne Thompson in 1990.) Working in the late 1980s in the vaults of Verve records, he discovered two hours of Charlie Parker performances and about an hour of Ella Fitzgerald live in Rome, none of which had ever been issued. He remastered and produced these materials for issue on CD. The Parker set includes Schaap's extensive notes, for which he received a Grammy in 1990. Schaap also wrote a biography of Parker for the complete set of Royal Roost broadcasts that he produced on Savoy, and he produced and remastered one of the Parker finds of all time: the club appearances recorded by Dean Benedetti, issued in 1990 on Mosaic.—Ed.

Lester Young was the most important soloist in the Count Basie orchestra and the most influential musician in jazz in the period between Louis Armstrong and Charlie Parker. He was also Billie Holiday's favorite musician. In the study of an individual of the magnitude of a "President," a great deal of emphasis is placed on the formative years. This is not always the case in biographies of jazzmen, as these are largely studies of music. They frequently jump in not at the birth certificate but at the jazz player's second birthdate, his first recording session. In Lester Young's case this would mean a cursory study of his first twenty-seven years, over 55 percent of his life. "Young Lester Young" is an attempt to salvage details about the most distant and least documented period of his life. In advance, I'd like to single out the research of Douglas H. Daniels, whose major finds must be published soon in a Lester Young biography, and Lewis Porter, whose remarkable reference work with musical analysis Lester Young *has been published by G. K. Hall.*

Lester Willis Young was born in Woodville, Mississippi, on Friday, August 27, 1909. No documents concerning his Mississippi origins have surfaced despite investigations by historians such as German researcher Diethelm Paulussen, who visited Woodville in 1976. Robert A. Perlongo mentioned Young's birth certificate in the May 1959 issue of *Metronome*, but the citation is more a figure of speech used to introduce Lester's birthdate. At present Eric Banks, a Mississippi specialist, is researching both branches of Lester's family, the Youngs on the paternal side, the Johnsons on his mother's side.

Many jazz reference works list New Orleans as Lester's birthplace. He did spend an important chunk of his childhood there and frequently referred to it as his hometown, so the mistake is understandable.

There has also been confusion concerning the birth year. Eddie Barefield, who was born December 12, 1909, and began his lifelong musical and personal friendship with Young in 1927, has always felt Lester was younger than he. Buddy Tate, another lifelong friend and sax section mate in the Basie band, stresses that Lester Young was a year older than listed and that the birthday party for Lester held at Birdland on August 27, 1958, was a celebration of Young's fiftieth birthday; furthermore, Tate states that an ailing Lester Young told him that he had made fifty and that was as far as he would go, that he didn't want to be old and feeble.

But the firmest evidence is in Lester Young's own words. In the legendary interview with François Postif (February 6, 1959), Lester Young announces that he was born in Woodville, Mississippi, and that the year was 1909. (Note: Lester Young died at age forty-nine on March 15, 1959, in New York City.)

The date of Lester's father's birth is much vaguer. Willis Handy Young was born in Thibodaux, Louisiana, probably in the early 1870s. He was called Billy, and sometimes his name crops up as William, but apparently he had a brother William (as well as another, Jacob, and two sisters, Mary and Martha). Mr. Young was a product of that brief period of black opportunity: Reconstruction. He majored in music at Tuskegee Institute. [There is no record of his studies at Tuskegee, but Lester, Lee Young, Paul Quinichette, Leonard Phillips, and others all recall having heard that he was there, so Schaap has chosen to include this information.—Ed.] He could play all the instruments, achieving notable proficiency on cornet and violin. Some family and friends believe Willis Young planned to become a music teacher, perhaps running a high school music program. Lee Young, Lester's younger brother, asserts that his father was actually a high school principal in Thibodaux, but no local records exist to back this up. In any case, *Plessy* v. *Ferguson*, the infamous 1896 "separate-but-equal" Supreme Court decision, eliminated most opportunities for a music teacher who was black. So Billy Young spent his life as a performer. He persevered as a teacher, however, training countless musicians and working as a choirmaster in various towns, schools, and churches.

The Young family was apparently from Louisiana. Lester's paternal grandmother ran a general store in Natalbany, Louisiana, and is remembered as being quite religious. The grandfather was a blacksmith, and Billy Young may have had some training in this trade. Billy Young and his sister Mary Young Hunter owned land in Hammond, Louisiana, less than ten miles south of Natalbany, although the purchase(s) may not have been made until the early 1920s.

Lester's father's early career is particularly hard to trace. He played in the traveling circus of Heck & Beck & Wallis. Other Youngs played there with him. Eventually Billy Young organized a family band, which backed minstrel shows, played carnivals and fairs, and toured the black theater circuit known as TOBA. (TOBA stood for Theatre Owners Booking Association, which was very Tough on Black Artists.) Occasionally the band would pull down a residency at a hotel or ballroom. Frequently the ensemble contained a few nonfamily players to fill essential chairs. Often, especially in winter, the Billy Young family would base itself in one town and work out of there.

Dates and sequences remain unclear. Lester's father may not have become a bandleader until 1920, after years on the road and a relatively settled period living near New Orleans in Algiers, Louisiana. The family arrangements are equally hard to establish. Apparently, Billy Young married Lizetta (maybe Lyzetta) Johnson about 1907. There's no way to know how Lizetta and Billy came to meet and marry, although it's tempting to speculate on a Louisiana connection.

Lizetta Johnson's family also came from Louisiana; Lizetta's sister and parents were born there. Mr. Johnson, Lester's maternal grandfather, was a farmer who moved to Woodville, Mississippi (Woodville is in the southwest corner of Mississippi less than six miles from the Louisiana border), where he worked or owned a farm. Lizetta, according to Lester, worked as a seamstress and school teacher, although it's hard to determine where or when.

Lester Young was their first child, and Lizetta was staying with her family in Woodville at the time of Lester's birth. That birth may have been a difficult one for Lizetta Young. This is possibly alluded to by Lester in the February 6, 1959, interview with Postif—"My mother was scared." If so, then it might explain why the infant Lester Young was in Shreveport, Louisiana, with his Aunt Martha (Billy Young's sister) when the 1910 census was taken. The next child was Lester's sister Irma, who steadfastly refuses to divulge her exact birthdate, but who states that it took place in her father's hometown of Thibodaux. [Schaap has recently placed her birthdate at July 18, 1912, as a result of a lucky call to her nursing home on July 18, 1988.—Ed.]

The next mystery is the move to Hammond, Louisiana. In 1913 it seems Lizetta Young took Lester (and presumably Irma) to this town, where the Young family may already have been landowners. Whether, when, and how much Billy Young or any other family members were with Lizetta and/or the children can't be verified. Billy Young may have spent a great deal of time on the road. Shortly after this period in Hammond, the family resettled in Algiers, Louisiana, just across the Mississippi River from New Orleans in what may have been an attempt to stabilize family life. But even during this stretch it is questionable whether Lizetta, Billy, and the children were always together.

During the Algiers–New Orleans stay, Billy Young worked in several prominent New Orleans bands. His best documented gig is in Algiers with Henry Allen's Brass Band—Henry, Sr., that is, Red's father. Also notable was the birth of Lizetta's and Billy's third and last child, Lee Young, who was born in New Orleans, or possibly Algiers, on March 7, 1917.

Despite these developments, things did not work out for Billy and Lizetta Young, and they were divorced about 1919. Billy Young took the three children into his family band, which included a new musician, Billy's second wife, Sara. Billy Young maintained his musical organization until at least the early 1930s when the family finally settled down in Los Angeles. Willis Handy Young was slowed by a stroke in late September 1936 but continued to make music at his church. He died on February 6, 1943.

After the parents' divorce not much is known of Lester's mother, Lizetta Johnson Young. She is known to have been living in Woodville in the early 1930s. In fact Lester visited her there. At some point she remarried and became Lizetta Gray. She also moved to Los Angeles about 1944. Leonard Feather spoke to her shortly after Lester's death. At that time Lizetta Gray made some perceptive comments about her son's shyness and how it contributed to his early death. She also spoke of a little

Lester dutifully attending church but being bewildered by and even a bit frightened by organized religion.

Although there is no record of Lizetta's death (or birth for that matter), she's undoubtedly deceased by now. As late as the early 1970s, Jo Jones used to speak of her in the present tense, although he always mistook her name for Mary.

As long as Lizetta and Willis Young's family was still relatively intact and living in Algiers, Lester got his elementary school education in that New Orleans area. His formal schooling came to an end when his father took him and his siblings on the road circa 1919. Lester was probably in the fourth or fifth grade.

Another New Orleans area student of that time, Shelby Ballott, offers us a fascinating sketch of what a young black child's education was like in that time and place. Shelby Ballott was born in New Orleans on February 15, 1910. He went to school variously in New Orleans, Algiers, and near his father's farm about 180 miles from New Orleans. He doesn't specifically remember any child or classmate called Lester Young, but he draws a blank at any names of schoolmates. Ballott recalls that he spent time in at least three different schoolrooms but can only describe one of them. His memories add important firsthand information and insight into what Lester Young's schooling was like nevertheless.

A black person was a second-class citizen in New Orleans; a black child's education was fifth rate, according to Shelby. The hierarchy of educational opportunity would have run like this: white private, first; white parochial, second; white public, third; black parochial, fourth; black public on the bottom. Ballott describes a three-room schoolhouse that had one room for all students in the first through sixth grades. Seventh and eighth graders used the other two rooms. One group of seventh and eighth graders would be high school bound. The non-high-school-bound group would be small, he remarks, since if you weren't going to high school, then you probably would already have dropped out before seventh grade. Good students and ambitious parents set their sights on entering one of the Catholic schools for blacks or on hooking in to one of the white parochial schools that offered blacks informal instruction. Shelby Ballott himself was so dissatisfied with his own public school education that he made sure to save money for his daughter's tuition at a Catholic school.

Mr. Ballott remembers three teachers: one was a Cora whose last name escapes him; one was a Jenkins whose first name eludes; and one was a popular and curvaceous person known as Miss Cruikshank. One thing Ballott points out favorably is that the teachers routinely used to keep in contact with pupils' parents. He also notes that classroom disruptions were rare, that discipline was high.

Of course we don't know that Lester ever had the lovely Miss Cruikshank talking to his mother, telling tales on him or praising some pedagogic progress. Yet Ballott's strokes are broad enough to give us a good picture of what Lester was getting—or missing—from his early schooling.

Whatever the appeals and disappointments of his regular school, the key aspect of Lester Young's New Orleans childhood is the fortuitous placement of a musical genius in the birthplace of jazz while that music was in its most creative period. Lester fell in love with hot music. Swinging rhythm thrilled him. The drums held a special attraction. Lester followed the New Orleans black brass ensembles as they marched and played through the streets of the city. When a New Orleans band had a nighttime gig, they'd advertise it during the day: the band would play in a horse-drawn wagon going through the town while announcements concerning the evening work were passed out. Lester had the job of handing out the flyers. Lester did this for the Henry Allen Brass Band and almost certainly for quite a few others in light of the probability that his father played for more than one ensemble during the Algiers years. In this way Lester doubtless heard every significant New Orleans jazzman, including Baby Dodds, Paul Barbarin, Freddie Keppard, King Oliver, Kid Ory, and the teenaged Louis Armstrong.

In this musical environment Lester began to play the drums. When he left the Algiers–New Orleans area about 1920, he held the drum chair in his father's band. In the early 1930s Lester Young spoke of ongoing New Orleans musical contacts, among them Joe Robichaux and Sidney Desdunes (as told to this writer by one Dr. Shaw).

Given the difficulty of following Lester's father's career, no events can be fixed with certainty, but it is quite possible that the Billy Young family band was forged just around the time Lester became a musician. The Young band was aided in no small way by Willis's second wife, Sara. Sara was from San Antonio, Texas, and she played many instruments, specializing on saxophones and the banjo. The Billy Young band and the family appear to have made Memphis their headquarters during the early 1920s. The unit consisted of Lester Young, drums; Irma Young, saxophone; Sara Young, saxophone and banjo; cousin Isaiah "Sport" Young, saxophone; his brother Austin "Boots" Young, saxophone, trombone, and other instruments; and Billy Young, cornet and violin. Everybody sang and danced as part of the show. During these years the father continued music lessons for the children. Lester said his father taught him trumpet and violin in addition to drums, but since he concentrated on drums, for a time he got away without learning to read music.

According to Jo Jones among others, Lester Young was an exceptional drummer for all musical styles, but especially for blues and jazz. Even so, when he reached adolescence he soured on drums because the time it took to pack them up was interfering with his post-gig socializing— particularly with the ladies. He switched to saxophone, garnering some rudiments with significant help from his sister Irma. Soon he was featuring hot choruses as part of the Billy Young band presentation.

Still, Lester couldn't read music much. On that score his father put him out of the band until he made himself a proficient reading musician. In the interim the hot element became even more vital to the Young family's music. That meant that when the prodigal son did return to the fold with his lessons learned, he got to reap a bit of revenge by outdoing the rest of them in technique and swing on the jazz-dance feature numbers.

In late 1923 or early 1924, a show that featured the Billy Young troupe closed in Warren, Arkansas. The family decided to winter in Warren and put on two shows each week in the town's auditorium. Billy Young discovered several young musicians in that town whom he coached during that season's stay. The family band left Warren in March 1924, and four of the young Arkansas musicians soon were part of the gang. They were a trombonist named Otto "Pete" Jones, who later married Irma; Jesse "Ham" Hamilton, who played E-flat alto horn and peck horn; and two brothers, Clarence Phillips on brass bass, and Leonard "Phil" Phillips, a cornetist whom Mr. Young switched to trumpet and who earned the second nickname "Deak" during this tour.

Leonard "Phil" Phillips, born in Warren on September 4, 1907, was initially a clarinetist. Phillips gave an extensive and extraordinary interview on the topic of Lester Young (conducted by Bryant Dupré for the Jazz Oral History Project housed at the Institute of Jazz Studies at Rutgers; the interview took place over the span of January 26 to April 8, 1983). His recollections when cross-referenced always speak the truth, and he is to be trusted and thanked when he is the only surviving witness to the developing genius of Lester Young.

Mr. Phillips joined the Billy Young outfit on April 15, 1924. He describes their gigging in carnivals, at fairs, and in theaters. This seems to be the kind of work the Young family had across the early 1920s. When Phillips arrived, the Youngs were working a carnival tour. They played the Kentucky State Fair in Lexington, got as far north as Indianapolis, as far east as Roanoke, and ended this carnival tour in Palatka, Florida, in November 1924. A harrowing racial incident, dimly recalled by Lee Young, is more clearly remembered by Phil Phillips. The Young carnival show arrived in Harlan, Kentucky. Apparently many in Harlan were not expecting the performers to be black, and coupled with a perennial violent racist element in Harlan, a lynchlike attack on the Young group sent them scurrying. And Lee Young claims it scarred his brother.

In Palatka, Willis Young began rehearsing the unit for a TOBA theater tour. In late November or December 1924, Young took his band to the legendary 81 Theatre in Atlanta, and week-long engagements followed in theaters in Greenville, South Carolina; Pensacola, Florida; Columbus, Georgia; Tampa; and then Lakeland, Florida. Next Mr. Young formed a minstrel show that toured from Lakeland, Florida, to Mobile, Alabama, where it folded. At this time, February 1925, Mr. Phillips took a better offer with Sidney DeParis, Sr., and was replaced in the Young family orchestra by none other than Cootie Williams. (DeParis was the father of the famous DeParis brothers.)

Performances by Billy Young's ensemble were already highly charged with jazz, and Lester Young was already the standout practitioner. It should be noted that everyone, including Lester, remembers the elder Young as being quite with it, someone who could swing on trumpet.

During Phil Phillips's first tour with the band in 1924 and 1925, Lester played alto saxophone. His bandmate asserts that he could double on other reeds, but that he only did so infrequently. Phillips can hear Lester in his mind's ear soloing on "How Come You Do Me Like You Do?" "Margie," "Bugle Blues," and "Way Down Yonder in New Orleans." On "Yes Sir, That's My Baby," Lester employed the then in vogue slap-tongue technique. A march tune, "Shouting Liza," was converted by the Young group into a jazz vehicle that was also a vehicle for the younger Young to really "get off." Phillips recalls Lester taking a lengthy alto solo, displaying his technique on this tune. From time to time, after the band completed a performance of "Shouting Liza," Lester's father would comment on the showing-off by threatening to slow his son down by putting him on tenor. But the enforced switch didn't happen.

The Young show as a whole also takes shape through Phil Phillips's memories. Lester, Irma, and Lee appeared in a singing and dancing trio. Lee was already playing some drums in the band, although he had not yet reached the age of eight. Little by little, Lee inherited Lester's percussion chair and ultimately had a successful career as a jazz drummer. A final point on the band of this period from Mr. Phillips: Willis Young kept his charges well supplied with good instruments—silver-plated ones were used on the carnival tours and gold-plated in the theaters.

During the years 1923–26 Lester Young made sure he got to check out all sorts of bands and musicians in live performance. He caught the name bands of Paul Whiteman, Vincent Lopez, Ted Lewis, Fletcher Henderson (perhaps during the summer of 1925 when Satchmo was in the brass), and Coon-Sanders, all in person.

During 1925 or 1926 Billy Young was able to expand his music productions. Two units now existed, one playing under Sara Young's leadership and the other under Mr. Young's. In the fall of 1926 Willis Young changed his operations. He gave up the band he was leading and consolidated the two bands into one unit that worked the show booked for Sara's band. They played from Carbondale, Illinois, to El Reno, Oklahoma, where the tour ended in November 1926. Then a most important development occurred. Willis Young reforged his ensemble into an eleven-piece jazz-dance band. They rehearsed extensively while working in El Reno and, perhaps, in Texas, too. Mr. Young had arranged for this new unit to move to Minneapolis, Minnesota. The family may have been or lived up there before (or was it Minneapolis, Kansas? or both?). [Schaap's point is that the family is not documented in Minnesota until 1926, whereas they are said to have visited the Minneapolis near Salina, Kansas, while touring.—Ed.] A big house was rented and all band members would be living in it. This band was billed as the Billy Young Jazz Band and also as the New Orleans Strutters. It was a major breaking away from the march band repertoire and the minstrel-carnival network (not to mention the racist South).

Lester Young was to be the new band's essential "hot man," but he almost blew the gig. Then seventeen, he had taken up with a woman named Clara. His father was determinedly against this union and in anger slapped his son. Lester reacted by running off with Clara, but not far, as he was found to be still in El Reno. Mr. Young apologized for hitting his son, and Lester rejoined the band on its last gig in El Reno on the eve of the departure for Minneapolis.

The Billy Young Jazz Band, a.k.a. New Orleans Strutters, worked in Minneapolis, Minnesota, from December 1926 to January 1928. Their first gig was a dance, apparently on December 1, 1926, as announced in a newspaper ad. They worked residencies at the Radisson and St. Paul hotels. There were many engagements at the South Side Ballroom. The personnel included Arthur Williams and Phil Phillips, trumpets; Otto

"Pete" Jones, trombone; Lester Young, alto saxophone, some C-melody and clarinet, occasional solos on soprano saxophone; Clyde Turrentine (he is not related to the famous Turrentine family), tenor and soprano saxophones; unknown, reeds; Gurvis Oliver, piano; Billy Young, tuba; Ray Jones (?), banjo; and Ben Wilkerson, drums. The eleventh piece might have been a second trombone. [This personnel comes from the Phillips interview. Phillips believed that Clyde Turrentine was the father of the famous saxophonist Stanley Turrentine, but Schaap has spoken with Stanley and with Clyde's son and found Phillips to be mistaken. Also, Phillips remembered one of the saxophonists as Ben Wilkerson, but Schaap interviewed Lee Young on WKCR radio by phone on August 27, 1988, and Lee was certain that Wilkerson was the drummer.—Ed.]

At this juncture came the first major influences on Lester Young since drums and hot New Orleans music had first enamored him: the sound of Frank Trumbauer's C-melody saxophone, the lines of Bix Beiderbecke's cornet improvisations, and the music of those two men in tandem, especially the creation of the jazz ballad. All these revelations came to Lester from the ultimate jazz teaching tool, the phonograph record. Earlier in the 1920s records had inspired Lester with profound indifference. There wasn't much he found on them that impressed him in terms of jazz. Not much jazz was on record in the early 1920s. Young found much more out by checking out the musicians and bands in the towns the Willis Young troupe visited. By December 1926 that record gap was closing.

Lester began his disc acquisitions after the move to Minneapolis. Once there with a firm base, there was less traveling, which also meant fewer bands to hear. Records had to become a more important resource. Moreover, by that time, the winter of 1926–27, a lot more jazz was making it onto 78 RPM discs that were newly utilizing microphones, rendering a better sound. At home in Minneapolis the trio of Pete Jones, Phil Phillips, and Lester Young would make their way to the record shop almost daily. In those days you could preview a disc in the store before purchasing. The three would buy a few records each time, so they built up quite a collection. In early 1927 that collection included many Armstrong Hot Fives (Lester learned Louis's solos and played them on his alto), various Red Nichols issues, Ben Bernie (Lester would hear Jack Pettis saxophone solos), and the Jean Goldkette band on Victor. These last offered glimpses of Bix Beiderbecke and Frankie "Tram" Trumbauer, but their names were not on the label.

During the winter of 1927–28, the Billy Young Jazz Band moved on to North Dakota, making their headquarters in Bismarck and staying at the Spencer Hotel. The Spencer had a music policy, and the house unit was a five-piece group led by Clarence Johnson.

The "hot" man in this band was a seventeen-year-old saxophonist named Eddie Barefield. [Barefield died on January 3, 1991.—Ed.] Barefield, from the Des Moines, Iowa, region, had turned to mail order records as early as 1923 to find out about saxophone and hot music. Eddie already knew about Bix and Tram. In his collection was a red-label OKeh 78, no. 40772. It featured two sides from Frank Trumbauer's first record date as a leader, February 4, 1927, with Bix as featured soloist. The coupling was "Clarinet Marmelade" with "Singin' the Blues," the first true ballad recording in jazz by virtue of Bix and Tram's solos.

Eddie Barefield, and presumably the trio of Phil Phillips, Pete Jones, and Lester Young, whiled away much of their time listening to jazz records in their rooms at the Spencer Hotel. One day, Eddie was listening to "Singin' the Blues" when a knock came at his door. Barefield opened his door and came face-to-face with a fellow his own age. He introduced himself as Lester Young, son of the bandleader Billy Young and alto saxophonist in that band. Lester said that he didn't mean to bother him but he had to know who the saxophonist was on the disc. Eddie Barefield called out Frankie Trumbauer and played the whole side for young Lester Young. The next three minutes were the most important in Lester Young's stylistic development.

Lee Young with Patricia Willard

The Young Family Band

Lester's younger brother Lee is an important witness to the early years of the family band. He became more serious about the drums when the family settled in Los Angeles, and he had a successful career with Lionel Hampton (1940–41) and with the Nat "King" Cole trio (1953–mid-1962). Lee had the unique opportunity, for a black musician, of working on Hollywood film soundtracks and even dubbed Mickey Rooney's drum parts in *Strike Up the Band*. More recently he has been a producer, for Motown Records and independently. He is also an accomplished golfer.

The present interview, previously unpublished, is part of the National Endowment for the Arts Jazz Oral History Project conducted at the Smithsonian Institution and the Institute of Jazz Studies, Rutgers University, where the project is housed. Lee Young was interviewed by Pat Willard, a jazz columnist and Ellington scholar. I have taken excerpts from that interview and have rearranged them to create a narrative flow. Ellipses indicate omitted text within an excerpt.

An articulate and forthright man, Lee presents a quite different personality from Lester. According to many he is more like his father than Lester was, but it's revealing that in this interview Lee says Lester was secretly the father's favorite. Since Lee was born on March 7, 1917, and was therefore eight years younger than Lester, he cannot be expected to remember his older brother's earliest years, and some of his statements are based on the family legends, which he heard rather than experienced. But these legends are worthwhile, and Lee has many memories of his own

Published by permission of Lee Young and the Institute of Jazz Studies, Rutgers University.

to contribute as well. Later in this volume he provides a picture of the band he led in 1941 and 1942 that included Lester.—Ed.

For further reading. See "The Lee Young Story," as told by Valerie Wilmer, *Jazz Journal,* January 1961, 3–5.

PATRICIA WILLARD: Can you trace your family back further than your own parents? Your own father?

LEE YOUNG: No, I can't. Yeah, wait a second now. Okay, gee, this is tough. There was a time when—it seems I remember when I was three or four; I don't think I was even five years old that I'm talking about now—that I remember my grandmother, you know. My grandfather was a blacksmith, okay, and my grandmother was an evangelist.

WILLARD: These are your father's parents?

YOUNG: Yes, my father's mother, you know, she was an evangelist, and my grandfather was a blacksmith, because my daddy used to talk about how hard he used to work so he could go to college, you know. And my grandmother—I just remember her—I think maybe I saw her once or twice, in a place called Natalbany, Louisiana, if that's the way you pronounce that. I understand that's not one hundred miles from New Orleans, but all I can remember, it sounds like to me it was called Natalbany, where they just had a store—you know how in the small towns where they just have a commissary or whatever they call them. That's all they had, was just the one store where you bought everything, you know, all of your supplies for whatever.

You know, when you're young, you're so foolish sometimes about, you know, what a child thinks, and I think the reason I ended up playing the different instruments was because I really didn't want to play, you know? No. I wasn't like Lester. I really didn't want to play the instrument. I wanted to be out playing baseball and basketball, you know.

Well, in our house you had to play an instrument or, you know, that was it. You had to do that. So I would say, "I want to play the trumpet"— you know, ever since I was a baby, "Do you want to play a trumpet?" You know, and the next day he [Father] would come up with a trumpet. And I was thinking he couldn't get these instruments because I thought he was buying them, you know, not thinking that he was a music teacher and he could go downstairs—go downtown, rather—to the music store and get an instrument.

And so it would be trombone, and he'd say, "You want a trombone? Okay, but you're gonna go to your room, and you're gonna practice the trombone."

So, I think that accidentally, really, I got my musical knowledge from thinking that I wasn't gonna learn, you know? But there was no way not to learn with my dad.

Oh, I left something out. Lester played drums first, you know?

WILLARD: Yeah, I know he did.

YOUNG: Did you know that? Yeah, he played drums first, and the only guy I've ever seen in my life—he was an individualistic person more than anyone I've known, I think. You know how he held his horn up in the air and how he turned the mouthpiece around.

WILLARD: I was gonna ask you, why?

YOUNG: I have no idea. He was away from us then. I don't know—

WILLARD: He didn't start playing like that?

YOUNG: No. When I saw him, that's what he was doing. I have no idea why he was holding it up in the air or upside down and that. But maybe it was things to come when he was a kid playing drums. Everyone would hold the drumstick between their forefinger and their thumb, because that's the way you're taught to hold a drumstick.

Well, he didn't do that. He held it between his forefinger and his middle finger. He didn't play anything with the thumb at all, and that's the way he held his drumsticks. But he held the left hand conventional—forefinger and the thumb. But the other, he held it between his forefinger and his middle finger. That's the way he held the drumstick. I have never seen anyone, you know, as long as I played drums after that, I never did see anyone ever do that.

So if he had stayed with the drums instead of the saxophone, he still would have had a uniqueness about him, you know.

WILLARD: Your father taught him drums?

YOUNG: Yeah, uh-huh. My dad taught me drums, also. He taught all instruments. He was an amazing man, you know. I didn't realize it until later.

WILLARD: Was Lester's first instrument the saxophone or drums?

YOUNG: Drums. My first one was saxophone.

WILLARD: And that was when you all played in the family band?

YOUNG: Yeah.

WILLARD: You mentioned that your mother played saxophone?

YOUNG: Yeah, she played baritone saxophone.

WILLARD: Your mother played baritone?

YOUNG: Uh-huh.

WILLARD: And which kind of saxophone did you play?

YOUNG: I played soprano first. And then I started playing alto, and then I played C-melody. You know, I went through everything, as I told you, you know.

We had a family band at one time, okay? We had cousins; let me see, my dad, my mother, my sister, my brother, and myself—and two cousins—and all of us played saxophone. It was a saxophone band. So some of that that you might see in some of the jazz books, where it says it was a saxophone trio, no, it wasn't a saxophone trio with Lester, my sister, and I. It was my mother, my father, and two cousins. One of them was called Cousin Sport [Isaiah "Sport" Young] and Cousin something, I don't know.

WILLARD: Boots?

YOUNG: Cousin Boots [Austin "Boots" Young], that's right.

WILLARD: Jimmy Talbot [Lee's nephew] told me that!

YOUNG: Jimmy Talbot tell you that? Well, Boots was his name. Well, it's a funny thing, there's a funny story about it. Boots was the one that— he played good saxophone, you know, and Lester, even as a kid, he loved the competition of playing his horn, and, you know, during this time they were wearing short pants.

And Cousin Boots was playing this dance, and Lester couldn't get in because he wanted to play—he wanted to play against him. So he couldn't get in because Cousin Boots had all the glory; everybody thought that he was really great.

And Lester got to the dance somehow. I don't know how he got into the dance, but he got into the dance and he went up on the stand and he took his horn out then, and he just absolutely killed him, you know. He just absolutely killed him, and I'll never forget how Cousin Boots was gonna whip him, you know, was gonna take his belt off and whip him. That was the time when my mother interceded and, you know, told him [Boots] it wasn't gonna happen because he said the kid embarrassed him. He [Lester] came up there, you know, and was blowing in on his gig, you know—I don't think they were using the term *gig* then, but that's, you know, whatever he said, that's what happened.

I'll tell you a little funny story about rehearsing with my dad. He used to write things up on the blackboard for you. And he had this yardstick. But Lester had just marvelous ears, you know, and it really did run in the family, you know, because I have relative pitch—you know, someone can play something, and I can whistle it back to them, or whatever, you know; I can do that now. But he was just uncanny, and he didn't like to read music. Well, Irma and I could read, and Lester couldn't read very well because he didn't like to read. He liked to get with the records, and he wanted to play with the records, but I'll never forget, my dad told him, "You got to learn to read or you won't get no job playing big." You got to read this thing. But my dad could play.

So Lester was, he was too quick for him, and so I think somewhere along the line my dad set a trap for him, because he didn't believe that Lester was really reading as fast as he was. So he used to write things up on the board for us to play, you know?

And we would—I would play it, Irma and I would read and play. And Lester would play it wrong, you know. And so my dad would pick up the horn and say, "How can you play it like that? This is the way it goes." Whatever, you know. And so he would give Lester the horn back, and Lester would play *ba ba dee doo dee*, right?

But he was putting his ear on him, see? And so then my dad wrote something else up on the board, and . . . Lester played it wrong. Then my dad took the horn and he played it and he said, "This is how it goes." *Ba ba doo dee doo da*, whatever, okay? So Lester picks up the horn and he says, *Ba da doo bee bop*, and he hit him over the head with the yardstick. He said, "I played it wrong. I knew you weren't reading!"

WILLARD: Jimmy [Talbot] said I should ask you how you felt about Boots's and Sport's influence on Lester. From what he said—Jimmy said that it was his impression that Lester was very impressed with their performance and their playing, and he took something from them into his own. . . .

YOUNG: Well, unlike Jimmy, I don't really know too much about that. I always saw them as adversaries, you know? My recollection of it is because it seems to me that Lester felt as though, and rightfully so, you know—he proved that he was right—that he was much better. And Cousin Sport or Cousin Boots, whichever one it was, they tried to hold him back, you know, he didn't feel as though—but that could be because of his zeal as a young person, you know, and so I don't know. Maybe they were helping him, and in his young mind he may have thought they were trying to hold him back, you know, as the saying goes, but I don't really think so. I think, if anything, I would probably lean toward what Jimmy was saying. But anyone who picked up a saxophone, you know [*pause*], Lester wanted some of it, as the saying goes—you know, he really wanted to see who was the better man. It would be just like a prize fighter or a wrestler.

WILLARD: You mentioned that you and Lester and Irma danced and sang, and you mentioned that you were doing comedy. Did Lester and Irma also do comedy, or was that strictly for you?

YOUNG: No, that was me. Lester would always be the straight man, you know, and I was the comedian because I was, I guess, more of a flake, it would be termed now, you know?

WILLARD: Did Irma give up music for good?

YOUNG: Yes, she did. Uh-huh.

WILLARD: And that was fairly young, wasn't it? When you went to Los Angeles [about 1930], right?

YOUNG: Right. Yeah, she didn't play any more, and then she started dancing and singing, and she worked quite a few places.

WILLARD: You mentioned a great long string of instruments that your father played, but you never mentioned drums. Was that just an omission, or—

YOUNG: Well, that was an omission, because I saw him play drums, too.

WILLARD: I figured that—well, he taught you, right?

YOUNG: Yeah, uh-huh. But I saw him play drums, too.

WILLARD: Okay. Do you know of any of the people who were in your father's band? I mean do you remember any names?

YOUNG: No, see—no. Because the thing, the band that I think that was probably the best band was in Minneapolis [in the mid-1920s], where he had a chance to go on the Orpheum circuit, I think. But he had eleven pieces, and they were gonna take the band and myself, you know, in front of the band, and Lester and Irma.

But they wanted him to cut two men out of the band, you know, and he was a high-principled man and he would not. And everybody was just dying to get on the Orpheum circuit, you know, that was the biggest thing that you could do in vaudeville then. But he wouldn't—I remember that he would not cut two guys from the band, and so they continued to do those little one-nighters up in Bismarck, North Dakota, you know, Devils Lake—they used to play all over the Dakotas, but I don't think there were any "name" people that we would know, you know, up in Minneapolis way. [In 1929 the Youngs toured through New Mexico. Lee Young continues:] From Albuquerque, I guess we went to Phoenix, Arizona, on the way to California, and so we stopped in Phoenix, and we used to play— and I started playing drums again, you know. . . . I started playing drums then in Phoenix, and we had the band. We used to play at a place called West Lake Park. And I think we used to play there three nights a week, and that's when Lester left. Lester left and went back to Kansas City, I think, because he—Lester was not a kid that you could chastise away like you could me. You know, parents learn—or they should learn—that you cannot treat, if you have three or four kids, you cannot deal with all of them in the same manner, you know. They all have different temperaments.

And I recognized that after I was grown, that Lester just—you could not whip him with a belt, because he must have run away from home ten or twelve times, you know? Because any time my dad would take off his belt and whip Lester, he would split. He was gone.

And I remember one time in the South he ran off to someplace in Oklahoma. And we were getting ready to go back to Minneapolis, and I don't think they'd seen him for seven or eight weeks, and my dad had just gone up to the window to buy the tickets for us to go back to Minneapolis, you know? And my mother was just crying because she was gonna leave Lester there and hadn't seen him in ages, and my dad went up to the window and says, you know, "Give me two halves and two wholes"—those were tickets, you know—you'd buy them in half fare, you know?

And so my mother said to my daddy to look around, and Lester was standing over by the door, and he said, "Make that three halves."

WILLARD: How old was Lester then?

YOUNG: I don't know, he was a young cat. He wasn't—he had to be very young, because we were going back to Minneapolis, right? That's what I said. And in Minneapolis, when I left Minneapolis, I was in the fourth grade, so it was during that time when he was very young. But he would run away if you hit him. But I wouldn't, you know. They needed to beat me, you know? They didn't beat me enough.

WILLARD: Why do you say that?

YOUNG: Well, because I was stubborn, you know. I was very, very stubborn. You got to be stubborn if you get beat for the same thing five and six times. But that's what I was saying, Lester—I think talking to him would have done it for him. Talking to me, though, wouldn't have done it for me. Never would have done it for me.

WILLARD: Did anybody ever find out where he had been and how he had gotten by for seven or eight weeks?

YOUNG: No. I got to tell you. See, he was the apple of my daddy's eye, no question about that. He was the apple, but when he would come back, everything would be okay. He never did question him—never questioned him. And you're talking about a time when men really would question their kids.

But being an educated man, I think it helped him not to really pursue it and start beating on him again; he wouldn't even discuss it with him—never did ask him. We never did know where Lester had been or what he had done. But that used to happen so many times—when he would come back, it was like he'd never been away. He just picked up where he left off.

WILLARD: How old was Lester when he left home? I don't think we really established that. Or, do you remember exactly?

YOUNG: I wouldn't remember exactly, because I would have to discern when was the first time he left home.

WILLARD: Well, for good.

YOUNG: No, well, not for good.

WILLARD: Well, if you remember how old he was when he first took off—

YOUNG: No, he—see, as I stated earlier, Lester used to run off every time my dad would raise a belt to him.

WILLARD: What would he do to upset your father?

YOUNG: Well, my father was a very strict man, you know, and he lived by the Golden Rule—that it doesn't have to be—that if you did anything that he told you not to do, you know, you would have to go and get "Greasy Jim." That was the name of his razor strap, you know. Well, I would go and get it and just stand up there and really take mine, but you couldn't do that to Lester, because he would leave home. I would say that the first time Lester left home he was probably eleven or twelve years old when he ran off from home.

WILLARD: And then when he left for good, he was about how old?

YOUNG: Oh, he must have been around eighteen; I don't think he was any older than that. But he left for good—the last time I think he ran off was in Salina, Kansas. Salina, Kansas—and the reason I can remember that was because we'd been to Dodge City, and I'd seen some football games, high school football games in Dodge City. And Hill City—I think there is a Hill City in Kansas—also, and we were playing all around there, Topeka and Lawrence and all those little places.

WILLARD: I asked you off the tape when we paused a few moments ago, if your father tried to change Lester's position with the drums when he held the drumsticks in a different way, with his right hand, and you said no, that your father always recognized him as being an individual. What did you say?

YOUNG: I think so. Yeah, I think that he must've recognized that he was different and he wanted to be different, and don't think that I profess that I knew this at the time. Since this time, I've had kids of my own, and this is what I'm saying. I believe that he recognized that there was something about Lester. Maybe he wanted recognition, why he held the sticks differently; maybe he wanted him to say, "Why don't you hold the sticks right?" You know, maybe he did and maybe he didn't, but whatever it was, he knew he was holding them wrong; but he was holding them wrong and playing right! You know? So which is—where do you stop? I think that if you're a teacher, sometimes what's conventional to you is unconventional to someone else, you know? So I don't know.

John Hammond

Lester Young

Young left the family band in 1928 to work with a bandleader named Art Bronson, returned to the family for several months, then went back to Bronson, and free-lanced from 1930 through 1933 with the legendary Blue Devils and the equally famous King Oliver, among others. Contrary to common belief, Young spent as much time in Minneapolis during his formative years as he did in Kansas City. He played in Minneapolis in 1931 and 1932, and again for most of 1934 and 1935, with Eddie Barefield and various local leaders including Leroy White and Rook Ganz.

The length of Young's stay with Oliver has been the subject of speculation. Young himself said it was "about a year" (see the interviews in Part Two), but that seems unlikely. In *"King" Oliver*, a monograph originally published by Walter C. Allen and Brian Rust in 1958 and thoroughly revised by Laurie Wright in 1987, Wright reviews the evidence and concludes that Young seems to have been in the Oliver band more than once. Perhaps when Young said it was for "about a year," he meant "on and off for about a year" or "for several tours, totaling about a year."

Early in 1934 Young joined the first band led by Bill "Count" Basie but accepted an offer from Fletcher Henderson in March of that year. He lived to regret the Henderson episode, as John Hammond recalls in this article. Hammond earned a reputation as the greatest talent scout in the record business. As you can read in his autobiography, *John Hammond on Record*, with Irving Townsend (New York: Ridge Press, 1977), over the course of fifty years, during which he was primarily associated with what is

Originally published in *Jazz: A Quarterly of American Music*, ed. Ralph Gleason, no. 3 (Summer 1959): 181–84. Copyright © 1959 by Ralph Gleason. Reprinted by permission of Mrs. Jean Gleason.

now CBS Records, he discovered and recorded an incredible list of artists, among them Billie Holiday, Aretha Franklin, Bob Dylan, George Benson, and even Bruce Springsteen. Most important for our purposes, he was the first to write in the international press about the Basie group that included Young, and he was responsible for their first recording and management deals. (At first it didn't work out quite as Hammond had hoped. Decca Records jumped in and signed Basie for the years 1937 and 1938, which is why Hammond rushed to record Young as soon as the band reached Chicago. But in 1939 Basie went with Hammond's company as planned.)

Here is Hammond's story of how it all happened. He begins with Young's stay in the Henderson band. Hammond's comments in the press of that time are quoted in my book *Lester Young.* Perhaps the most impressive are from his column dated January 23, 1937, which appeared in *Down Beat,* February 1937. The subheading of the article reads "Lester Young, World's Best Tenor Man." Hammond continues:

> The other night Benny Goodman, Basie, Lester Young, Joe Jones, Buck Clayton and Harry James got together in a small Harlem joint and jammed from two-fifteen to six in the morning. The music was something tremendous, for every one distinguished himself. But one conclusion was inescapable: that Lester Young was not only the star of the evening but without doubt the greatest tenor player in the country. I'll stick my neck out even further: he is the most original and inventive saxophonist I have ever heard. . . . This afternoon Lester Young, Walter Page, Buck Clayton, a certain clarinetist, Joe Jones, Freddie Green and Billie Holiday are all recording with Teddy Wilson up at Brunswick [Records], and I will be disappointed indeed if this is not the best date of the year.

(By the way, that first session of Holiday and Young together, and Goodman, is usually dated January 25.)—Ed.

For further reading. Another article by Hammond, covering the same ground as this one but in different ways, appeared in *Jazz and Blues Monthly,* August 1973.

There is a big story to be told about the life and death of Lester Young, and the person who could tell it would be Jo Jones, his one real confidant. If this article seems to rely on the word and memory of Jo, it is for the simple reason that Lester was either unwilling or unable to communicate with anyone of a different hue.

For the last twenty-five years I have known Lester, and for the first seven I was nothing less than a worshipper at the shrine. In 1934 I heard his audition with Fletcher Henderson's orchestra, and I supervised his first recording session in 1936 (with Jones-Smith, Inc., on Vocalion) and most of his subsequent ones with Teddy Wilson and Billie Holiday. In 1939, when Basie's Decca contract expired, there were all the Vocalion-OKeh-Columbia sessions with the big band, plus such special discs as "Lester Leaps In" and innumerable pickup sessions behind vocalists. Those were the years when Lester was the perpetual innovator and faultless soloist.

The first time I heard of Lester was in 1933, when Fletcher Henderson returned from a midwestern tour. Smack had been having trouble with some of the prima donnas in his band, and he told me of a group of musicians he had heard who had just quit Bennie Moten. He was toying with the idea of firing his whole orchestra and using Basie's men as the nucleus of a brand new band. Nothing ever came of it, however, partly because of the dire state of the music business and mostly because his only assets were his soloists, among whom were Hawkins, Red Allen, and Higginbotham. Fletcher did vow that he would bring in "that strange young tenor man" at the first opportunity.

Within six months the time came when Hawkins quit and followed Benny Carter to London and a contract with the BBC. Harlem musicians had already decided that Chu Berry was the logical replacement, but Fletcher played his hunch, borrowed some money, and brought Lester to New York. He arrived one day in 1934, came up to the Cotton Club, where Smack was rehearsing and auditioning—hoping to replace Cab Calloway—and flopped. That wonderful tone that is so admired today was swallowed up in the reed section and barely audible in solos. The other musicians urged Fletcher to send him back immediately, and within a couple of weeks Lester was back scuffling with Basie, while Chu Berry was blowing with Henderson [temporarily, until Ben Webster was hired—Ed.].[1]

In the fall of 1935 Benny Goodman was working the Congress Hotel in Chicago, and I was spending my time organizing recording sessions for English Parlophone in that city. Basie's band of nine men was broadcasting nightly from the Reno Club in Kansas City over W9XBY, and one Saturday I tuned them in for three solid hours during a "spook" dance. It was the most exciting, inventive band I had ever heard, and Lester was only one of several superlative soloists: Buster Smith, Jack Washington, Lips Page, and of course Basie himself.

I soon found out that the band was on the air every night from 1:00 to 1:30 and managed to leave Goodman a bit early so that I could tune in my car radio and be ravished by the Basie sounds. Lester's solos had a cohesion and architecture that were unique in my musical experience, and I realized that much of his inspiration came not only from the rhythm section but from the background riffs that always sounded fresh and improvised. Unlike the New York experience, Lester was speaking a language common to everyone else in the band, and this was the secret of his authority and invention.

When finally I reached Kansas City and listened to the Basie band night after night, I could see and hear that Basie was just about the ideal leader: unobtrusive yet firm, capable of providing the greatest possible stimulus for soloists. It is a fact that none of these original Basie musicians were ever again to play with the same freedom, once they tried to make it on their own.

Musicians at the Reno Club played a sixty-hour week: eight to four, except on Saturday, when the "spook dance" extended the time to eight in the morning. But these hours were not enough for Lester, who would jam with Pete Johnson at the Sunset and the wonderful Everett Johnson at the Panama Club on Eighteenth Street. Wherever he played he was great, but it was always the combination of Basie, Jo Jones, and Page that stimulated him the most.

In the fall of 1936 a Greyhound bus pulled up outside a Kansas City dance hall, where Basie and Duke Ellington were having a battle of bands. The bus was headed for Chicago and the Grand Terrace for Basie's first MCA job as a big (fourteen pieces, including Jimmy Rushing) orchestra. Two of the original stars, Lips Page and Buster Smith, had already pulled out, and only some of the replacements and additions were top flight. Fortunately for Basie, Buck Clayton was actually an improvement over Lips, while Herschel Evans on second tenor was the greatest competition conceivable for Young. The band may have been raggedy, intonation atrocious, and reading substandard, but the excitement was there just as long as there were no arrangements to confuse the musicians.

Lester made his first recording date two mornings after the disastrous Grand Terrace opening. [Since the opening was November 7, this supports the current dating of the recording session at November 9, 1936.—Ed.] He cut four sides with Basie, Page, Jones, Tatti Smith (Buck had a split lip and couldn't blow a note), and Rushing on two vocals. Looking back at it now after nearly twenty-three years, it is still my most memorable session, where absolutely nothing went wrong and four masterpieces resulted. Lester's solos in "Lady Be Good," "Shoe Shine Boy," "Evenin'," and "Boogie Woogie" stand up today with the greatest of all his recorded output.

It was in New York that Lester finally came into his own. Although there were many musicians and fans who preferred the more orthodox tone and style of Evans, Young had his passionate admirers. Among them was Billie Holiday, who met him first at one of her Brunswick sessions under Teddy Wilson's name. Their styles fitted, as did their tastes in smoking (the session was nearly canceled when one of the top American Record Company officials walked in and sniffed the air suspiciously). My enthusiasm for him knew no bounds, but I was not alone in finding it next to impossible to carry on a conversation with him. His world was a special one, and I was never to be a part of it.

After four glorious years with Basie, winning polls and praise from everywhere, Lester quit Basie and formed a small band with his brother Lee. Two more different personalities never came from the same family. Lee was a clean-living family man with a modest musical talent, and he had but little in common with the more famous "Pres." The band opened at Café Society Downtown, with which I was connected, and there were some mighty soloists in it: Sir Charles Thompson on piano, Red Callender, bass, and a fine California tenor man, Bumps Myers (whose name is inexplicably omitted from all the encyclopedias of jazz). After a couple of hours all of us were yearning for the incomparable Jo to come and sit in, but the Basieites were on the road, and there was to be no rescue. Later on in life Lester learned the trick of not listening to a long list of inferior percussionists with whom he worked, but in these pre- and early war days he was most sensitive. The band left the Café after a couple of disastrous weeks, and it was immediately obvious that "Pres" had none of the qualifications for being a successful leader. (It is only fair to point out that Lee has been doing a fine job with Nat Cole for more than ten years and sounds vastly different from his days at the Café.)

A few months before he was inducted into the army in 1943, Lester returned to Basie for the last time and also made the wonderful film short for Norman Granz and Gjon Mili, *Jammin' the Blues*. His army career was a disaster from start to finish, much of his time being spent in the guardhouse at Fort McClellan, Alabama, and Camp Gordon, Georgia. He came back to civilian life more suspicious and less communicative than ever, and I rarely exchanged more than a few words with him until a few months before his death in March.

Norman Granz always remained one of Lester's most fervent boosters. I can remember Norman in the late 1940s taking him to the Museum of Modern Art and serious drama, but there is no record as to how fruitful these excursions were. "Pres" was always too much of an artist to pander to the JATP crowds, and it wasn't much fun for him to play second to Flip and Jacquet in the various tours. He made innumerable recordings for Norman's Clef and Verve labels, but the zest and invention of the old days were pretty well dissipated.

For many years Young's health was precarious. He refused to go near a dentist despite constant pain from his teeth; his liver was practically destroyed from immoderate drinking; and there were other medical problems too complicated to go into here. According to Jo Jones he was the kindest of men, who knew only how to talk through his horn.

To me, Lester Young was one of the very few improvising giants in jazz—and the most creative reed player of my ken. Together with Charlie Christian he was a creator who enlarged our musical perspectives, even though lacking in formal training and basic education. If ever there was a musical genius, it was he.

Editor's Note

1. This story has been told differently. Walter Allen, the author of the extraordinary research work *Hendersonia: The Music of Fletcher Henderson and His Musicians* (Highland Park, N.J.: By the author, 1973), agrees with Hammond that Young came from Kansas City to New York for rehearsals before there were any performances, and then went out on tour. But Young and such musician friends as George Dixon maintain that he went directly to an engagement with Henderson in Detroit on March 31, 1934, and then traveled with the band until they reached New York. Some discussion of this appears in my *Lester Young* (Boston: Twayne Publishers, 1985), 11–12.

The length of the stay is also at issue. Hammond says "a matter of weeks," but Allen suggests that Young probably stayed until July, given that Young was mentioned (favorably) in the press about Henderson as late as June 16 and that no replacement is known until July. Phil Schaap has recently added a new wrinkle. When he interviewed guitarist Lawrence Lucie, who joined the band on April 29, 1934, he asked him for memories of Young. Lucie surprised Schaap by maintaining that Young had already left and that he distinctly remembered the band members talking about the whole experience. This would mean that Hammond was right about it being only a few weeks. The press reports could have lagged behind the reality.

Hammond notes that one reason for Young's failure with Henderson was that his tone didn't blend with the saxophone section. Benny Morton, in an unpublished interview with jazz critic and historian John McDonough on January 19, 1980, suggests another reason. Morton was a superb trombonist who played with both Henderson and Basie, and he notes that going from Basie's band to Henderson's "was like going from grammar school to college. Most bands in those days played in pretty much the same keys—B-flat, C, E-flat.

Fletcher's book was E-natural, D-natural, D-flat, B-natural. A guy would come in there and he'd have to play notes he'd never played. It was all written down. You had to read good. Basie's band was looser—used the player's ear and talent. That's why Lester was so important to Basie."

So, perhaps Young was a bit uncertain playing his parts in the Henderson band, which would have made him sound even less acceptable to the other members, since his style was suspect already. To win them over he would have had to read perfectly and solo with confidence, and apparently he did neither.

Lee Young with Patricia Willard

Lester's Style:
The Lee and Lester Young Band

Young left Basie before a recording session of December 13, 1940, creating a stir of rumors. Young himself was cryptic on this matter. Later in the *Reader,* when François Postif asks Young why he left, he slyly replies, "That's some deep shit you're asking me now." The most complete explanation can be found in *Good Morning Blues: The Autobiography of Count Basie,* ed. Albert Murray (New York: Random House, 1986), 244–45:

> Somebody put out a very weird tale about how Lester had to leave the band because he was absent from the record date on Friday the thirteenth. As a matter of fact, the [*Chicago*] *Defender* actually ran a story on it with a headline that was two columns wide:
>
>> LESTER YOUNG LEAVES BASIE: . . . According to sources close to the "Jump King of Swing," Lester was "fired" when he allegedly refused to show up for a recording date that took place on Friday the 13th. Lester is said to have asserted that Friday the 13th was definitely no time for music.
>>
>> Basie became enraged at this bit of insubordination and immediately handed Young, who was one of the mainstays of his powerful sax section, his notice after waiting for him several hours in the recording studios. [A similar story ran in *Down Beat,* and Young's wife of that time, Mary, wrote a letter to the editor disputing it.—Ed.]
>
> I don't know who put that out, but it was pretty ridiculous. In all of those years that I knew Lester, I never heard anything about him being superstitious until somebody made up that story. The truth of the matter was that he wanted to go out on his own and see what he could do with a little group

for a while. And I really think another thing was Herschel's death. He had really wanted to leave right after that happened, and the longer he stayed right on in that same situation, the harder it was for him to get over it. . . .

And there was also one other thing that made him decide to leave when he did. By the beginning of December the band wasn't really doing too well financially. We were still working, but there were a lot of miles between gigs, so we were not really making any money. The problem, as I saw it there, was the way we were being handled by MCA [booking agency]. . . .

We did reach an agreement with MCA for the time being, but in the meanwhile Lester had finally split, and that was why he didn't make that next recording session, which was on Friday, December the thirteenth.

Young's silence and seeming bitterness about the split with Basie suggest that we may still not know the whole truth. In any case, Young didn't do very well on his own, and in May he moved to Los Angeles to join his brother Lee's band. The band had various names, among them Lee Young's Esquires of Rhythm and Lee and Lester Young's Isle of Capri Combo. Here Lee tells the story of that band, continued from his oral history at the Institute of Jazz Studies. But first he speaks at length about Lester's trips to the West Coast during his Basie years, and his thoughts about his brother's musical style. (I have rearranged these excerpts for continuity.)—Ed.

PATRICIA WILLARD: When Lester came back here to town [Los Angeles] after he left Basie, did you—did he—was he any different than he was before? You hadn't seen him for how many years?

LEE YOUNG: Oh, no, I hadn't seen him—no, he was very different to me because, you know, I hadn't seen him since I was quite a kid. No, he came back once before that. My dad was ill once when he was in Kansas City with Basie [September 1936], and Basie's chauffeur and Basie's car, you know, Basie let Lester have the car with the chauffeur to come out and see my dad. Now, that was the first time I had seen Lester as an adult, you know.

And I was asleep upstairs, and my mother brought him upstairs, and she said to me—you know, Lester had a very high voice, you know, and my mother said, she touched me and woke me up and said—"Lee, do you know who this is?" And I looked up, and I said, "No, who is it?" And she said, "This is Lester!" And Lester looked at me, and he said, "Oh, look at

how big he is!" I said, "Listen to his voice. He sounds like a girl!" That's
what I woke up saying. You know, about your brother, I said, "He sounds
like a girl," you know, with that high voice he had. So that was the only
time and he was here.

WILLARD: Was he here very long, or just—

YOUNG: He stayed about ten days, I think, and he brought a dog
with him, I think—you know, he loved dogs. As you can see on my desk
there, we really love dogs, love animals, and he brought a dog; he always
had a dog, but he always gave them the darndest names. This dog he had,
it was a Belgian police dog, all black, and his name was Tonics, you know,
because he used to have a musical saying, "Get your tonics together," so
he named this dog Tonics. He always had strange names for them.

WILLARD: Did he have a dog on the road with Basie?

YOUNG: No, I don't think so. But they lived in Kansas City, see, and
that was their headquarters. But he left the dog here with me, and when
he was here, that's when I was saying our voices were so similar, even
though I was trying to make fun of him. I didn't realize that my voice has
the same timbre as his. The dog would think that I was Lester a lot of
times, so he left this dog with me, and this dog tore up three suits and
shirts, and I took the dog out, which is Watts now, but there was nothing
out there years and years ago—there was nothing out there but just trees
and all that—and I took the dog way out there and let him loose, even
though I loved dogs, I let him out of the car, and we never did see Tonics
since.

And my mother would say, "What happened to Tonics?" And I
would say, "I don't know. I have no idea what happened to him."

YOUNG: I think that you wanted some input on what I thought about
Lester from the time that I had seen him when we were quite young in
Minneapolis, when Frankie Trumbauer was his idol—what changes he
may have made?

WILLARD: Yeah, well, how he evolved from that point. . . .

YOUNG: His style, I can't say about that; I don't know where he came
up with it, because I was not around, you know, during that time. But
when he came to us [in 1941] and joined the small group that I had, he
was well established, he was well known, he made many, many records
with Lady Day and Teddy Wilson, and he did a couple of things with
Benny Goodman.

WILLARD: Was his approach to improvisation similar at the time he
left home, or—

YOUNG: Well, no; I don't—

WILLARD: Was he improvising then?

YOUNG: Oh, yeah, he could always improvise, but at the time he executed an awful lot. He played a lot of fast things; as I mentioned earlier, Frankie Trumbauer and Jimmy Dorsey and those people had things like "The Bouncing Ball" [a feature for Paul Whiteman's saxophone section written by Trumbauer, recorded in 1934—Ed.]. Well, that was like running a lot of scales, and that's what he used to do. You know, he used to run all over the horn a lot, but I think when he went to the tenor—and this is just my assumption; I don't have any way, we never discussed it—I imagine it maybe was a larger instrument, and he felt as though it wouldn't sound right for him running up and down the tenor, because maybe he thought it was more mellow, I don't know, but he did change considerably.

But Lester played the way he was; that's the way I think. He was a very soft-spoken man, and he was an extreme introvert. You know, he was extremely introverted. He was not out at all. Very few people knew him. I'm positive of that.

WILLARD: You mean he was always like that, even when he was very young?

YOUNG: As a child. Yes, as a child. But of all the people that have written things about Lester that I have read, I only know one that really captured him, that made me, you know, as his brother, sitting down reading it, thinking that that person really got to Lester, got to know Lester—and that was Ralph Gleason.

When Lester passed, Ralph Gleason, I read something that Ralph Gleason wrote about Lester, and I never have been able to read it again, you know, because if I read it, it really breaks me up. [Gleason's piece appears later in this volume.—Ed.] But he was one person that—he sounded like Lester had told him everything that he said, because, you know, Lester used a lot of slang and he had his own language, and only the people that he really cared for, that he allowed them to understand him, you know?

WILLARD: I understand he used to say things that rhymed with what he really meant?

YOUNG: Uh-huh. Yeah, he did. Well, he did, because he just—

WILLARD: And that his friends knew what he meant by hearing the rhymes.

YOUNG: Yeah. Well, he would give out nicknames, but they were names—

WILLARD: Do you remember any of them?

YOUNG: They were names of endearment, you know, like, well, you know about Lady Day; that's been stated many times that he gave her that name. I don't know, you know?

But like we had a little trumpet player [in 1941], you know—some little guys act like little men, and . . . other guys, they would say, "He's a cute little man, isn't he?" Well, Paul Campbell was a little fellow, and Lester used to call him "Ripty Gipty," so, you know, I guess he would come up with many things that way.

About his playing—I'll tell you what he would do at sessions. He loved to play jam sessions and loved not to know the tune. You know? And during the sessions, a lot of times, if you were playing a tune the instrumentalist—the soloist—didn't know, well, it was fashionable for the pianist to turn around and say, E-flat-seventh, you know, D-flat, C Major—he wouldn't want that. If he didn't know the tune, he'd say, "Don't call the chords to me. Just play the chords, and I'll play." And I'd seen him do it many a time, you know; they just started playing, and he didn't know it, but he would play it. But he would say it confines you too much if you know it's a D♭7, you know, you start thinking of the only notes that will go in that chord, and he would say that's not what he would hear. He wanted to play other things and make it fit. And he did. And I think most of the great musicians could do that, you know? So that's what that was all about.

To me, if you listen to any records where Lester played solos on ballads, he's a very melodic musician, and he was one of the very few jazz musicians that, if he were to play "These Foolish Things" or—what were some of the other things he used to play?—"Polka Dots and Moonbeams," he would, the first chorus, he would always play the melody, you know, then he would work around the melody, you know, when he would start his improvisation.

But I was in New York once, and Norman Granz was gonna do a session with him, and I told him, you know, I said, "I'd like for you to do one song on the session for me." And he says, "Well, what do you want me to do?" And so we went across from Birdland—there was a big music store right across the street from Birdland, so we went in there and started looking at sheet music, and I found a song that I wanted him to do. I wanted him to do "Come Rain or Come Shine" because that was the way I had heard him, and I knew when he played with us, the most requests that Lester got was playing ballads, you know, such as "These Foolish Things" and "I Can't Get Started." There was one thing that he did with Lady Day—oh, "The Man I Love"—just a beautiful solo, but the type of solos that I'm speaking of that he did with the melodies, you always knew what he was playing.

And if you go back and get the records where he is doing "These Foolish Things" and "Talk of the Town" and "I Can't Get Started," the layperson would always know what he was playing, and I really think that's why he was so well known among the lay people, because I think they related to what he did, because they could understand; he didn't play over their heads. Like in later years, when bebop first came in, the people didn't know what the musicians were playing, you know, that was really just for musicians, you know, and even some of the musicians didn't understand it at the time.

But I really think that the guy really did play melodic, and he played beautifully, and I just don't think that. If he ever had a chance to record with strings and that sort of thing, I think you would have seen what the guy could do. But I don't think he was really given a chance because he was recording, and someone was recording him that I thought was very narrow in his musical taste.

WILLARD: The way that he played around the melody so that it was recognizable, was that his preference of the way to play, or was he playing to specifically communicate?

YOUNG: No. Well, now he didn't—no, his music was not—it just happened that way. But his music was a very personal thing with him, and I really think that Lester played to please Lester. If you go back and hear some of the stories, which I had to read about, when he was replacing Coleman Hawkins with Fletcher Henderson's band, you know, and I think you can read some of the liner notes I read where he was saying that Fletcher's wife would try and get him to play like Coleman Hawkins.

WILLARD: Yeah, and play him Coleman's records.

YOUNG: Yeah, playing Coleman's records—so [he] was never into that, you know. He was an individual, and he was a stylist; you know, he set the style, and I think when people like that—Louis [Armstrong]—Louis was a style setter, a trendsetter, and I think that we've had many of them in the music business, and they are all individuals, and you can't turn them around, because it's just meant to be, I think.

But he—I think my preference was to always hear him play the beautiful things, because, you know—and I loved to hear him play in the harder keys, but just to play in B-flat and, you know, it makes the instrument sound the same. Where can you go? You know, playing eight-bar blues—that's what they were playing, the twelve-bar blues, or whatever they would play, they'd try to mix them up, but still blues are blues.

When he started recording with—and I will say with Norman Granz—I think the things that he was doing really were almost demeaning, because it did not show the scope of the man as a musician.

WILLARD: Uh-huh.

YOUNG: Because the man that was recording him, he was into blues, you know, so he wanted you to play some B-flat blues and because that was about what he could understand.

[Here we continue with Lee's account of his band with Lester in 1941 and 1942.—Ed.] After Hamp [Lionel Hampton's band], I came back home, and I formed a band with Red Callender, Bumps Myers, Paul Campbell [on] trumpet, [and] Louis Gonzales on guitar. And Arthur Twine was playing piano.

And we used to rehearse five days a week. And then Lester quit Basie, and we were working at a place called Billy Berg's. . . . But a funny thing happened. Lester came out. Now, I told you—or I stated earlier—that we had separate locals, so everybody imagined, because Lester was my brother, when he came out, he was gonna join the band, that I was gonna get rid of Bumps Myers. Well, now, Bumps was really, you know—everybody in L.A. loved Bumps, you know, big smile, infectious smile, and he was a big guy, but really, just like a little chubby bear or something. But a nice man. But I had no intention of axing Bumps. What I ended up doing was having two tenors, one trumpet, and a guitar, you know, which is a real big sound that people didn't believe.

But we had a lot of arrangements made for them, and we used to rehearse six days a week, I think it was, and we would learn one arrangement per day, you know? . . .

So they [the musicians union] wouldn't allow Lester to play with the band when he first arrived, and they told him that he had to appear as a guest. He could play three sets a night, but he had to play on the floor, he couldn't play on the bandstand with the band. . . . He would sit out back all night on a milk box waiting to come on, and we would play a set. We would play three sets a night, and then we would introduce Lester Young, and he'd come out and stand in the middle of the floor and play three tunes. He couldn't play but three, and then he would play nine songs a night [three in each set].

Well, then, they made him do this for six weeks, while he put his transfer in [to the Los Angeles local of the union], and after that, then he could play with us.

But the West Coast musicians—they didn't know too much of what was happening on the East Coast, you know? And maybe it was because of the trains or the covered wagons or whatever we had at that time. But Bumps—everyone felt as though Bumps Myers . . . would really blow Lester away, because they always had their favorites, but it took them about a couple of sessions to understand what he [Lester] was about. It was just absurd. Didn't anyone realize how absurd it was until they played together, because, as I told you what he did about his cousin, you know, he would have to establish that he was the President. It was a good name for him, really, because you know, he kind of lived up to it.

We had a very good band, because—I'll tell you who made the arrangements for us—Gerald Wilson was making arrangements for us, Dudley Brooks, and Billy Strayhorn.

WILLARD: Oh? Was Strayhorn—

YOUNG: Yeah, Strayhorn was here, and the reason he was making arrangements for us was because Duke Ellington was in town with the show, "Jump for Joy"—the "Jump for Joy" was downtown at the Mayan Theatre. Was that in forty-one?

WILLARD: Uh-huh.

YOUNG: Okay. So the band that we had was quite unique because they had not started using guitars playing parts, so we had four-part harmony, and this was why Gerald and Dudley and Billy Strayhorn wanted to write for us, because we had—which is a big sound—we used a trumpet, two tenors, and guitar. And you voice that properly, and you have a big sound; and we did have a big sound.

As a matter of fact, we made so much noise out here, they heard about it back east, and they brought—Barney Josephson brought us back there to work Café Society [in New York in September 1942]. [Young told Phil Schaap that Josephson first heard the band on a CBS broadcast.—Ed.]

WILLARD: Oh, did you ever record with this group?

YOUNG: Never did. Well, it was a ban [on recordings]; it was something, and just a terrible time, because it seems when we really were into it, there was a ban on recording, it seems to me, during that time. [Although the band never went into a recording studio, about ten titles, some incomplete, have turned up from broadcasts and other sources. These were first reported in my book *Lester Young.*—Ed.]

Jimmy Rowles with Lewis Porter

The Lee and Lester Young Band

Lee Young (see p. 38) talked about the first band with the pianist Arthur Twine. When Twine died suddenly of a heart attack, he was replaced early in 1942 by Jimmy Rowles, who continues the story of that band in this previously unpublished interview. Rowles, a superbly creative jazz pianist, played with Lee and Lester Young in Los Angeles from February until late August or September 1942, when he accepted an offer to join Benny Goodman's band to replace Mel Powell (who had replaced Jess Stacy). A charming raconteur, Rowles surprised and delighted me with a phone call on June 1, 1989, and told me this story.—Ed.

When I was in Spokane, when I started out, an Indian guy that I went to school with made me listen to Teddy Wilson. And in half of a minute I made up my mind that's what I wanted to do. First he played me the Benny Goodman trio, and so I started buying those, and the lady in the store was a real knowledgeable lady—one of the very few in Spokane. And she tipped me off to all kinds of things. She got me started on the Teddy Wilson Brunswick records with Billie Holiday. At that time Chu Berry was on some of them. You know, the "Blues in C Sharp Minor" [1936] and things like that. And then she comes out with "A Sunbonnet Blue" [1935] and those things, and I started listening to Ben Webster. And then I started subscribing to *Down Beat,* and I found out about Ben Webster and Teddy Wilson recording with Bob Howard and Willie Bryant and all these records, and she'd send away and get me all this stuff. So I had stuff on Lester Young with Count Basie. I had the Jones-Smith records [of November 1936], and I flipped out because I didn't know who that was. And then she told me about Count Basie, so Boom!—I'm in, you know! I knew most of Lester Young's choruses note for note by the time I went to work for him. I still play some of his choruses note for note. To me, I think one of the greatest tenor solos I ever heard in my life to this day is "Time Out" [Basie band, 1937]. After Herschel's introduction and Pres comes in, that's it! The whole thing is marvelous! I'll bet when they got into that thing on the job, they must have played that for hours. I just played that for my wife the other night, I got an album—four sides of those Decca Records [MCA 4050], you know? And, man!

I'm from Spokane, but Marshall Royal came through Spokane, and I played for him—he told me to go to Seattle. There's nothing in Spokane. I met Ben Webster in Seattle. After I came to Los Angeles from Seattle, I used to play at the 331 Club on Eighth Street here, between Vermont and Western. Art Tatum used to play there, Nat Cole, Slim [Gaillard], and Slam [Stewart], and he [the owner] hired me to be an intermission piano player there. Then all of a sudden I get this call from Billy Berg. Now, Billy Berg was a beautiful guy; he was incomparable as far as a nightclub owner. He was like Max [Gordon] down at the Village Vanguard.

So, Billy Berg wanted me to come out—I think Slim and Slam told him about me. He was forming a band with Slim and Slam and Lee and Lester Young [all together in one band]. And they got Bumps Myers brought in there, and a trumpet player from out here named Jake Porter, who I'd never heard. I did not know anything about Arthur Twine [the pianist in the group during 1941]. He's in a picture I've got of the band. I don't know—he had a heart attack, and I replaced him. But nobody ever asked any questions; all of a sudden it was a thing that was just happening, where they incorporated the band into Lee and Lester Young and Slim and Slam. So, I started writing arrangements for this little band. And we went to work in a place called the Capri Club, at Pico and La Cienega, [opening on February 24, 1942]. That Capri Club was his first club, that I know of. We worked there, and we also had the Spirits of Rhythm with Leo Watson and Teddy Bunn on the bill. With them they had Doug and Wilbur Daniels. Wilbur played the bass, and Doug played the tiple and the trumpet. It was a calypso type—an awful lot of calypso music. And they used to raise hell up there, and Eddie Beal was playing piano with them. Now, we had Bumps Myers and Pres, and Lee was playing the drums. Leo Watson played the drums with the other group. Lee and Lester were so different. Lee would go across the street and get a milk shake; Pres always had a bottle of liquor in his pocket.

One day the Capri ended its music policy. Nobody knew about this having happened; the next night all of a sudden I came to work and there's a jukebox in the middle of the floor. But all of a sudden a week later Billy Berg had bought this Trouville Club, one short block east of Fairfax on Beverly Boulevard. And we went into that club, and that switched everything around. Slim and Slam worked alone, and [bassist] Red Callender joined our band, plus a Mexican fellow named Louis Gonzales—guitar player. And the trumpet player's name was—I used to call him Squeegie—Paul Campbell. Paul Campbell was from St. Louis, and he had played with Basie—I don't know how much, but he had been there. [Actually Cydner "Paul" Campbell played with Basie later on, from 1951 to 1953.—Ed.]

We started playing like that, and Slim and Slam played alone as a duo, and the Spirits of Rhythm played alone, and Eddie Beal stayed with them. We also had Joe Turner singing the blues, and Marie Bryant dancing. And Barney Bigard came in and joined us for a while. He played with the Spirits of Rhythm. It was a pretty wild club! And Norman Granz came in there with no socks and tennis shoes, and he was practically broke. He was in there, you know, just hanging around, he hadn't even started with his jam sessions. Yeah! I knew him before he had a nickel to throw around. [By July 1942 Granz began his career in jazz by producing Sunday afternoon jam sessions at the Trouville.—Ed.] Later Billy Berg bought a club on Vine Street where Bird and Diz played in 1945.

We were broadcasting almost every night. I would love to hear some of that stuff. It seems like I heard a couple of dubs, like acetates. One was an arrangement of "Broadway." Slim was the announcer. He used to say things, when we'd come on the air, things like, "I want everybody to fall on out here and get your boots laced up." All of his talk. He called Dizzy Gillespie "Daz McSkip n' Voutie." And Lester used to love that. He incorporated that into his own stuff, which made him triply hard for other people to understand. Well, I remember sitting down with him at a table, and he and I would converse, and, well, you know, he'd just say things. And I knew what he was talking about, but nobody else knew what he was talking about. Unbelievable, little things, and yet it was all English and it was no profanity. But nobody knew what he was talking about. All women were "hats." He used to say, you know, like, "I see you're wearing a new hat." And he'd be talking about the girl, the woman—of whoever he was talking to—he'd be talking about her. And the whole conversation would go down about her, and she didn't even know what they were talking about. He had "skull caps" and "Mexican Hat Dance." He had numbers like 143 and 369 that stood for sex phrases and swear words. White people he didn't like were Orrin Tucker or Tommy Tucker instead of something that rhymed with that!

We used to play "Imagination." There are two tunes Pres really liked, but we didn't play them—" 'Tis Autumn" and "Mandy Is Two." I've got me a little picture that was taken at the time that Billie Holiday was singing with us. [Actually, it predates Holiday's visit; see the photograph section.—Ed.] I remember when she showed up. She was there every night, and we rehearsed every day.

When I joined Benny Goodman, I had to leave that Lester Young group. And then they came to New York to work at Café Society Downtown in September 1942. That was the job I was supposed to go to with them. He offered me so much money—I was only making forty dollars a week, and Benny comes up with a hundred and a quarter. And they were gonna start off with a picture, you know [appearing in a Hollywood movie, *The Powers Girl*]. So I couldn't afford to turn this thing down, because I didn't know what I was gonna make in New York, and my wife was pregnant, so I had to watch my cues. But when I did go to New York, I went down to the Society down in the Village to see them, you know, and Clyde Hart took my place. There were no piano parts! Very, very little. Well he learned the tunes quick. Yeah, he really jumped right in there. I always admired him. I knew him when he was with Stuff Smith [touring from 1936 to 1938].

Mike Nevard

I'll Take Flip Any Time!

During the 1940s Young was changing as a person and as a musician. By the time he first toured Europe in 1952, he was highly controversial. On his return there in 1953 (Young also went back in 1956 and 1959), Mike Nevard reviewed what he saw as "years of deterioration" in Young's music and personality. The Nat Hentoff piece that follows this one gives a more sympathetic portrait of Young's personality in later years, and in Part Three we present several essays defending the music.—Ed.

Lester Young is no longer the President. The mantle of honor has slipped from his shoulders, and his greatness lives only in the past.

Lester—probably the biggest influence in jazz outside Armstrong—now plays a pathetic parody of the "cool" style he inspired. While his countless minions carry the message, Pres sits back in a throne, held up only by the reverence of his more blinded admirers.

Lethargy

His lackluster showing at the Gaumont State did not come as a revelation. It was the culmination of years of deterioration.

Reprinted from *Melody Maker,* March 21, 1953, 5.

His records started going off in the mid-forties. The individual personality that had sparked his playing paled, and the bright fluency of ideas that he translated so subtly became dreary and lifeless.

In February 1951 Edgar Jackson reviewed some Lester sides recorded in 1944 and said: "What had been the languorous ease of complete relaxation had come dangerously near to sounding like the lethargy of tiredness."

Last year, in Paris, the change was even more marked. Lester played with Jazz at the Philharmonic, and I described his playing as "extremely indifferent."

Empty Shell

A week later Steve Race caught up with the unit in Brussels and wrote: "I was too disappointed in Lester's playing to think of anything but how disappointed I was. According to unimpeachable but unprintable authority. Lester is in the middle not of an off-day but of an off-decade. He's now the ex-Pres."

Let us face it. Lester Young is out of office. Onstage he is a big empty shell of a man. Offstage he is a whisky drinker who makes a lot of witty remarks.

Our first glimpse of him this year was at London Airport on JATP-Day (March 8), when he glided through the barriers like a Sandeman advert, his bland expression half-hidden by the shadow of a sinister black hat.

He boarded the [Melody Maker] coach and sat zombielike in a rear seat. When the rest of the boys piled out at Buckingham Palace, Lester remained in his seat. His wife brought him a new bottle of whisky.

Twenty minutes later the other fellows returned with their cameras swung open on their paunches. Lester looked slyly at Granz's Contax.

"That little eye can't see far, can it?" he inquired dryly.

At the hotel he made straight for bed. Later, he arrived at the theater and found his dressing room already besieged by fans. They brushed past Flip, Barney, and Oscar to see Pres. And all day they were there.

Such a seething mass gathered that Granz had to clear the corridor to get his men through to the stage.

When Lester finally walked on the stand, the crowd gave him their biggest ovation. He stood there, gnawing his lip. And when he sidled up to the mike, head cocked to one side like a fondled spaniel, we hoped the Lester of old had returned.

He hadn't. Lester had finally handed his Jazz at the Philharmonic supremacy to Flip Phillips, the hard-blowing Herdman from Long Island.

And the critics' acclamation of Flip was gratifying to one who went overboard about his kicking tenor three years ago. Then, Flip—like Wardell Gray—was ready to take the tenor crown away from the maudlin pupils of the cool cult. Today, Flip blows with even more verve and enthusiasm.

The Roads

It was gratifying, too, to find my 1950 raves about Oscar Peterson, then "an exciting new pianist," being endorsed by almost every man, woman, and child in the State audience.

Peterson and Phillips are indicative of the swinging, uninhibited men who are thrusting their way into the pliable ranks of the coolies.

The cool school, which has sidetracked so many talented jazzmen, has lost its novelty. For was it ever anything else?

A lot of our more narrow-minded musicians—and even critics— have spent much of their time since Jazz at the Philharmonic played its historic London date telling all and sundry that British musicians could do all that Jazz at the Philharmonic did.

Poppycock!

To add ignorance to ignorance, they state that Jazz at the Philharmonic wasn't modern.

Poppycock again! Bop isn't the all and everything of modern jazz. There's room for the cool and hot schools to take their separate roads.

And I know which road I'll take. I'll follow Flip while the intellectual sheep walk in step behind the zombie who was once President.

Nat Hentoff

Lester Young

After Lee and Lester Young worked in New York for a while, they went their separate ways. When Billy Young died in 1943, Lee went back home, and Lester continued to free-lance around New York. He worked for a while with the Al Sears USO band that appears in a rare photograph in this volume, touring armed forces bases. At the end of 1943 he rejoined Basie, playing at the height of his powers on a few studio recordings and on numerous radio broadcasts (many of which are now on bootleg LPs). But the war finally caught up with him, and he was drafted in September 1944 and inducted on September 30.

Nat Hentoff has been one of our most astute writers on the arts and on politics since the early 1950s, and his piece on Young from *The Jazz Makers* still stands as one of the best on Young's life and personality. It also helps to complete the story of Young's life during and after World War II. The abridgment that follows, approved by Hentoff, avoids redundancy with the preceding articles by shortening the review of Young's early career, and it eliminates some quotations from articles reprinted elsewhere in the *Reader* by Feather, Harris, and Hentoff himself. Parenthetical interpolations in quoted passages are the author's.

Hentoff provides revealing background on Young's army experience. More recently, the transcripts of Young's court-martial were turned up during John McDonough's research for his revealing booklet to the Young boxed set in the Time-Life Giants of Jazz Series, and he published the army story in greater detail in a *Down Beat* article of January 1981. Even with the release of this data, there are still some mysteries. Why wasn't Young placed in a band as many musicians had been, such as his friend Buck Clayton? Did he really sit in with the army band anyway, as claimed by Jimmy Cheatham and others? Did the officer who arrested him really see a photo of his wife, Mary, and was this an influence behind the arrest? In addition to marijuana and barbiturates, did Young really concoct a homemade still to make a type of liquor? (There is a tantalizing mention in the army files of two bottles found among Young's effects that contained a strange pink liquid that "smelled like rubbing alcohol.") Once Young was placed in detention, did he really sneak out and play with the band on a regular basis? Did he ever conduct that band, as Zoot Sims once claimed?

One question continues to nag: Since the army's own investigation declared Young unfit to be a soldier, why didn't they just let him go? We see now that there is no logical answer to this question. The army just functioned under its own mysterious logic, and it was devastating to Young.

Another point will be discussed in Part Three, namely, the widely held opinion that the army experience destroyed Young's musicianship. This romantic view is strange enough, since common sense alone tells us that musical skills are not destroyed by life experiences, short of physical catastrophe. In any event, listening to Young's recordings after the war easily disproves such statements.—Ed.

For further reading. The fifty-two-page booklet that came with the Time-Life three-record set of Young (Giants of Jazz Series, 1980) includes two pieces well worth reading: a newly researched biography by John McDonough, with rare photographs, and comments on each recording by trumpeter Richard Sudhalter, who is also coauthor of an important Bix Beiderbecke study.

Billie Holiday awarded Lester Young his nickname. "When it came to a name for Lester," she said in one of the few mellow pauses in her autobiography [*Lady Sings the Blues,* chap. 4], "I always felt he was the greatest, so his name had to be the greatest. In this country kings or counts or dukes don't amount to nothing. The greatest man around then was Franklin D. Roosevelt and he was the President. So I started calling him the President. It got shortened to Prez."

And Prez (or Pres) it has remained. In one sense Pres's term—
among musicians—is not likely ever to run out. It is not that he has or
ever had unanimous recognition from his peers as the nonpareil jazz
tenor. There are those who prefer Coleman Hawkins; there are younger
men who look to Sonny Rollins; and several other tenors have had their
determined bands of constituents.

Yet Lester Willis Young has continued to be Pres to nearly all insofar
as he has personified consummate relaxation in the act of creative improvisation. The relaxation may sometimes have been more apparent
than real; some feel that in recent years it has occasionally approached
resignation.

But the memory and occasional present power of Pres invariably
evokes a particular musical effect—pulsating ease. He has several corol-
lary achievements of major importance in the evolution of jazz; and these,
of course, contribute to his stature. A large part of the essence of Pres,
however, is the flowing quality of his phrasing, his rhythmic development,
and even his tone. In the process of sustaining this uniquely muscular
ease of playing, Lester, as French composer-critic André Hodeir has
noted, was also greatly if perhaps unwittingly responsible for "a new
conception of jazz."

Off the stand, without a horn to speak through, the ease of Pres has
frequently turned into a fiercely shy, unpredictable independence. An
independence of movement, of speech, of dress. An independence that
for many years was stubbornly self-destructive.

A booking-agency executive has said bitterly of Pres: "He's an aloof
goof. He's in a world all by himself. He's oblivious to people. I don't think
he regards people as anything. I'd talk to him and all he'd say was 'Bells!'
or 'Ding! Dong!' I finally decided I'd go to Bellevue if I wanted to talk to
crazy people. So he's a talent! He's a nut!"

John Lewis, who was Lester's pianist for several months, disagrees:
"Lester is an extremely gentle, kind, considerate person. He's always
concerned about the underdog. He always wants to help somebody. It is
true that he doesn't like unpleasantness and that he'll avoid it if he can,
but isn't that true of most of us?

"The basic mark of Lester," Lewis adds, "is that he's always young;
he stays young in his playing and in his person. Some people are always
crying for love and kindness; but Lester doesn't cry. The way he seems to
see *being* is: 'Here we are. Let's have a nice time.'"

Lester, it is true, does not *cry* for love and kindness. But he has
searched for them for a long time while trying to look as if he weren't

looking. And he spent many of his years in a forest of petrified emotions, petrified into surface numbness by gin and pot, behind a mask that was only removed before those he trusted. And he trusted very few.

Where and how the first crack in his sense of security began to widen is difficult to trace. But in going back to his beginnings and to his growth as a jazzman, there is illumination to be found concerning the growth of a significant part of jazz itself. And while Lester, more than most of us, will probably always be seen quite differently by quite different people, a unified perspective of his life in music may help outline him somewhat more clearly as a man, as an intently casual individualist for whom the self-expression of jazz has been a life-sustainer.

Lester Willis Young was born in Woodville, Mississippi, August 27, 1909. The family moved to New Orleans and remained there until Lester was ten. . . .

At ten, Lester joined his brother Lee and his sister Irma as all three went to live with their father, who had left New Orleans. "He took us to Minneapolis, where we went to school. During the carnival season we all traveled with the minstrel show, through Kansas, Nebraska, South Dakota, all through there."

He began at ten as a combination drummer and handbill carrier. "I played drums until I was about thirteen but quit them because it was too much trouble to carry the traps and I got tired, too, of packing them up. I'd take a look at the girls after the show, and before I'd get the drums packed, they'd all be gone. So I switched to alto." . . .

Lester has been entirely self-taught except for basic lessons from his father. "He wrote out the scales for me when he got me an alto, but I'd get to listening to a lot of music, and I'd goof off and play everything but the scales. My sister was a better reader than I was. She played saxophone, too, and so did my brother Lee. I always played by ear. Whatever she would play, I would play a second or third part to. One day my father spied me. He had my sister play her part alone, and then he had me play my part alone. I couldn't play a note. He put me out of the band and wouldn't let me back in until I could read. That hurt me real bad, so I practiced every day and was back in the band in about six months. I was about thirteen. (Author's note: he has also said another time he was sixteen when he was temporarily expelled from the family band.) Pretty soon I could cut everybody and I was teaching other people to read." . . .

Another view of Lester's father comes from Ben Webster, who also became an important jazz tenor. Webster was playing piano in Amarillo in the late twenties "when Lester Young's father came to town along with Lee Young to pick up a piano player. I took the opportunity to ask Lester's father if he needed a sax player. He said he did, and I told him I didn't have an instrument. He laughed and said he'd find an instrument for me. Then I told him I couldn't read. He really fell out laughing then but told me he'd teach me. So I went to Albuquerque with the Youngs, and for three months Lester's father taught me how to read. He was a very good musician. I remember Pres used to sit and practice with me every day, and he'd try to help as much as he could."

For Lester the carnival seasons continued. "I was raised up in a carnival, a week in each town. I liked it, but in the wintertimes my father wanted to go down South. I didn't like the idea, and I'd run away." . . .

"I ran away and went to a cop, who asked me whether I could take care of myself. I had nothing but the clothes on my back. But this fellow Art Bronson from Salina, Kansas, who had [a band called] the Bostonians, accommodated me." . . .

At this point the exact pattern of Lester's subsequent band alliances is as hazy as are the memories of the principals of the story, some seven of whom were interviewed in this connection. Lester remembers spending some time around Oklahoma City, where, incidentally, he met Charlie Christian. "We used to go out in the alley and jam." He then apparently went back to Minneapolis and worked around there for a while. It was in Minneapolis that Lester joined Walter Page's Blue Devils. Page concurs that he picked Lester up in Minneapolis and feels it was before Lester played with [King] Oliver.

About 1930–31, Page remembers, he went to a "joint" in Minneapolis where he heard a group that wasn't very good except for the tenor. He talked to Lester, and Lester left with him that night, staying about ten or eleven months. John Hammond recalls hearing Lester with Oliver about 1933, presumably after his stay with the Blue Devils. . . .

Jo Jones relates a story that neither Lester Young nor Walter Page remembers of one night when Lester was with the Moten band and tenor Herschel Evans was with Basie. Lester was growing bored, Jones recalls, with having to play sedately in Moten's band at the Harlem club [in Kansas City] with too little chance to solo, while Evans preferred the added money that being with Moten would bring. So, the story goes, they switched jobs. Later, said Jo, Lester went back to Minneapolis when times became tough.

Lester and Basie remember differently. Both agree that Lester first joined Basie as a result of a telegram Pres sent from Minneapolis. "I had heard of him before," Basie recalls, "but he didn't play with me until that wire. It was a strange and convincing wire." . . .

Some time before he joined Basie an incident occurred in Kansas City that had a sequel. While working with Bennie Moten and George Lee, Lester had had his first chance to hear the Fletcher Henderson band, which was traveling through town.

"That was the time I first heard (Coleman) Hawkins. I'd always heard so much about Hawk—he was from St. Joseph, Missouri—and while I was working at the Paseo Club in K.C., Fletcher Henderson was in town. I ran over to dig him between sets; I hadn't any loot, so I stayed outside listening. Herschel was out there, too.

"Then one night Fletcher said his tenor man hadn't showed up, and wanted to know if there was someone around that could blow. I went in, read the book—clarinet part and all—blew Hawk's horns, then ran back to my own job at the Paseo."

In 1934, after Lester had joined Basie, the Basie band was in Little Rock when Lester received an offer of more money from Fletcher Henderson if he would join the Henderson band. Coleman Hawkins, the dominant tenor stylist of the time, had left Henderson to go to Europe. Lester went to New York and auditioned for Henderson at the Cotton Club.

John Hammond was there. "I thought he was the greatest tenor I'd heard in my life. He was so different. There was a terrific scene. The guys in the band all wanted Chu Berry to replace Hawkins because Chu had a sound like Hawkins. They complained that Lester's tenor sound was 'like an alto.' Buster Bailey, Russell Procope, and John Kirby outshouted me that day," says Hammond.

It is Hammond's recollection that Lester soon went back to Kansas City, but Lester and Mrs. Leora Henderson, Fletcher's widow, state that Lester was with the Henderson band for from six to eight months. It was a painful period for him. . . .

Back in Kansas City, Lester worked [briefly] with Andy Kirk ("He was wonderful to work for") and then returned to Basie. One night, Lester remembers, Basie asked him if he'd mind if Herschel Evans were to rejoin the band. Lester said he didn't, and from then on there were two tenors with Basie, which may have been the start of the two-tenor "battle" that was later to become a prevalent phenomenon in big jazz bands.

Lester first began to attain a significant reputation with Basie when the band moved on to Chicago and farther east and Lester began to make records. Several critics and musicians feel, in fact, that Lester did a key percentage of his most creative and influential (in retrospect) work while with Basie. . . .

While in Kansas City, Lester had experienced his formative years, and they may also have contained many of his most enjoyable hours musically. There was little money to be made then in music in Kansas City. In 1934 Lester was earning about $1.50 a night at the Reno Club working from 10:00 P.M. to 5:00 A.M. And in the summer of 1936 he was only making a dollar an hour more. But there were strong compensations.

Kansas City in those years was a nonstop jam-session after-hours town, and a man could play at these sessions as long as he had something to say. There were tenor battles of the titans, often with Lester Young, Herschel Evans, and the late Dick Wilson of the Andy Kirk band confronting each other.

Mary Lou Williams has written of a characteristic 1934 Kansas City jam session [in *Melody Maker,* May 1, 1954, 11]: "The word went round that Hawkins was in the Cherry Blossom, and within about half an hour there were Lester Young, Ben Webster, Herschel Evans, Herman Walder and one or two unknown tenors piling in the club to blow. Bean (Coleman Hawkins) didn't know the Kaycee tenor men were so terrific, and he couldn't get himself together though he played all morning. I happened to be nodding that night, and around 4 A.M., I awoke to hear someone pecking on my screen.

"I opened the window on Ben Webster. He was saying, 'Get up, pussycat, we're jammin' and all the pianists are tired out now. Hawkins has got his shirt off and is still blowing. You got to come down.' Sure enough, when we got there, Hawkins was in his singlet, taking turns with the Kaycee men. It seems he had run into something he didn't expect. Lester's style was light, and . . . it took him maybe five choruses to warm up. But then he would really blow; then you couldn't handle him on a cutting session.

"That was how Hawkins got hung up. The Henderson band was playing in St. Louis that evening, and Bean knew he ought to be on the way. But he kept trying to blow something to beat Ben and Herschel and Lester. When at last he gave up, he got straight in his car and drove to St. Louis. I heard he'd just bought a new Cadillac and that he burnt it out trying to make the job on time."

Lester kept up his after-hours vocation in New York when the Basie band moved east. In her memories of New York during the thirties, in *Lady Sings the Blues* [chap. 4], Billie Holiday writes that it was at a jam session that she first met Lester Young.

"From then on," she continues, "Lester knew how I used to love to have him come around and blow pretty solos behind me. So whenever he could, he'd come by the joints where I was singing, to hear me or sit in. I'll never forget the night Lester took on Chu Berry, who was considered the greatest in those days. Cab Calloway's was the biggest band and Chu Berry's was one of its big sounds.

"Well, this night Benny Carter was jamming for a session with Bobby Henderson, my accompanist. And then there was Lester with his little old saxophone held together with adhesive tape and rubber bands. Chu was sitting there and everybody started arguing as to who could blow out whom, trying to promote a competition between Lester and Chu.

"Benny Carter knew Lester could shine in this sort of duel, but for everybody else the end of the story was considered a pushover: Chu was supposed to blow Lester right out of the place. Chu had this pretty gold horn, but he didn't have it with him. Benny Carter wouldn't let that stop him. He was like me, he had faith in Lester. So he volunteered to go and pick up Chu's horn. He did and came back.

"And then Chu Berry . . . suggested they do 'I Got Rhythm.' . . . (Lester) blew at least fifteen pretty choruses, none of them the same, and each one prettier than the last. When the fifteenth one was down, Chu Berry was finished. . . .

"Chu's gang were die-hards, and they were sick. All they could say to console themselves was that Chu had a bigger tone. What the hell that meant, I'll never know. What difference how big a tone is or how small, as long as Lester's line was moving in that wonderful way, with those chords, changes and those notes that would positively flip you with surprise? . . . There ain't no rule saying everybody's got to deliver the same damn volume or tone.

"But anyway, this talk about a big tone messed with Lester for months. And me too. So I said, 'What the hell, Lester, don't let them make a fool of us. We'll get you a big horn with big fat reeds and things and no damn rubber bands around it holding you back. We'll get us a tone.'

"So every time Lester could get a dime together he'd get him some more reeds and start cutting them up all kinds of different ways. He got him a new horn, too, and thought that would end him up with a big fat growl. But his tone never got any bigger. He wasn't meant to sound like Chu and he soon gave up trying."

And Jo Jones remembers how Lester always loved to jam. "There were thirty days in Chicago in 1936. Lester and I were with Basie at the Grand Terrace, and Roy Eldridge would pick us up in front of the Terrace after work every night, and we'd jam from four until ten or eleven in the morning. We'd often wind up with just the three of us playing."

Although the necessary confines of the Basie band didn't allow a constant jam-session spirit, there was one presence in the Basie band that particularly spurred Lester to keep challenging himself.

Herschel Evans, a tenor from Texas, was cofeatured on that horn with Lester in the band until Evans died in 1939. Evans was a remarkably sensitive, powerful soloist with roots in Coleman Hawkins.

"Herschel Evans," Jo Jones recalled for *Hear Me Talkin' to Ya* [ed. Nat Shapiro and Nat Hentoff (New York: Rinehart & Co., 1955), 309], "was a natural. He had a sound on the tenor that perhaps you will never hear on a horn again. As for the so-called friction between him and Lester, there was no real friction. What there was was almost like an incident you would say could exist between two brothers. No matter what, there was always a mutual feeling there. Even in Lester's playing today, somewhere he'll always play two to four measures of Herschel because they were so close in what they felt about music. I was always a sort of go-between between them. I roomed with Herschel, and I had a liking for Pres and I was always trying to get them together in a cafe or in a restaurant booth. It was some childish thing that had started it—I never knew exactly what. It may have started in part that night Coleman Hawkins came to Kansas City with Fletcher Henderson and Herschel, Lester and Ben Webster played for him.

"That night, Herschel played all over the horn—played it the way it was supposed to be played because Hawk was his idol. You couldn't say anything bad about Hawkins to Herschel. Some of that friction between Herschel and Pres may have had something to do with that night and with Hawkins. Lester, you know, has always been an unlimited soloist, and he was still playing at the session when everybody else was finished.

"And then, too, there was something about tone. Hawkins had a full tone and Herschel's was full, too. But Lester's tone was different. It was lighter. Some people would tell Lester that he didn't have a good tone, that he should change his tone. And that would cause friction. These people never think in terms of the physical features of an individual and how each one has different physical characteristics and that these make him play the way he does play."

Billie Holiday illuminates the Evans-Young ambivalence further

[*Hear Me Talkin' to Ya,* 310]: "Pres and Herschel Evans were forever thinking up ways of cutting the other one. You'd find them in the band room hacking away at reeds, trying out all kinds of new ones, anything to get ahead of the other one. Once Herschel asked Lester, 'Why don't you play alto man? You got an alto *tone.*' Lester tapped his head, 'There's things going on up there, man,' he told Herschel. 'Some of you guys are all belly.'" . . .

Recently, Jo Jones returned to the subject: "In a way they were almost like twins. When Herschel died, it was like part of Lester had died. The difficult thing was to keep him in the band after Herschel died. Their rivalry wasn't a vicious thing. Herschel wanted Pres to get what he felt was the *tenor* sound, but he wouldn't change. As for the band, the more musical rivalry we could get, the more distinctively things kept going."

And Jimmy Rushing adds: "Basie used to like to make them angry. He'd make one follow the other. They'd turn their backs on each other and play like mad."

Rushing's sidekick, altoist Rudy Powell, discloses: "You know how Lester first started holding his horn at that forty-five-degree angle he used for so many years? When he first joined the band, he said, 'Herschel is playing so much, nobody is paying any attention to me.' So he held his horn a different way."

Perhaps the most traumatic event in Lester's life was his army experience. A friend of Lester in Chicago says: "He once told me how he got in. He kept getting notices as to when and where to report; and later, urgent telegrams. Finally, he said, someone from the draft board came down to the club where he was playing at the time and 'grabbed me off the stand and took me away!' In that last sentence, he may have been speaking figuratively, although I'm sure he wasn't too happy to go into service."

The fifteen months in the army turned into a nightmare.

A musician, a close friend of Lester who was also stationed at Fort McClellan, Alabama, tells the story. "First of all, Lester didn't get into the band. The warrant officer was from Atlanta, Georgia. He said he wouldn't select Lester for the band because 'he'd be hard to manage.' Now that was absurd. Here was a man who had broken no rules doing something he disliked, soldiering. He certainly wouldn't be apt to break any if he had been put to something he wanted to do so much. He'd already been throwing hand grenades in the mud, and he wasn't hard to manage *then.*

"Anyway, we had a sympathetic captain, a twenty-four-year-old drummer, and a sergeant major who also understood Lester, his sensitivity, and how difficult it was for him in the army. There was a move underway to have Lester discharged because of 'maladjustment to the confines of the army.' Lester, meanwhile, went into the hospital for minor but painful rectal surgery. He was returned to the company, and to relieve the postoperative discomfort, he was given pain-deadening pills."

When he had entered the hospital, according to one version, Lester had filled out the usual forms and, with characteristic ingenuousness, had answered, "Yes" to a question as to whether he smoked marijuana. After his discharge from the hospital, a search was conducted of his belongings.

In charge of the search was a major from Louisiana who was Jim Crow. In going through Lester's locker, the major found the pills. He also found a picture of Lester's wife. Lester's wife (they have since been divorced) was white. The major also knew of the plans to obtain a discharge for Lester.

The major brought charges against Lester. The exact nature of those charges has been difficult to find, but they were connected with the pills and with Lester's admission on the questionnaire concerning his use of pot. The feeling of the captain and the sergeant and Lester's friends was that the major was primarily driven by prejudice, but pot was also found.

The trial resulted in a one-year sentence. Lester was remanded to the detention barracks at Camp Gordon, Georgia. (He later recorded "D. B. Blues.") An intimate of Lester says: "Lester has yet to talk in any detail of that year. He'll say a few words once in a while, but then he'll stop. It was a horrible time.

"He did a wonderful job of rewinding himself when he was discharged, but he was very bitter. He didn't say anything, but he acted out certain things."

When he was finally separated from the army, Lester refused to appeal his case. He just wanted out. He came back to Los Angeles, began playing, headed his own unit, and began touring with Jazz at the Philharmonic.

Among other scars, the army experience had made him more suspicious.

One promoter, an honest man, gave Lester a large sum of money one night after a particularly successful concert a few months after he had left the army. Three weeks later Lester called the man in California and charged him with having stolen his money. The promoter flew back to Chicago, found Lester very high, impossible to reason with. "How much did I steal?" "You know, about one thousand dollars or something." "All right, here it is," and the promoter left in disgust. He's still not sure why he gave him the money except that he wanted to be done with the whole affair.

The story sounds apocryphal, but the action is entirely characteristic of this particular promoter.

In the years since, Lester has traveled the nightclub circuit with small combos, usually a quintet, toured with Jazz at the Philharmonic and the Birdland All-Stars throughout the States and Europe. He has also recorded prolifically for Norman Granz.

As of this writing, Lester is probably in better condition—physically, emotionally, and musically—than he has been in several years. He lives in a small, comfortable home in St. Albans, Queens, with his lovely considerate wife, Mary, a nine-year-old son, Lester Young, Jr., and a new daughter, Yvette. He enjoys his family, and the ties remain strong during his long travels. While strolling in Paris recently, Lester had his picture taken before a huge statue at the Museum of Modern Art and immediately had it sent to his son.

Since a hospital stay in the winter of 1955, Lester has played consistently well and with a strength and confidence that had often been missing in the previous decade. There are several musicians who feel he has long passed his creative apex of the Basie years and the early forties. Others are moved no less by his horn now—at its best—than they were then. They are, to be sure, moved in a different way, but they're convinced he can still be an unusually distinctive, eloquent improviser.

Lester had gone to Bellevue in the winter of 1955, knowing with what must have been an awful awareness that the effects of having been almost constantly high on gin and marijuana for a long time were finally impossible for his body, his nervous system, to ignore. The period of self-appraisal his illness made mandatory has apparently resulted in a Lester Young whose personality is more integrated, whose fears and insecurities are more under control, if not conquered.

Pres still wears a mask, although it is more often a cheerful one than the familiar phlegmatic, almost somnolent face and posture with which he faced strangers, particularly white strangers, for many years. His voice remains soft; he speaks slowly and with deliberation when he's serious. In his frequent teasing, good-humored moods, his tone can be lightly mocking, though almost never malicious.

With strangers he is courteous but still guarded. Lester is a fairly large man, but the primary physical quality he projects is a looseness, an ease of movement.

A Swedish writer whose house Lester visited several times a few years ago, wrote: "As soon as I tried to get him to make statements on musical problems, Lester changed the subject. What nightclubs were there in Stockholm? Could one make a round-trip to Paris in one night and could one get 'schnapps' there? . . . In his wide-brimmed hat and down-to-his-feet overcoat, he reminded me quite a bit of 'the wolf dressed as a sheep' . . . but he is really a lost child."

A young girl in Chicago grew to know him somewhat better. She is not a musician but spends much of her time with musicians, and many of them trust her. "About Lester," she says, "once I had made known to him my own personal attitudes on various things, he would take it into consideration, not by strictly conforming but by not pressing *his* divergent attitude on those things. This fell into his overall philosophy that he expressed as 'to each his own.' I don't recall that he ever forcefully tried to talk me—or anyone that I observed—into anything or out of anything."

Another perspective on Lester is that of George Wein, a Boston jazz-club owner. George also plays piano and occasionally will work with an attraction at his club. When Lester Young was booked for a week last year, Lester had not been told that the boss would be playing piano.

"It was the first set of the first night," recalls Wein. "No customers were in the place yet. I got up on the stand with the rhythm section. Lester wouldn't. He sat on a chair by the bandstand, waiting until I played. It was like an audition. I played one chorus, two choruses, three. Finally he said, 'You and I are going to be all right, Pres.' He calls whomever he's working for, a club owner or a promoter, 'Pres.' Fellow musicians he addresses as 'Lady.'

"I have a feeling," Wein concludes, "that if Lester hadn't liked my playing, he would have walked out. The week's work wasn't as important as working for a week with a man whom he could get on musically."

With regard, however, to being on time, Lester is very conscientious. "He's of the old school," says his manager Charlie Carpenter, who has been with him for ten years. "He feels obligated professionally to be on time. In fact, Al Cooper, who used to promote concerts around New York, once said, 'The one thing you have to worry about Lester is he gets to town too early.'"

There is a famous (or notorious, depending on who tells it) story about Lester that has been much changed in the rerelating of it through the years. Most people tell it to prove how "eccentric" Lester is. But his manager tells it to show how self-compelled Lester is to make time.

"It was in 1949," says Carpenter. "Lester had missed a train in Washington because he'd fallen asleep in the station. He was due in New Bedford, Massachusetts, for a one-nighter. Instead of waiting for the next train, he became panicky. He hired a taxi to Newark, chartered a plane to Providence, and then took another taxi to New Bedford. I think it cost him at least $250. He was an hour late and worked three hours overtime for nothing.

"About Lester being aloof," Carpenter goes on, "he's very sensitive and he's been hurt so much through the years with people telling him about his tone and his style and with many personal problems complicated by a lack of being understood that he feels if he says nothing, then he won't get hurt."

Jo Jones, who has been close to Lester for some twenty-six years, adds: "Lester never did a malicious thing. He's very sensitive. Anything that hurts a human being hurts him. He's very sincere. When he meets phonies, he makes himself scarce. He's also religious. I remember in the Kansas City days when we were all traveling with Basie, we'd go to a different church every Sunday. Basie would play organ; Jimmy Rushing would sing. We weren't doing that to bribe the people in the community. That's the way we were.

"Lester doesn't like unpleasant situations, but he'll break up a fight if he can. They ought to send him to the UN; he's that kind of person. To avoid his own conflicts, he'd always grab his horn and go out and play. We had facilities for jamming then. Anything he wanted to say, he'd say on his horn. He spent most of his time playing in those years."

One of Lester's problems through the years has been a fear of doctors, and Jo has been one of the very few people who have been able to break through Lester's obstinacy on the subject. "There was a time when his teeth were practically falling out of his mouth until I got him to a dentist. Another time I had to take him to see about his tonsils."

Some of those who have been associated with Lester claim he has no interests aside from music, and one goes further to claim he hasn't much intellectual capacity for any other subject.

Jo Jones disagrees. "He has depth. He used to read a lot of comic books, but that doesn't indicate lack of intelligence. He's very interested in baseball, too. He's definitely a Giants fan, and he keeps abreast of other sports. He can discuss practically anything."

Young pianist Bobby Scott, with whom Lester became friendly during a 1956 Jazz at the Philharmonic tour, adds: "He's bright, very bright. A lot of his trouble in communicating is the vernacular he uses. A lot of people just can't understand him." (Norman Granz tells of the times Lester used to try to pretend to speak a foreign language. "It was gibberish, but he did it with a straight face and with conviction.")

"Lester," Bobby Scott continues, "is an avid sports fan, and we also talked a lot about music. A few other musicians of his era don't keep their ears open. But Lester has always had his open. He's very broad. He may vote for Harry Edison in a poll, but that doesn't stop him from listening to Miles Davis. He hears everything. He wants to. I had records on the tour with me, and he was always on me to play them. Modern records—Bird, Milt Jackson, Bud Powell, Jimmy Giuffre.

"As a person," Bobby adds, "I'd say he's pretty pure. I mean goodhearted. To me he can almost be like a father image. He was encouraging. He took an interest. He used to bother me about my right hand and said I wasn't playing enough with my left hand. He'd ask me about my 'left people,' as he would put it."

While in England in 1953, Lester met a young English modern tenor, Ronnie Scott. He spent time and a considerable amount of patience teaching Scott his fingering secrets, how to achieve two different sounds from the same note.

A man for whom Lester has toured and recorded frequently has yet another view of Pres: "I knew him in 1941 in Los Angeles. I'd see him a lot. I'd go to rehearsals of the first band he and his brother Lee had. I've never known two brothers who were more completely antithetical. They profess to love each other, but I don't think they really get on. They never ran together.

"Lee, for example," the promoter continued, "runs a boys' club, is a wonderful golfer, basketball player, an all-round athlete. I don't think he ever got high in his life. He's been with Nat Cole for a long time now and is a thoroughly consistent musician. Lester is undoubtedly the genius of the two.

"He's been a strange guy as long as I've known him. I remember watching Lester walk to a rehearsal. He was a block down the street. They were waiting for him. Lee yelled, 'Hurry up, Lester.' But Lester dragged his horn on the sidewalk and took his time. You never could rush him. We've been with him with planes to make, curtains going up. I've never seen him make a hurried move. Coleman Hawkins once told me: 'I think *I* can get relaxed, but I don't know anyone who can get as relaxed as *he* can.' The way I heard his troubles in the army was that he just wouldn't do anything."

A French writer, Frank Tenot, who spent some time with Lester in

Paris, observes, "Lester expresses himself with a minimum of gestures, words, notes."

"He's a loner," the promoter says. "On our tours we'd all check in at the same hotel. But he'd wind up in one of his own. 'I'll go for myself,' he'd say. And it was always a colored hotel.

"Except for the time he was in the hospital, there was no period when I knew him when he wasn't high. You could wake him up in the middle of the day and he'd be high. As for his drinking, he'd go for strange combinations. Gin with a sherry chaser. Courvoisier and beer. He could drink incredible quantities of liquor, more than anyone I've known. And he wouldn't eat. I remember one tour when he'd gone four days and we had to force-feed him. I think he has a strong death wish."

"He didn't always drink," explains a musician who knew Lester well in the Basie band. "A lot of people go in for drinking as a substitute companion. And he happened to acquire a taste for one specific drink, gin, and stayed on that. Now he's happy with a half-pint of Henessey's that he can sip at during the night."

"He has a lot of phobias," says the promoter. "When I knew him well, he couldn't sleep unless the radio was on full blast and the lights were on. I've never seen him in a dark room. He's frightened of life. But fear turned him into a lotus eater. He lived in a lassitude. Not his playing though, not in those years. He had a vigor then that the 'cool' modernists today haven't approached.

"There was sometimes a resentment in him. The people who have been with our show a long time take pride in our grosses. But Lester would come to me with glee and point out what a competing show had done. 'They smothered you in Minneapolis!'

"He'd get into business problems. He either can't or won't read a contract. Once, he got into a tax jam, and I had to save his home for him. And later, when he had himself put into Bellevue, I sent his wife money. Yet when we talked about his going on my tour after he got out, he first agreed to his usual $750 a week. Then he talked with his manager, called back and asked for $850. That was OK. Ten minutes later he called and asked for $950. OK. Finally he said he'd have to have $1,000. That was very strange conduct for him. Anyway, we had a blowup, and he made another tour instead.

"The thing with him is that if anything's making him unhappy, he'll walk away from it. If he's bugged on a session, he'll pack up his horn and go. He won't face up to things. On a European tour he came to me in Paris in the middle of the night and said, 'Please give me my money, I'm not happy. I want to go home.' I didn't and he was all right the next day.

"I said he was a loner. Like on the bus, his was always the last seat. He never dressed in a room with the rest of the guys unless that dressing room was the only one there was. At Carnegie Hall they would have to open up the symphony room so he could have it by himself. He almost never mixed socially with the group. The other guys would always pair up and run for girls. But not Lester. His relationships with women seemed strange to me. Those I saw looked alike. Same size. Fragile.

"The only guys he would pair up with on the tour would be the misfits. The few weirdos. One of them, a drummer, was a guy whose playing he didn't like. But he hung around with him.

"Another thing is he won't write. At least, he was the only guy on any of my tours for whom I had to make out his own immigration slip with his name and passport number.

"He does have a great pride in being a musician. He has a great tolerance for a wide variety of music, too. He could probably tell you Perry Como's latest record.

"Lester likes to be different; he apparently needs to be. Like the ridiculous things he'd eat: buttermilk and Cracker Jacks. There was a period, too, in which he was affecting effeminacy although he's never been a homosexual. At one point he had let his hair grow so long in back, it fell in natural curls, and he was going to put ribbons in it. We had to stop him.

"Anything that's weird attracted him. Anything that's weird and different he buys. He used to wear his hat backward. Then he started wearing the porkpie hat that's become identified with him. He would always wear dark clothes, black or dark blue. I once took him to Brooks Brothers, selected and paid for some suits, but he never picked them up.

"There's also something masochistic about him, I feel. At one time a business associate was cheating him. He knew it, but he kept him. Another time a guy who was part of his entourage was playing Uncle Tom to some white girls. 'Look at him Tomming,' Lester said in disgust. But he never said anything to the guy."

"He was always different," Jimmy Rushing and Rudy Powell remember. "If he'd follow a guy's solo, you'd think he'd go one way, but he'd always go the other. He always did the opposite. He could play an odd note, and you'd think, 'Gee, he'd better leave it alone because now it's going to be all wrong if he goes on with it.' But it wasn't. He'd always have another note next to that one to slip into. He played on a note like you would play a word."

"Lester sings with his horn," Billie Holiday wrote [*Lady Sings the Blues,* chap. 6]. "You listen to him and can almost hear the words. People think he's so cocky and secure, but you can hurt his feelings in two seconds. I know, because I found out once that I had."

"Everyone playing an instrument in jazz," Jo Jones comments on the same theme, "expresses what's on his mind. Lester would play a lot of musical phrases that were actually words. He would *literally* talk on his horn. That's his conversation. I can tell what he's *talking* about in 85 percent of what he'll play in a night. I could write his thoughts down on paper from what I hear from his horn. Benny Goodman even made a tune out of a phrase Lester would play on his horn—'I want some money.'

"But Lester also has continuity," Jo emphasizes. "He tells a story. A lot of the little kiddies today aren't saying anything. They'll start talking about Romeo and Juliet and in two measures, they're talking about William S. Hart."

Nearly all musicians who have worked and traveled with Lester agree that, as John Lewis puts it, "Lester has a subtle and playful sense of humor."

"He's always a lot of fun," says Jo Jones. "There's always something going on, never a dull moment when he's around."

The seeming conflict between Pres as an introvert and as a humorist may be resolved in the realization that by making people laugh, by using his unique gift for language-sketching to amuse, Lester can feel he is accepted. By his wit he can shore up his ego and gain pleasure from the exercise of an unusual skill.

"He's always performing," says Bobby Scott. "He does it for other people. Without him on that one tour I made with Jazz at the Philharmonic, I might have shot myself."

Lester is most renowned avocationally for his ability to select nicknames that stick. Billie Holiday was christened Lady Day by Pres. "Lester was the first to call Mom 'Duchess'—and it turned out to be the title she carried to her grave. Lester and I will probably be buried, too, still wearing the names we hung on each other after he came to live with us.

"Back at the Log Cabin (where Billie worked in Harlem in her early time in New York), the other girls used to try and mock me by calling me 'Lady,' because they thought I thought I was just too damn grand to take the damn customers' money off the tables. But the name Lady stuck long after everybody had forgotten where it had come from. Lester took it and coupled it with the Day out of Holiday and called me 'Lady Day.'"

Pianist Charles Thompson is now irreversibly Sir Charles because of Lester. Bobby Scott became Bobby Sox on the tour they worked together, and bassist Whitey Mitchell, since it was World Series time, was dubbed

Whitey Ford. And Harry Edison has been Sweets since 1936 because of Lester.

It's likely that Lester originated much of the onomatopoetic "rooney" material on which Slim Gaillard later expanded. And he is credited with having originated the widely used phrase (among Negro musicians mostly), "I feel a draft," which can mean the detection of Jim Crow in a person or a general feeling of not being wanted for other reasons.

Lester's way of inviting a sideman to take another chorus may be, "Have another helping." If he'd like you to take three choruses, he's apt to advise, "Have a trio."

Pres has also been known to slip into song during a set at Birdland, slyly enjoying the effect. And he has been known to engage in water-pistol battles with members of the Basie band at Birdland.

As for his verbal wit, the pleasure of others in this aspect of Lester's humor may be deepened for some by their feeling that he respects their intelligence enough to expect they'll understand his highly idiomatic subtleties. The softly deft humor that is Lester's basically is an expression of personality that, whenever possible, seeks fun and warmth and the security of communication among soul brothers, to use a current term among jazzmen. . . .

Occasionally, depressed by colleagues who honk and by the easy rise they get from audiences, his own performances have suffered. Once he played France with Jazz at the Philharmonic, and French editor Charles Delaunay recalls: "The first time he came over with JATP [in 1952] his short, mediocre stage appearance disappointed nearly every one of his fans. But pianist Henri Renaud and a few other musicians managed after the concert to take him to the Tabou, where he sat in with the local band and really *blew*. There we discovered that Lester could still blow when he wanted to, when he was in a proper environment or mood." And another night, in the warming empathy of a French jazz club, following a formal concert, Lester was seen dancing for hours. . . .

In Paris, during a JATP tour, Lester spent his free time for five days sitting in with French jazzmen and finally played all night from 2:00 A.M. on.

Wrote Frank Tenot: "Lester and Barney Kessel were the two musicians of the JATP troupe that year who played as much as they could. . . . One night Lester said, 'There are too many people at the concerts and I don't think my music interests them; they've come for something else. I bore them. I prefer to play before those who like my music.' "

Tenot concluded: "Lester Young has never gone commercial. What Louis Armstrong, Dizzy Gillespie, Charlie Parker have not been able to avoid, Lester Young has not tried yet."

Lester Young's insistence on being Lester Young has resisted more than commercial pressures. Ralph Gleason has written: "Lester Young was himself when all pressures were on him to be something else. The way he chose to go was the way everyone else chose, eventually." . . .

Young is aware that he has influenced so many of the young modern tenors. Bill Simon wrote: "Oddly enough, while there were some Lester followers during his Basie period, his influence didn't really catch a firm hold until the late forties. Then it did so emphatically, virtually obliterating (author's note: for a time) other tenor styles. The Woody Herman band, with its 'Four Brothers' sax section, actually at first consisted of four tenor saxophonists, all playing with Lester's sound. To fashion that sound, Woody at times employed such men as Stan Getz, Zoot Sims, Herbie Steward, Al Cohn, and Jimmy Giuffre. Others in the idiom included Paul Quinichette (called the 'Vice Pres' and often indistinguishable from Lester whom he followed into the Basie band), Allen Eager, Brew Moore, Dexter Gordon, Wardell Gray, and such latter-day stylists as Arno Marsh, Dave Pell, Bill Perkins, Bob Cooper, Warne Marsh, and alto saxophonists Lee Konitz and Paul Desmond."

Konitz's tribute to Young, as reported by Barry Ulanov [*A History of Jazz in America* (New York: Viking Press, 1952), 328], was eloquent: "The sound of Lester Young on the old Basie records—real beautiful tenor saxophone sound, pure sound. That's it. For alto, too. Pure sound. How many people Lester influenced, how many lives! Because he is definitely the basis of everything that's happened since. And his rhythmic approach—complex in its simplicity. How can you analyze it? Shall we tag some words on it? Call it polyrhythmic?"

Charlie Parker, *the* influence in modern jazz, claimed not to have been influenced by Lester, but said that in his formative years, "I was crazy about Lester. He played so clean and beautiful" [*Down Beat*, September 9, 1949, 12]. It's interesting to note that when Charlie Parker first began to attract attention among New York musicians by his playing at Monroe's Uptown House, "They began to talk about Bird," according to Kenny Clarke [*Hear Me Talkin' to Ya*, 354], "because he played like Pres on alto. . . . We thought that was something phenomenal because Lester Young was the style setter, the pace setter at that time. We went to listen to Bird at Monroe's for no other reason except that he sounded like Pres. That is, until we found out that he had something of his own to offer."

"Have any of the younger tenors," Lester was once asked, "said anything to you about your having influenced them?" "No," said Lester, "none have. I hear a lot of little things from what I play, but I never say anything. I mean I hear a lot of little riffs and things that I've done. But I don't want it to sound like I think I influenced everybody."

The problem, George Wein once pointed out, is that "his imitators have played so much of him, he sometimes doesn't know what to play." . . .

Lester has always encouraged younger modern jazzmen pragmatically. Trumpeter Jesse Drakes worked with him for a long time, and more recently Art Farmer and Idrees Sulieman have played trumpet with him. John Lewis has been his pianist, and Gildo Mahones was a later Young pianist.

"He never put the kiddies down," Jo Jones says.

" 'I've got to give the kiddies a gig,' he'd tell me before a record session," Norman Granz adds. "So we'd have to use his people. Afterwards, he'd sometimes admit the records weren't as good as they could have been if we had used better-known guys."

Lester is not as laissez-faire as he sometimes appears on stand. On the matter of solos for his sidemen, he is more generous than some leaders. But he has firm ideas of what he wants. . . . "On a date I play a variety of tempos. I set my own tempos, and I take my time." . . .

"That's what I especially noted, playing with Lester," says George Wein. "He very seldom played the same song at the same tempo. It would change from night to night."

"Another thing about Lester," contributes Jo Jones, "is his choice of tunes. He's often a year or a year and a half ahead of everybody else. He catches something on the radio he likes, and he starts playing it—like "How High the Moon." He and Marlowe Morris were playing it at Minton's before it became so widely popular in jazz. He was the one who first started playing "Polka Dots and Moonbeams" and "Foggy Day" again. He finds things that have meaning to them, and soon, other people are playing or singing them again."

Lester spends much of his time at home listening to the radio or watching TV. He keeps up with popular records. . . .

Even when abroad, according to [French critic] Frank Tenot, "as soon as Lester arrives in a hotel, he has a radio installed. He can't do without music."

One of the best analyses of Lester's style and of the permanent effect he has had on the direction of jazz was written by Ross Russell in the

April 1949 *Record Changer:* "Lester was the first to junk the machine-gun style of Hawkins, with its reliance on eighth note-dotted sixteenth patterns. This is the phrasing method of Sedric, Berry, Webster, Wilson and Young's Basie section mate, Herschel Evans. Lester used more notes and less notes than his predecessors, but abundances were balanced against bareness within the structure of his solos.

"In his solo on *Lady Be Good* (small-band version), Young employs a bare ten notes for the first four-bar section. A classic stylist would have doubled the amount. These ten notes are set with lapidarian skill in the rhythmic and melodic framework. The opening phrase, so succinctly stated, leads to longer and complex improvisations upon the melody, the whole of which is a masterpiece of economy, subtlety and logic.

"Lester's musical thought flowed, not within the accepted confines of two or four-bar sections, but more freely. He thought in terms of a new melodic line that submitted only to the harmony of the original as it reworked the melody into something fresh and personal.

"Harmonic sense that enables a jazzman to improvise readily is a talent. Melodic vision of Young's quality is a mark of genius. His example and that of the Basie band restored to the jazz language a tool which had been dulled by improper usage.

"Lester Young's chord and bar changes are arranged with such adroitness that the listener is frequently not aware of them until after they have fallen. Lester's method is to phrase ahead—to prepare for and gracefully lead into the next change several beats before its arrival. To be able to move so freely, in and out of the harmonies with an ear so keen and a step so sure, to always come out on the right note and the right beat— this is a mark of genius. Jazz had known nothing like it since the first daring improvisations of Louis Armstrong.

"As an innovator of harmonic change Lester employed the light polychrome orchestral palette of the Debussyians. Lester's spirit was pleased by the sound of the sixth and ninth intervals which lie adjacent to the dominant and tonic notes. It was typical of his subtle and inquiring nature to play just off what the ear expected and thereby extend musical structure on a horizontal plane.

"Lester added variety to the melodic line, but he knew well how to balance the parts. He is complex, but he is never complicated. Wild crescendoes are contrasted with hammering repetitions, iridescent multi-note passages with sections where notes are massed like blocks. Short statements lead to long flowing sentences. Lester's solos are replete with dips and soaring flights, surprises, twists, hoarse shouts and bubbling laughter. The holes—and, like Basie, Lester leaves many—are deliberate and meaningful. The dry bite of the attacking notes, the fatness of the slurs and periods—all are parts of the deliberate style of a master virtuoso of the tenor saxophone.

"Like all of the giants, Lester possesses a tremendous beat. He is one of those rare musicians who can swing an entire band. The massive swing of the Basie orchestra became even more exciting when Lester soloed. Very often, when he had the first solo, as on *Taxi War Dance*, Young would divest the opening statements of all but their rhythmic elements. Here Lester underlines the first and third beats, giving greater emphasis to Jo Jones's high-hat accents, which fall on two and four. In rhythmic language, this solo develops a $\frac{4}{4}$, a $\frac{2}{4}$ and a $\frac{3}{4}$ pattern simultaneously and results in rhythmic complexity that goes beyond that of any contemporary. No one before him, neither Armstrong, nor Morton, nor Hawkins, had created melodic lines as rich in rhythmic interest as did Lester Young.

"New Orleans bands achieved this rhythmic complexity collectively. The quality deteriorated during the following period when jazz emphasized romantic and individualistic tendencies. Lester Young, the arch-romantic, recreates this quality in an individual style.

"Lester's insistence on the rhythmic priorities of jazz came as a tonic to a music which was drifting away from the drive of early New Orleans music. Lester did more than reaffirm these priorities. He replenished the stream polluted by the arrangers and thus made possible the even more complex rhythmic developments of the bebop style. . . .

"Lester's detachment was unshakable. He always seemed to be in a world of his own. . . . The Lester Young style is essentially romantic. It is uninhibited and relaxed, sensitive, imaginative, deeply subjective. . . . Less disciplined than Hawkins, he is none the less a musician whose product is orderly and structural. But these qualities—balance and unity of parts, clarity of concept—lie beneath the surface, under the luminous texture of notes.

"When Lester first appeared on the jazz scene he had command of a completely integrated style. . . . It was as if he had been planning a frontal attack on orthodoxy for years.

"The roots of Lester's style extend in many directions. On one side they are indisputably in the reed tradition of the early clarinetists who emphasized the melodic and lyrical qualities of jazz, and thought in terms of the blues scale. . . . But Lester draws equally from sources of a much different nature—Debussyian harmony . . . and the spiritual qualities which are attached to the white jazz tradition of Bix Beiderbecke and Bud

Freeman, both of whom Young listened to during his early period. . . . It is this synthesis of opposing attitudes and ideologies—the profound tradition of the blues combined with the infusions of European harmony and white romanticism—that gives Lester Young's music its special appeal. The various materials are combined in a style which has no eclectic qualities, but is fused, integrated, and intensely personal. . . .

"(The young tenors who came to be influenced by Lester) were in revolt against the orthodoxy of the Armstrong-Hawkins school of jazz, with its powerful vibrato, emphatic periods, lusty intonation, rigid harmonies and severe solo architecture. What they admired in Lester Young was his lighter and purer tone, his broader harmonic concepts, his greater extension of the solo line—with the resultant freedom from its bar divisions—his . . . more lyrical style . . . his melodic gifts, inventiveness, and above all, his tremendous swing."

Sidney Finkelstein in discussing Lester's freedom from bar limitations, points out in *Jazz: A People's Music* [(New York: Citadel Press, 1948), 73]: "This freedom from strict bar limitations is not unknown to other music, but is a reassertion of a basic truth of music, a 'humanization' of music. . . . The great recitative, chanson and madrigal art of early musical centuries shows a similar flexibility, and interplay of beats" (as do, he goes on, the songs of Mussorgsky and Charles Ives).

Along with the flexibility, humor, warmth, and relaxation of Lester's playing, the blues have always been present in his work, [both the] "blue" tonality and the coursing virility that its rich tradition connotes. On occasion, there has been a completely individual evocation of sadness in Lester's playing. "There is a poignancy," Norman Granz feels, "in the bending of the notes that is peculiarly, especially his."

In an image that "makes it" musically as well as visually, Barry Ulanov has described one key aspect of Pres's style ["The Four Men Who Made Modern Jazz," in *Jazz 1950: The Metronome Yearbook,* ed. Barry Ulanov and George Simon (New York: Metronome, 1950), 19–20]: "His phrases were longer than the traditional riff; when at a loss for fresh ideas, he would extend his statements by hanging on to one or two notes, in a kind of auto-horn honk that gave his solos a quality of cohesion; his lines hung together, even if suspended precariously from a single note. And how they swung!"

Further insights into Lester's style can be found in André Hodeir's *Jazz: Its Evolution and Essence* [(New York: Grove Press, 1956), 69, 119, 161, and 238]: "(Sometimes Lester) sacrifices everything else to swing, concentrating all his rhythmic powers on one or two notes repeated at greater or lesser length. . . .

"Young's veiled sonority and his almost imperceptible vibrato, which tends to disappear completely in quick tempos, brought into being an unprecedented musical climate, the first fruit of the revolution begun by men like Carter, Goodman, and Wilson. . . . The indefinable charm that is all Lester Young's own comes chiefly from his astonishing muscular relaxation. Good jazzmen have always had to be supple, but Lester has gone beyond being merely supple to achieve a kind of relaxation that has become something of a cult among his disciples. . . .

"(He can sometimes effect) a thorough, essential renewal of the melodic raw material and its emotional content. . . .

"Lester Young took over the element of relaxation at the high degree of perfection to which Armstrong and Hodges had brought it and carried it even further by developing muscular relaxation and suitable rhythmic conceptions."

As for the quality of Lester's rhythmic mastery, John Lewis, in discussing ways of varying and developing the jazz potential for improvisers, said: "If you have a melodic design that is strong enough, you can build on that design and on the accompanying rhythm patterns without relying on any particular harmonic progression. This is especially true if there is enough rhythmic character. Lester Young has been doing this for years. He doesn't always have to lean on the harmonic pattern. He can sustain a chorus by his melodic ideas and rhythm. The chords are there, and Lester can always fill out any chord that needs it, but he is not strictly dependent on the usual progression.

"That's why he needs first-rate musicians to play with him. This is something you can't tell a musician. He has to know and feel it."

Frank Tenot has written of the fact that the relaxation of Lester's playing does not preclude his ability to project tension, that half of the tension-release equation that propels nearly all artistic achievement for the creator and for those with whom a communication is established.

A less realized part of Lester's musical equipment has been his clarinet playing. Except for a few sides with Basie and several solos on a series of Kansas City Six sessions for Commodore, Lester's clarinet does not appear on records. Yet the few solos extant indicate to several listeners, this one among them, that Lester could have been as important and influential a creator on clarinet as on tenor. . . .

Lester Young, in transitory summary, is a musician who has found emotional sustenance in jazz and has helped provide that essential nutrition to many others. A man who has often found it difficult to articulate his feelings verbally, Lester has been able to make his emotions, thoughts, inside humor, and sadness—his life experiences—meaningful to others and perhaps clearer to him through his horn.

The result has been a continuing enrichment of a significant part of the whole of the jazz language, for Lester's story has proved more universal than he himself might have imagined.

In telling so personal, so introverted a life tale, Lester has communicated enduringly to listeners throughout the world; and he has marked hundreds of younger musicians, men who have taken parts of his speech, adapted it to their own needs, and in the process have made Lester's voice a permanent part of the sound of jazz.

Allan Morrison of *Ebony*, who has known Lester well for seventeen years, recently tried to summarize his feelings about Pres: "There are really two Lesters—prewar and postwar. You can tell by just listening to his playing. In jazz more than any other way of music, a man's music will reflect the man, his thoughts, his emotions.

"Those who knew Pres before the war felt deep changes in him when he returned from the army. His experiences in the Southern army camps embittered, soured, changed him profoundly. He had been a boy in the South, so he had known the cruel humiliations of Jim Crow as only a Negro in the South can. He came out of the South early in life with distrust of whites and a loathing for second-class citizenship.

"The years barnstorming with his father's band and later in Kansas City were freewheeling and gay. Lester laughed and loved and lived it up. Life was one long romp with little time out for serious reflection or depression. He was a happy man, bursting with vitality and constantly visiting beyond the pale. He ran unfettered and confident in his strength and stamina. The prewar years stimulated him and gave him seemingly endless opportunities for self-indulgence and release.

"He was one of the great dissenters of his own jazz age, the man who took the 'wrong' turning, and ended up the most pervasive personality of his time. He turned his back on Hawkins and told the jazz world that he was going to be himself and they could take it or not. He found his own voice, and, in a wonderful way, he expressed it eloquently and with increasing power between 1933 and 1942.

"His army service was marked by tragedy, tension, appalling indignities, spiritual and physical torture. When he came out of it, his spirit was twisted and sore, and he hated with an intensity he had never before known. He deeply distrusted practically all whites and realized as never before the injustice and inhumanity under which Negroes in the South lived. And not only in the South. A feeling of revenge lingered in him for years.

"Whether or not he knew it, his spirit had been defaced. His postwar music showed it and conveyed moods that had been alien to him before. He became withdrawn, less forceful, hesitant, often pitifully unsure at times. For a while, in 1946, when he grossed close to $50,000 working for Norman Granz and captured many new admirers, he seemed about to reclaim his former glory. But it didn't last. The reasons were more than commercial. Two marriages failed, and he gathered and sustained deep hostilities to people he felt had wronged him. He remembered hurts, slights, defeats.

"He accepted the fact that the postwar world was much different from the one he had known in the happier thirties. He made his adjustment and peace, but it was more of a surrender. He knew he could never return to the world he had known.

"In the past decade Lester has often aligned himself in his choice of sidemen with those who were working for musical change, evolution in jazz. I once heard him turn down an offer to play with a group of ex-Basie musicians and reconstruct the style of that era for an album. 'I can't do it,' he said. 'I don't play like that any more. I play different; I live different. This is later. That was then. We change, move on.'

"His children have softened and gladdened him, and given him a new grip on life. But he often remains a man drifting sadly through a world he fears and dislikes."

Whitney Balliett

Pres

Balliett's article could have been placed at several points in this book, but it seems to make sense at this juncture, because, like Hentoff's, it is a compilation of memories about Young's personality at various stages of his life. Balliett's writing on jazz for *New Yorker* magazine has long been admired for its elegance and musicality. He has an uncanny ability to capture the look of a jazz musician or the sound of his horn with a few well-placed words. This piece on Young portrays him through Balliett's prose and through the reminiscences of pianist John Lewis, who met Young as far back as 1929 and worked with him in the 1950s; pianist Jimmy Rowles, whom we met earlier in this volume; singer Sylvia Syms; fellow saxophonists Buddy Tate and Zoot Sims; and composer Gil Evans. To avoid redundancy I have edited out a few paragraphs that review Young's basic life history, with Mr. Balliett's kind permission. The closing quote from the Postif interview is taken from the version published as "Lester Young: Paris, 1959," *Jazz Review*, September 1959, 10.—Ed.

Very little about the tenor saxophonist Lester Young was unoriginal. He had protruding, heavy-lidded eyes, a square, slightly oriental face, a tiny mustache, and a snaggletoothed smile. His walk was light and pigeon-

Originally published in the *New Yorker*, February 23, 1981, 90–100; reprinted in *American Musicians: Fifty-six Portraits in Jazz* (New York: Oxford University Press, 1986), 234–40. Copyright © 1981 by Whitney Balliett. Reprinted, slightly abridged, by permission.

toed, and his voice was soft. He was something of a dandy. He wore suits, knit ties, and collar pins. He wore ankle-length coats and porkpie hats—on the back of his head when he was young, and pulled down low and evenly when he was older. He kept to himself, often speaking only when spoken to. When he played, he held his saxophone in front of him at a forty-five-degree angle, like a canoeist about to plunge his paddle into the water. He had an airy, lissome tone and an elusive, lyrical way of phrasing that had never been heard before. Other saxophonists followed the emperor, Coleman Hawkins, but Young's models were two white musicians: the C-melody saxophonist Frank Trumbauer and the alto saxophonist Jimmy Dorsey—neither of them a first-rate jazz player. When Young died, in 1959, he had become the model for countless saxophonists, white and black, most of whom could play his style better than he could himself. He was a gentle, kind man who never disparaged anyone. He spoke a coded language, about which the pianist Jimmy Rowles has said, "You had to break that code to understand him. It was like memorizing a dictionary, and I think it took me about three months." Much of Young's language has vanished, but here is a sampling: "Bing and Bob" were the police. A "hat" was a woman, and a "homburg" and a "Mexican hat" were types of women. An attractive young girl was a "poundcake." A "gray boy" was a white man, and Young himself, who was light-skinned, was an "oxford gray." "I've got bulging eyes" for this or that meant he approved of something, and "Catalina eyes" and "Watts eyes" expressed high admiration. "Left people" were the fingers of a pianist's left hand. "I feel a draft" meant he sensed a bigot nearby. "Have another helping," said to a colleague on the bandstand, meant "Take another chorus," and "one long" or "two long" meant one chorus or two choruses. People "whispering on" or "buzzing on" him were talking behind his back. Getting his "little claps" meant being applauded. A "zoomer" was a sponger, and a "needle dancer" was a heroin addict. "To be bruised" was to fail. A "tribe" was a band, and a "molly trolley" was a rehearsal. "Can Madam burn?" meant "Can your wife cook?" "Those people will be here in December" meant that his second child was due in December. (He drifted in and out of [at least] three marriages and had two children [from the last one].) "Startled doe, two o'clock" meant that a pretty girl with doelike eyes was in the right side of the audience.

Eccentrics flourish in crowded, ordered places, and Young spent his life on buses and trains, in hotel rooms and dressing rooms, in automobiles and on bandstands. . . . Young's father, who could play any instrument, had organized a family band, which worked in tent shows in the

Midwest and Southwest. Young joined the band as a drummer and then switched to alto saxophone. An early photograph shows him holding his saxophone in much the same vaudeville way he later held it. . . . Young quit the family band when he was eighteen and joined Art Bronson's Bostonians. During the next six or seven years, he worked briefly in the family band again, and at the Nest Club, in Minneapolis, for Frank Hines and Eddie Barefield. He also worked with the Original Blue Devils and with Bennie Moten, Clarence Love, King Oliver, and, in 1934, Count Basie's first band. . . .

Soon after going with Basie, Young was asked to replace Coleman Hawkins in Fletcher Henderson's band, and, reluctantly, he went. It was the first of several experiences in his life that he never got over. Hawkins had spent ten years with Henderson, and his oceanic tone and heavy chordal improvisations were the heart of the band. Jazz musicians are usually alert, generous listeners, but Young's altolike tone (he had shifted to tenor saxophone not long before) and floating, horizontal solos sounded heretical to Henderson's men. They began buzzing on him, and Henderson's wife forced him to listen to Hawkins's recordings, in the hope he'd learn to play that way. Young lasted three or four months and went to Kansas City, first asking Henderson for a letter saying that he had not been fired. Two years later, he rejoined Basie, and his career began. The pianist John Lewis knew Young then: "When I was still very young in Albuquerque, I remember hearing about the Young family settling there. They had a band and had come in with a tent show and been stranded. There was a very good local jazz band, called St. Cecilia's, that Lester played in. He also competed with an excellent Spanish tenor player and housepainter named Cherry. I barely remember Lester's playing. He had a fine, thin tone. Then the family moved to Minneapolis, and I didn't see him until around 1934, when he came through on his way to the West Coast to get an alto player for Count Basie named Caughey Roberts. Lester sounded then the way he does on his first recordings, made in 1936. We had a lot of brass beds in that part of the country, and Lester used to hang his tenor saxophone on the foot of his bed so that he could reach it during the night if an idea came to him that he wanted to sound out."

Young's first recordings were made with a small group from Basie's band. The melodic flow suggests Trumbauer and perhaps Dorsey, and an ascending gliss, an upward swoop, that Young used for the next fifteen years suggests Bix Beiderbecke. Young had a deep feeling for the blues, and King Oliver's blues must have settled into his bones. He had a pale tone, a minimal vibrato, a sense of silence, long-breathed phrasing, and an elastic rhythmic ease. Until his arrival most soloists tended to pedal up and down on the beat, their phrases short and perpendicular, their rhythms broken and choppy. Young smoothed out this bouncing attack. He used long phrases and legato rhythms (in the manner of the trumpeter Red Allen, who was in Henderson's band with him), and he often chose notes outside the chords—"odd" notes that italicized his solos. He used silence for emphasis. Young "had a very spacey sound at the end of '33," the bassist Gene Ramey recalls. "He would play a phrase and maybe lay out three beats before he'd come in with another phrase." Coleman Hawkins's solos buttonhole you; Young's seem to turn away. His improvisations move with such logic and smoothness they lull the ear. He was an adept embellisher and a complete improviser. He could make songs like "Willow Weep for Me" and "The Man I Love" unrecognizable. He kept the original melodies in his head, but what came out was his dreams about them. His solos were fantasies—lyrical, soft, liquid—on the tunes he was playing, and probably on his own life as well. The humming quality of his solos was deceptive, for they were made up of quick, virtuosic runs, sudden held notes that slowed the beat almost to a stop, daring shifts in rhythmic emphasis, continuous motion, and often lovely melodies. His slow work was gentle and lullaby-like, and as his tempos rose his tone became rougher and more homemade. Young was also a masterly clarinetist. In the late thirties he used a metal clarinet (eventually it was stolen, and he simply gave up the instrument), and he got a nudging, murmuring sound. He and Pee Wee Russell resembled each other somewhat and were the most original clarinetists in jazz.

Young bloomed with Basie. He recorded countless classic solos with the band, giving it a rare lightness and subtlety, and he made his beautiful records accompanying Billie Holiday—their sounds a single voice split in two. Late in 1940 Young decided to go out on his own, as Coleman Hawkins had done years before. He had a small group on Fifty-second Street for a brief time, and went West and put a band together with his brother Lee. The singer Sylvia Syms hung around Young on Fifty-second Street as a teenager: "Lester was very light, and he had wonderful hair. He never used that pomade so popular in the forties and fifties. He was a beautiful dresser, and his accent was his porkpie hat worn on the back of his head. He used cologne, and he always smelled divine. Once, I complained to him about audiences who talked and never listened, and he said, 'Lady Syms, if there is one guy in the whole house who is listening— and maybe he's in the *bathroom*—you've got an audience.' His conversation, with all its made-up phrases, was hard to follow, but his playing never was. He phrased words in his playing. He has had a great influence on my singing, and through the years a lot of singers have picked up on him."

Jimmy Rowles worked with Young when he went west: "I don't know when Billie Holiday nicknamed him Pres—for 'the President'—but when I first knew him the band called him Uncle Bubba. Of all the people I've met in this business, Lester was unique. He was alone. He was quiet. He was unfailingly polite. He almost never got mad. If he was upset, he'd take a small whisk broom he kept in his top jacket pocket and sweep off his left shoulder. The only way to get to know him was to work with him. Otherwise, he'd just sit there playing cards or sipping, and if he did say something it stopped the traffic. I never saw him out of a suit, and he particularly liked double-breasted pinstripes. He also wore tab collars, small trouser cuffs, pointed shoes, and Cuban heels. In 1941 the older guard among musicians still didn't recognize his worth. They didn't think of him as an equal. He was *there*, but he was still someone new. And here's an odd thing. His father held a saxophone upside down when he played it, in a kind of vaudeville way, so maybe Lester picked up his way of holding his horn from that. Whichever, the more he warmed up during work, the higher his horn got, until it was actually horizontal."

The Young brothers played Café Society Downtown in 1942, and, after stints with Dizzy Gillespie and the tenor saxophonist Al Sears, Young rejoined Count Basie. He was drafted in 1944, and it was the second experience in his life that he never got over. There are conflicting versions of what happened, but what matters is that he collided head on with reality for the first time, and it felled him. He spent about fifteen months in the army, mainly in a detention barracks, for possession of marijuana and barbiturates and for being an ingenuous black man in the wrong place at the wrong time. He was discharged dishonorably, and from then on his playing and his personal life slowly roughened and worsened. John Lewis worked for Young in 1951: "Jo Jones was generally on drums and Joe Shulman on bass, and either Tony Fruscella or Jesse Drakes on trumpet. We worked at places like Bop City, in New York, and we traveled to Chicago. He would play the same songs in each set on a given night, but he would often repeat the sequence the following week this way: if he had played 'Sometimes I'm Happy' on Tuesday of the preceding week, he would open 'Sometimes I'm Happy' this Tuesday with a variation on the solo he had played on the tune the week before; then he would play variations on the variations the week after, so that his playing formed a kind of gigantic organic whole. While I was with him, I never heard any of the coarseness that people have said began creeping into his playing. I did notice a change in him in his last few years. There was nothing obvious or offensive about it. Just an air of depression about him.

"He was a living, walking poet. He was so quiet that when he talked each sentence came out like a little explosion. I don't think he consciously invented his special language. It was part of a way of talking I heard in Albuquerque from my older cousins, and there were variations of it in Oklahoma City and Kansas City and Chicago in the late twenties and early thirties. These people also dressed well, as Lester did—the porkpie hats and all. So his speech and dress were natural things he picked up. They weren't a disguise—a way of hiding. They were a way to be hip—to express an awareness of everything swinging that was going on. Of course, he never wasted this hipness on duddish people, nor did he waste good playing on bad musicians. If Lester was wronged, the wound never healed. Once, at Bop City, he mentioned how people had always bugged him about the supposed thinness of his tone. We were in his dressing room, and he picked up his tenor and played a solo using this great big butter sound. Not a Coleman Hawkins sound but a thick, smooth, concentrated sound. It was as beautiful as anything I've ever heard."

Young spent much of the rest of his life with Norman Granz's Jazz at the Philharmonic troupe. He had become an alcoholic, and his playing was ghostly and uncertain. He still wore suits and a porkpie hat, but he sat down a lot, and when he appeared on the CBS television show "The Sound of Jazz," in 1957, he was remote and spaced out. He refused to read his parts for the two big-band numbers. (Ben Webster, who had been taught by Young's father, replaced him.) When he took a chorus during Billie Holiday's blues "Fine and Mellow," his tone was intact, but the solo limped by. The loving, smiling expression on Billie Holiday's face may have indicated that she was listening not to the Lester beside her but to the Lester long stored away in her head. The tenor saxophonist Buddy Tate drove down with Young from the Newport Jazz Festival the next year: "I first met Lester when he was in Sherman, Texas, playing alto. A little later, I replaced him in the first Basie band when he went to join Fletcher Henderson. He didn't drink then, and he didn't inhale his cigarettes. He was so refined, so sensitive. I was with him in the second Basie band in 1939 and 1940, and he had a little bell he kept on the stand beside him. When someone goofed, he rang it. After the 1958 Newport Festival, I drove back with him to New York, and he was really down. He was unhappy about money and said he wasn't great. When I told him how great he was, he said, 'If I'm so great, Lady Tate, how come all the other tenor players, the ones who sound like me, are making all the money?'"

The arranger Gil Evans knew Young on the Coast in the forties and in New York at the end of his life: "Solitary people like Lester Young are apt to wear blinders. He concentrated on things from his past that he should have long since set aside as a good or bad essence. The last year of his life, when he had moved into the Alvin Hotel, he brought up the fact that his father had been displeased with him when he was a teenager because he had been lazy about learning to read music. But maybe his bringing that up at so late a date was only a vehicle for some other, present anger that he was inarticulate about. Sometimes that inarticulateness made him cry. A long time before, when I happened to be in California, Jimmy Rowles and I went to see Pres, who was living in a three-story house that his father owned. We walked in on a family fight, and Pres was weeping. He asked us to get him out of there, to help move him to his mother's bungalow in West Los Angeles. We had a coupe I'd borrowed, so we did—lock, stock, and barrel. Those tears were never far away. I was with him in the fifties in a restaurant near Fifty-second Street when a man in a fez and robe came in. This man started talking about Jesus Christ, and he called him a prophet. Well, Pres thought he had said something about Jesus and 'profit.' He got up and went out, and when I got to him he was crying. I had to explain what the man had said. I don't know where he got such strong feelings about Jesus. Maybe from going to church when he was young, or maybe it was just his sense of injustice. He couldn't stand injustice of any kind. He had a great big room at the Alvin, and when I'd go up to see him, I'd find full plates of food everywhere. They'd been brought by friends, but he wouldn't eat. He just drank wine. One of the reasons his drinking got so out of hand was his teeth. They were in terrible shape, and he was in constant pain. But he was still fussy about things like his hair. He had grown it so long at the back, and finally he let my wife, who was a good barber, cut it. At every snip, he'd say, 'Let me see it. Let me see it,' before the hair landed on the floor. It was amazing—a man more or less consciously killing himself, and he was still particular about his hair."

The tenor saxophonist Zoot Sims, who listened hard to Young in the forties, also saw some of this harmless narcissism: "We roomed together on a Birdland tour in 1957, and one day when he was changing and had stripped to his shorts, which were red, he lifted his arms and slowly turned around and said, 'Not bad for an old guy.' And he was right. He had a good body—and a good mind. Lester was a very intelligent man."

Young died at the Alvin Hotel the day after he returned from a gig in Paris. He had given François Postif a long and surprisingly bitter interview while he was in France, and perhaps wittingly, he included his epitaph in it: "They want everybody who's a Negro to be an Uncle Tom, or Uncle Remus, or Uncle Sam, and I can't make it. It's the same all over: you fight for your life—until death do you part, and then you got it made."

Dan Morgenstern

Lester Leaps In

Although he continued to tour and record, Young experienced troubled times in the mid-1950s. He needed to be hospitalized for a brief spell because of his heavy drinking and other health problems. By 1958 his touring schedule had been drastically curtailed. Marshall Stearns and Nat Hentoff, two writers who felt particularly close to Young, arranged to feature him at a party in honor of his thirty-year career. The party, given on Monday, June 2, 1958 (not on Young's birthday as often stated), was covered by Dan Morgenstern.

Morgenstern, director of the Institute of Jazz Studies, Rutgers University—the largest jazz archive in the world—is one of the leading jazz historians, and his help is acknowledged at the front of virtually every publication on jazz of the past twenty years, including this one. Moreover, he may be the only leading writer on jazz who is universally liked by the musicians! The author of hundreds of informative liner notes and booklets for recordings, Morgenstern is the winner of four Grammys for these efforts. He wrote the text of *Jazz People* (Englewood Cliffs, N.J.: Prentice-Hall, 1976), which earned him an ASCAP-Deems Taylor award, and has written scores of articles on jazz criticism, history, and on individual artists (including interviews).

Morgenstern was born in Munich in 1929 and reared in Vienna. His father, a Polish Jew, was a critic and novelist in Vienna whose close friends included the composer Alban Berg. When Dan was eight, the family fled

Germany and became separated: Dan and his mother lived in Denmark, then Sweden; the father made his way to New York City, where the family was reunited in 1947. Morgenstern immediately involved himself in the jazz scene. By 1961 he was editor of *Metronome*. Then he edited *Jazz* magazine, and from there went to *Down Beat,* serving as editor from 1967 to 1973. He has been at Rutgers since 1976.

Morgenstern delicately captures some of the ambiguity of the occasion, which was heightened by the precarious health of Young and pianist Bud Powell. Near the beginning he refers to Young having been recently "in a Parker mood" (incorporating a reference to the 1948 recording "Parker's Mood")—meaning that Young, like Parker, had been accused of self-destructive behavior. Morgenstern has a soft spot in his heart for this article, as he explained in *Down Beat* before the version here reprinted: "The fact that Lester Young read it, liked it, and told me so at what was to be our last encounter remains a highlight of my writing career. It is here dedicated to his memory." (All ellipses in this piece are in the original—I have not made any cuts.)—Ed.

This piece was written in 1958. It appeared, in somewhat different form, in the British magazine Jazz Journal *in August of that year. Lester's picture was on the cover. I gave a copy to drummer Willie Jones, who was then with Lester, and he liked it well enough to pass it on to Prez. This was at the time of what was to be Lester's last appearance in New York, at the Five Spot, and I went down to hear him. When Willie spotted me, he asked if I would like to come "backstage" and meet Prez. Would I! Prior to this I had been around Lester, had exchanged formal "how do you dos," but had never really talked with him. There was about him that presence—like a glow—which some who are touched by greatness have. One heard talk, in those days, that Prez was very "far out" and that it was difficult to communicate with him. Well, here was Prez, and he was warm, gentle, and fully aware (more fully than most of us will ever be) of what was going on. He was pleased with the story, which made me (I had just recently begun writing about jazz) as happy as a kid on his birthday. We talked a little about music and about life. Prez was looking forward to his impending trip to France—although he said that he needed some rest. When he came back to New York, I should give him a call ("You know the Alvin, don't you?") and we would get together. We shook hands, and Lester said in his soft New Orleans drawl: "What's your name again . . . Dan? . . . that's a date now, when I get back . . . I won't forget."*

Lester did come back, but there was to be no time for him to keep any date but that final one in the morning hours of March 15, 1959. Now, I want to share with you a memory of a moment in the life of a great musician and rare human being.

Monday night is jam-session night at Birdland. The regulars are off, the admission is lowered, and there is no minimum at the tables. Newly formed groups and lesser-known musicians are given a hearing. There may be a few "names" present, but more often than not they appear in supporting roles. There may be drum battles, flute battles, and unusual instrumental combinations.

On this particular Monday night, however, there was to be something else, something quite different. There was to be an anniversary party for Lester Young, given to celebrate his "Thirty Years in Showbusiness." The guest of honor, who was to appear with a group of his own choosing, was reportedly in a Parker mood—three weeks earlier he had opened and closed at Small's Paradise uptown on the same night. Lester, after arriving late, had fallen asleep on the bandstand. (Or so they said—later, one discovered that he had suffered a mild heart seizure.) It was said that he had the "No Eyes Blues," and bad. Thus it was a noble and missionary gesture that Marshall Stearns and Nat Hentoff, the sponsors, Morris Levy, the club owner, and Symphony Sid, the master of ceremonies, were making. In the world of jazz such gestures are rare; more attention is paid to the dead than to the troubled living.

Would Lester be there? And if he did come, would he stay on his feet? And if he did stay on his feet, how would he sound?

And Lester came—graceful sleepwalker; Prez hat and Lester face; beat but on the scene.

The house is full. The Lester Young Quintet is on stand—a young band, as Lester's bands have always been. A promising supporting cast: Curtis Fuller on trombone, a young hard bopper but not looking hard at all; Nat Pierce on piano, the unbilled member of Count Basie's Home Runners; Doug Watkins on bass, very young but already a name; Willie Jones on drums, even younger but a veteran of the Bohemia and the Charlie Mingus club. Lester Young mounts the stand. The downbeat is soft, the tempo medium. "Pennies from Heaven" is a haunted song. Not a mild summer rain this, but a gray November drizzle. The pennies are few, worn thin and smooth. The tone is choked, the phrasing halting—not from inability but from pain. The last note dies, and Lester looks up from a troubled dream. Silence. The faces of the musicians who have backed him, so gently, so sympathetically, are intent and serious. Then the applause: warm and strong and friendly—the applause of a jazz audience.

"Mean to Me" is not a lament but a quest—climbing in uncertain terrain, gaining a foothold, and finally reaching solid ground where one can walk once more. And Prez smiles, and the young band, having helped to bring on that smile, are in turn turned on. From then on it's walkin' and talkin'. Having prayed, Prez is now ready to preach. "Up 'n Adam" jumps. The master begins softly, gaining in volume and heat with each consecutive chorus (can one speak of "choruses" where there is unbroken continuity?), coming up shouting like the old Prez (did they say he was no more?) and suddenly there is a new, astonishing Prez as well!

Behind him, cool Doug Watkins, elegant in his double-breasted Ivy League suit, new in approach as well as clothes, is coming on like Slam Stewart's little brother, singing, bowing, and having a quiet ball. Shy Willie Jones, knowing how to drum softly yet hotly, knowing how to join the party without slamming the door, pawing the chicks and grabbing all the whisky, uncorks a drum solo that has a message and that is to be just the first in a triad of uniquely original excursions into time and timbre. And Nat Pierce is laying down the right chords in the right places as if he's there to help, striding out on his own, too, with his soul in the right place. And Prez—Prez walking over to whoever is speaking his piece, saying, "yes," "aha," "yeah"; digging everybody, saying, before taking it out, "Catch me somewhere along the way"; and going out with a Louis ending, while someone shouts, "Yeah, Prezerini," and there is some handclapping going. And when it is over, everybody is happy—Sid beaming from inside for a change, and Prez hugging his horn as he retires to his corner.

The other group makes its appearance. Alto, three trombones, piano, bass, drums—and four music stands. "In a Mellotone," by Duke Ellington. But where is Duke, where are the mellow tones? It's loud, man, and I do mean loud! Yet it is hard to hear anything. The alto has heard Bird, but only when he spoke in anger or frustration. The 'bones have heard J. J.; but have they heard Teagarden or Vic or Dicky? Machine gunners all: chief gunner, triple-tongue gunner, and burp-gun champ. There is no attempt at contrasts in mood or volume, and had there been, they would have been effortlessly demolished by the perpetual drum solo being played behind it all. And everybody blowing so long—oh, baby, how long! Everybody drumming, nobody singing; everybody driving, nobody swinging . . .

Off go the music stands, and Lester Leaps In. Horn up high, tempo solid, rhythm gentle but firm behind him. And then the stop-time thing; stop time; suspend time—go around it, behind it, in front of it—always on time and on to time. Lester leaping in and bouncing back, spiraling up like a diver in reverse, joining time and space in sound. I Got Rhythm and a Unified Field Theory, too. Can Prez still blow? Oh, baby!

The house is warm as down home now. "'Waterfront,' Prez baby," someone calls out when the last leap has returned us all to earth, with four bars of half-speed for gentle landing. The plea in the voice is explicit. "*Right* now," says Prez, gentle wailing Prez who has just made Curtis Fuller blow like you know he never blew before—maybe didn't even know he could. Prez covers the waterfronts, all of them. He covers them with a tenor saxophone sound that vibrates right through everything and everybody—as if the ocean were inside of us and Prez playing from in there, making us all his sounding board, bringing on the message from so deep within himself that it merges with all around him as he and his instrument have merged.

Almost without pause Lester glides into "Tea for Two"—fast, fast, but unhurried. Surging like a river, like blood through the veins . . . runs and cascades of notes, and notes whole and sustained: systole and diastole, that good old tension-relaxation riff: not one *and* one, but tea for two, me an' you . . . tea for we. And all so quickly from mind to mouth and hands . . . time and tone and chords and changes; no time to polish and revise, choices made and determining other choices, music once and for all in the making and the hearing. Here, hear and gone. (Sometimes grooved into wax immortality, the ephemeral made permanent—but how often when it is right, like this?) Tea for two, all for you, *right* now and gone—but leaving a message behind.

The music stands return: rattle 'dem 'bones, crash that cymbal . . . off we go! To where? To Lostville: too much sound and no true fury. Good hands, good skill . . . good will? Yes, but also frustration. Tense, not relaxed; alone, not together. Not together is not jazz.

LET'S GO TO PREZ! The sponsors and their guest having arrived amidst the 'boning, we are now ready for the ceremony. Lester is on stand, perhaps wanting to blow. But parties must proceed on schedule. Big cake and champagne brought in. Lester attempts cake-cutting ritual from stand. Impossible. Descends into space between stand and front table. Big cake. Lester blows out candles, smiles, shakes hands. Symphony Sid announces members of party. Includes a Dr. Cloud. Nice name for doctor. Lester cuts cake. Birdland cameragirl, instructed by official-looking gentleman, takes picture. Pop! goes flashbulb. The band watches. "He didn't look up," says cameragirl, plaintively. Lester plays a few bars of "I Didn't Know What Time It Was." Dr. Stearns breaks up. "Got the message?" asks Prez. Picture is ordered retaken. Lester picks up knife, makes like cutting cake, looks up and says, "Cheese." Flashbulb goes pop. Success! A toast. Bubbly and exchange of pleasantries. Lester is perfect gentleman. Excuses himself. Climbs back on stand. Party is attentive, but some late arrivals seem vaguely reminiscent of philanthropists at a benefit. Prez beats off "There'll Never Be Another You." It is nostalgic: wistful and tender but somehow removed. A part, who can say which, of the whole Lester is no longer involved. The spell is breaking. During trombone solo, distribution of cake commences. Guests at front table on left begin conversing. Not loud, but it spreads. Nat Hentoff is digging Lester. The party was a wonderful idea. The cake should have been cut later, the guests should have come earlier. Doug Watkins plays his first plucked solo of the evening. Prez and the band deliberate next tune. Familiar face appears on stand; Symphony Sid announces well-known drummer who asks to sit in. Willie Jones leaves stand slowly. Prez starts "Jeepers Creepers." Fantastic tone. The new drummer is a little stiff. He is louder than Jones, but not as sensitive.

And now something very strange is about to occur. A familiar figure is being shown to a front table. In brown suit, red shirt, and budding beard, Bud Powell seats himself. He hunches over. He digs Lester. He *digs* Lester. Thirty seconds pass. Bud leaps from chair to stand, gives Nat Pierce a hug, and takes over at the piano bench. It was a rather gentle hug, to be sure, but quite sudden. Nat, sitting at Bud's vacated table, looks as if he had seen a ghost. Lester, too, has seen him, but it is reflected only in his playing. In mid-solo he searches for Bud, but Bud is hard to find. Prez plays three choruses under strain, but he will not hurt Bud's feelings. And now Bud solos. He is trying to play everything he can hear. The fingers cannot always follow, so he sings. He sings a weird song, yet he is happy— he is possessed. Lester gazes upon Bud and gradually withdraws into himself. He shows no displeasure, only sadness. From the "bleachers" a little man is watching with an indescribable expression on his face. His name is Erroll Garner. He has been present since early in the evening, but he did not leap up on the stand. Where he lives that isn't done. Bud goes into a locked hands passage that gains coherence, but he is interrupted by the entry of the drums. A long, loud drum solo ensues. Bud, leaning over the piano, appears to dig it. Right now, he digs everything. Lester raises and lowers his horn, silently moves his lips, and politely waits the drummer out. He enters with the release and takes it out. He then talks into the microphone for the first time. "Ladies and gentlemen," he says, "I would like to introduce my trombonist, Curtis Fuller. He will play a slow-motion number for you." He acknowledges the sporadic applause and steps down.

The blues begin. Fuller is caught out twice by Bud's introduction. Then he just moves in, and Bud falls into line. His playing is much clearer now. He no longer sings, and he has adopted his characteristic pose: legs crossed, smile fixed like a mask. His solo is moving. He understands and perhaps is sorry; he just wanted to play with Prez. Fuller plays much better than any of the music stands. Perhaps he is angry.

Prez sits at the musicians' table, far to the left of the bandstand, where he also sat earlier between sets. His companion is a young lady dressed in black. She did not participate in the cake cutting. The official party is restless. Nat Hentoff is digging Curtis and Bud. The tempo doubles. I think of "Up 'n Adam." How long ago was that? Prez will play no more tonight. It is too late. The music stands return. The party arises, bids Prez good night. They should have come earlier. They did a great thing. I will never forget the celebration of Lester Young's thirtieth anniversary in show business. Some business. Quite a show.

Robert Reisner

The Last, Sad Days
of Lester Willis Young

Shortly after Lester Young's death, Robert Reisner wrote this touching
article giving a picture of the artist's private life during his last months. It
is especially valuable for the information from Dr. Luther Cloud, a psy-
chologist (or perhaps a psychiatrist, as he is identified here) who was
called in by jazz historian Marshall Stearns—the founder of the Institute
of Jazz Studies—to help Young. (You may remember that Cloud was at
the Birdland party reviewed by Dan Morgenstern.) Cloud tried in informal sessions to find out what emotional and psychological issues lay
behind Young's drinking, which had become clearly self-destructive by
1955. Some of his observations as recorded here are quite revealing.—Ed.

*(Editor's note: If Lester Young's influence was widely understood, the motivations,
the way of living, and the inner thoughts of "Pres" were not. There were many
misconceptions about Lester Young the man, and New York jazz writer Robert
Reisner would like to see some of them cleared up. In this blunt but strikingly
perceptive article, he recalls an evening spent with the musician and Dr. Luther
Cloud, a prominent psychosomaticist, only a few weeks before Young's death.)*

It was a large room in a hotel heavily tenanted by jazz musicians. Pres
owned a private house out in St. Albans, in Queens, on Long Island, but

he loved the lights of the city and preferred to be in the center of things musically.

Lester's one large window directly overlooked Birdland, and sometimes for as long as six hours or so in the evening he would sit in a chair staring down at the busy scene, a scene he had at one time completely dominated.

In Pres's room the phonograph ran continuously, maybe even when he slept, and on the night of my visit it was Frank Sinatra's output that was piled on the changer.

The room was bare, except for the usual hotel furniture. There was a picture of both his mother and father on his dresser—alongside his tenor saxophone, which was out of its case. A large, black porkpie hat (he wore it in the Gjon Mili movie short *Jammin' the Blues*) hung on the wall.

Dr. Cloud asked Pres how he happened to settle on that type of hat. Lester replied that he had once seen some Victorian pictures of ladies wearing hats like that, with ribbons hanging from them, as part of their riding habits. Their style appealed to him, so he had had one made especially for him. I asked the price, thinking he must have spent quite a sum. Pres's usual laconic answer to matters pertaining to business was "some change from twenty dollars." This was revelatory for Pres, who usually limited his answers to "bells" or "ding dong."

When Dr. Luther Cloud, a longtime friend and psychiatrist who visited and counseled Lester about once a week, asked him how he was feeling, Pres answered, "I'm cool, but I don't feel a draft." When Lester felt a draft, it meant he detected racial prejudice or unfriendly surroundings.

This was to be Lester's night for being an injustice collector. He poured out a stream of poetic profanity against the enemies he claimed were maligning him.

He hadn't been working often during the past months, and it hurt. Dropped as a casual remark was, "It's kind of bitter when all your disciples are working and you get a job once in a while." He complained of a snarled contract he was currently involved with and observed, "Things are bad, all the popes are dying." He wondered if it was because he had always had a longing to be different, not only in his playing but also in his speech, mannerisms, and dress.

I asked him about his friendship with the late Charlie Parker. He clammed on the subject as though it were some terrible secret. He did say that Bird had told him, "The kids coming up really have it made because they can pick up from the TV." Lester himself had two children, a boy of eleven and a girl two years old.

One thing that irritated Pres more than anything else was allegations by certain people who did not know him that he was a junkie or an invert. Neither charge nor rumor was true. As he put it, "I never even auditioned."

Dr. Cloud mentioned the fact that actually Pres was extremely needle shy. On one of his trips to Europe, he had bribed a doctor (not Dr. Cloud) to fake a vaccination. Dr. Cloud had a difficult time getting him vaccinated before his last crossing. The doctor had done the vaccination himself after convincing Pres it wouldn't hurt.

The bad rumors about Young may have derived from the famous story regarding "D. B. Blues," a well-known original recording Pres made for Aladdin back in 1947, after getting out of the army. It was based on Lester's only experiment with a strong drug.

While in the service in Georgia, he was in a period of desperate boredom. He rigged up a small still to concoct a weird brew consisting of grain alcohol, liquid cocaine (he had exchanged all his chocolate bars to get this stuff from a dental assistant), and fruit peels. This drink was capable of elevating your rank from a humble private to a space cadet. When the still was discovered, he was confined to detention barracks for [several] months. Thus "D. B. Blues"—meaning "Detention Barracks Blues"—was born from an actual experience.

Lester was vehement when he referred to the charges of homosexuality. "I wish people didn't fool with me, if they do I can fool them right out of their minds." He liked to affect the mincing walk and mannerisms of the invert, but it was a sort of stylistic joke or parody, like his love for the porkpie hat. Dr. Cloud substantiated the fact that Pres was straight on both counts.

I left the room that night feeling that Lester Young was the spiritual leader of the hip world and the quintessence of cool. One cannot truly have experienced jazz unless he has heard and understood "the President."

POSTSCRIPT—I talked to Dr. Cloud after Pres's sudden death at 3:00 A.M. on the morning of March 15, a few hours after returning from Paris. He died of heart failure, as does everyone with a heart. The cause was really a combination of malnutrition and cirrhosis of the liver.

The trip to Europe had not been a success. The *Melody Maker* in England mentioned a letter they had received from a club owner in Paris.

Lester walked into the club the night before he was to open. Stan Getz was playing his closing night, but Lester and Stan did not play together at the Blue Note that night, as was usually the case. Pres just sat at the bar sipping whisky and listening.

Pres was scheduled to play four weeks at the Paris Blue Note and then expected to join the JATP unit for more European concerts. He was too sick to play the last week in Paris. Basie boys who saw him said he hadn't been eating at all. This was partly because Pres rarely got enjoyment from food. He loved the heavily spiced food of New Orleans, which he didn't get often.

Dr. Cloud said Lester had wanted to get home fast because he knew he was dying. When he disembarked from the plane, he clenched his mouth so hard with the pain that his lips were bleeding.

A few hours later the man who held his tenor sax at a forty-five-degree angle for long solos (a habit he started back on the crowded bandstands of Kansas City so he would not hit the fellow in front of him) was so weak he could hardly lift a cigarette. He missed the ashtray when he reached for it.

Graham Colombé

Presidents Ain't What They Used to Be

Colombé's compilation of interviews with black musicians who worked with Young eloquently dispels the notion that Lester was always a taciturn, mysterious character. Pianist Sadik Hakim (formerly Argonne Dense Thornton), who toured and recorded with Young in 1946 and 1947, begins by saying that Young was a delightfully informal boss, and all the speakers remember him as a remarkable wit. The other musicians are drummer Connie Kay and pianist John Lewis, who worked for Young at separate times in the early 1950s before they ended up together in the Modern Jazz Quartet (MJQ), and drummer Jo Jones, Young's compatriot from his Basie days.

Graham Colombé is a college teacher in England who writes occasionally about jazz. He became interested in jazz as a teenager, and one of his first loves was the *Jazz Giants '56* album with Lester Young. He is also a songwriter who fondly recalls writing a song for Salvador Dalí, who was present at its performance.

Colombé told me, in a letter of June 12, 1989, that the name Lester Young opened doors: "All the musicians were very helpful once Lester's name was mentioned. John Lewis left Ronnie Scott's (where the MJQ was appearing) because the doorman wouldn't let me in, and came round the corner, for a coffee he probably didn't want, just to answer my questions. And Jo Jones would probably not have met me at all if it weren't for Lester."—Ed.

Originally published in *Into Jazz* (London), April 1974, 8–10. Copyright © 1974 by Graham Colombé. Reprinted by permission.

For further reading. The complete Jo Jones interview—most of which is not about Young—appeared in *Jazz Journal,* December 1972. Bassist Gene Ramey, who worked with Young primarily in the 1950s, usually has a little to say about Young when he is interviewed. For example, there are a few relevant paragraphs in *Jazz Hot* 174 (March 1962): 20–23, 28 (interview, in French, by François Postif), and in the Oral History interview at the Institute of Jazz Studies, Rutgers University.

The four people whose comments follow were interviewed separately, but it seemed on the whole more effective to intercut their remarks. In this context some of Jo Jones's statements, which have been published before, appear in a new light.

Sᴀᴅɪᴋ Hᴀᴋɪᴍ: When I was in Lester's band, he wasn't like a leader at all. He'd invite us into his room, and he'd be sitting there in his shorts with some music on the radio or record player. He'd always have music—any kind. Louis Armstrong was a favorite of his, but he'd listen to Charlie Parker and Dizzy Gillespie, too. We'd go in and sit down, and he'd give us something to drink and smoke, you know. Occasionally there'd be someone Lester didn't like in there, and we'd have to go through a big routine. Anyone he didn't like he'd call "Von Hangman," and he'd whisper to me or someone, "Von Hangman is here—we'll have to go out." So he'd tell this guy we were going out and we'd go with him and say good-bye, and then we'd go round the block and right back in again!

Jᴏ Jᴏɴᴇs: When we were along with Pres and all these other musicians, we didn't have time to think about this stuff, and I've told guys a lot of times, "Please do not get caught up in all this social crap."

Hᴀᴋɪᴍ: People used to make fun of him because they didn't understand him—they thought he was strange. At one time they were calling the band "Lester Young and His Six Faggots." Lester didn't chase after women every night like some guys, but every now and then he'd call up a woman he'd known some time before. He'd say, "I'm going to call up a way-back," and he'd go and see her.

Jᴏɴᴇs: Sensitivity? Here he was—Lester Young. Very sensitive. Lester loved human beings.

Hᴀᴋɪᴍ: He had a name for everybody. He called me "Lady Dense." [Dense was his middle name.—Ed.] I used to have the records I made with him, but after traveling around so much they got misplaced, left in different people's houses, and I hadn't heard them in years till I came back here to England. They were fun to hear again. I like "No Eyes Blues" and "Jumpin' with Symphony Sid" the best. It seems that what I played made more sense than on the others.

CONNIE KAY: I was working in the Bronx, and I knew the piano player, in fact I knew all the guys, in Lester's band at the time. He had a sextet with Jesse Drakes, Leroy [Jackson] and Junior Mance, and a guy named Jerry [Elliott] from Pittsburgh and Roy Haynes. And Roy Haynes quit. So Junior Mance and Leroy told Lester that they knew a drummer, and Lester told them, "OK, get him." But I knew Lester before I worked with him, and when I got the job Lester didn't know that I was the drummer they were getting, because he didn't even know I played drums. I knew him through a friend of mine who was in the army with Lester, and we used to go by and visit Lester every now and then and sit down and talk about army days, but he never knew I played drums. The first job I had with him was in Philadelphia, and I went down to Penn Station to get on to the train. Lester was standing up there, so I walked up to him and said, "Hey, man." I said, "Lester, what're you doing, standing up here?" and he said, "Well, I'm waiting on the drummer." So I said, "I'm the drummer," and of course he was very surprised!

Lester's was the last regular group I worked with before joining the MJQ, but it wasn't a permanent job. Twice a year he'd cut out and play with Jazz at the Philharmonic, and he'd do a solo so at that time the band would be laying off. I did a lot of free-lance work—record dates, playing in Birdland and with other bands—until Lester came back. Then we'd work a few clubs.

We never rehearsed anything. He never said anything to me about how I should play, so I guess he was satisfied because I kept the job. Lester never played over three choruses on anything. If he played four it was very unusual. There were times when I wanted him to play more, but he wouldn't. He'd always leave you wanting more rather than play all night till you'd get tired of hearing him. Charlie Parker was the same way—play two or three choruses and stop. These guys who stand up here and take fifteen or twenty choruses, man, after a while it gets monotonous. They play themselves out.

GRAHAM COLOMBÉ: It seems to me Jesse Drakes wasn't a good partner for Lester, musically.

KAY: We had a manager called Charlie Carpenter, and Jesse Drakes was the straw boss of the band. He was really more Charlie Carpenter's man than Lester's. If it had been up to Lester, he would have had somebody else, but that's the way things are.

JONES: At one time in Lester's life they said, "Lester don't sound like he used to." I said, "Who is he playing with?" That was the object of making the '56 record [with Jones and Teddy Wilson]. How the hell do you think I would sound playing with a bunch of high school kids?

KAY: Lester was nice—a sweet guy. We were good friends. I used to drive Lester to work every day. I was more or less his buddy, like when we went out on the road, we'd hang out together. A lot of things he said were funny, but they were funny in a serious way. Nothing he said was just funny—but he had funny ways of saying something that was serious.

JONES: When he and I talked, the way we talked nobody knew what we were saying. They never did.

KAY: When I first joined the band, I didn't understand his language, but after a while I understood, and I used to talk it, you know. In fact when I first joined the quartet, I used to talk it; it took me a while to get out of it, and Milt and Percy didn't know what I was talking about. Of course John had played with Lester.

JOHN LEWIS: I was in Birdland in Lester's group in 1950, but I knew him long before that. He and his family lived in the town where I grew up [Albuquerque], when I was small, about thirteen or fourteen. [Actually, Lewis would have been almost ten.—Ed.] So I heard him before he joined Basie. His family had a family band, and they landed in Albuquerque, New Mexico, and stayed there for a while. And he played there.

So I enjoyed playing with him later because of all the nostalgia—he knew my family and so forth.

KAY: Lester was sort of a shy person, you know. The only time he would like a crowd of people was when he was playing. He didn't like to go to restaurants because he always had the feeling somebody was looking at him. You know, somebody was talking about him, that kind of thing. He'd start eating, and if he saw somebody—they might not even be looking at him—but if he thought they were looking at him, that would ruin his whole meal. He'd say, "Come on, man, that cat is dragging me," and he'd put on his coat and he'd split. The cat might not even have been thinking about him. It was a mental thing.

He wasn't a nervous person—he just had that phobia about being around people other than people who'd come to hear him play. When we played a nightclub, you wouldn't see Lester at all except on the bandstand. When he'd come off the bandstand, he'd go in the dressing room, and he'd stay there till it was time for him to go back out again. If any of his friends came by, they'd go and have a few drinks with him in the dressing room, but you wouldn't see him sitting at a table with somebody or standing at the bar.

Was Lester depressed? Lester was depressed like all black musicians in the States that are talented and not appreciated, man. If you're not strong enough, it'll get to you. You go around the world and you see how other artists are appreciated and accepted and you wonder. Here's a guy who's talented, who's considered a genius, and what is he getting out of it? He's got to work like a dog to keep two cents in his pocket and feed his family and keep a roof over his head. And you see people less talented, and they're out there making it.

JONES: I do not understand why they take the black man who's the originator and take the imitator and give him this much money. Tex Beneke, "The World's Greatest Saxophone Player" in *Down Beat* and *Metronome!* He wouldn't have lasted as long as a snowball in hell in a Kansas City jam session.

KAY: When Lester died, I was surprised and I wasn't. I knew the way he was going he wasn't going to be around too long, but it hurt me that he did die. Lester's biggest fault was that he wouldn't eat. He'd drink all day and wouldn't put anything in his stomach. I used to go out and get him a steak dinner and bring it back to the room and put it down—and it would stay there. He'd send me out to get it; it wasn't that I forced it on him or anything. He'd say, "Go to the restaurant and get me so-'n'-so . . ." and then he wouldn't eat it. Actually the last couple of years of Lester's life I didn't see him that much—just once in a while. I'd hear he was playing somewhere and go by and say hello. The last few years of his life he had cut out from his wife and kids, man, he was living by himself, and that didn't help either. When he was with his wife, she'd make him eat, but after he left he was staying in a hotel by himself.

JONES: I had to bury Lester. Nat "King" Cole and Lee were coming in, but Lee just called me and said, "You got it," and his mother came. . . . It was a strange thing—every Saturday Lester wouldn't come out. We had a thing going about Saturdays. He checked into the Alvin Hotel, and he'd be upstairs, right across the street from the Birdland. There was a little bar next door, the Magpie, and when I'd got through doing some things downtown, I'd come in and get a drink and "Cheers" to him, you know, and then he'd hit double, meaning take another one. So I'd take another for him, drink his drink. I'd say, "Give me another, I'm drinking Lester's drink," and then I'm gone.

That Saturday I drove right in front of the hotel. Seems like I'm heading east, and the hotel's right here. I stop in front of the hotel and say, "Jack, I'm going to pick up a paper then go home." It's 2:30. He's upstairs dying. I was right downstairs. I got the paper, went home, put my feet up, looked at the sports page . . . Brrrrrring! Lester Young's dead. Back across town, and there he was, his hat and his horn. His wife was there, and there was a girl in shock, a very good friend of Lester's who just worshipped him. She said she'd wanted him to go to bed, and he said he wouldn't unless he had a drink. So she got a tall glass of water and poured a drink in there, to stretch it out. He got it and just laid down . . . Bam! Gone.

LEWIS: Lester was a very original artist and a very great artist, and he represents far more than any of his imitators can ever understand, because if you only hear the records and don't know the man and where the music came from or what's behind it, it's another thing altogether. His playing was a tremendous adventure all the time. There was always surprise, and he was a virtuoso, one of the great virtuosi of jazz. There are not that many that are great musically as well. He also represented a new kind of person in the American community, which later evolved as something we call "cool" or "hip." He was a poet, too, a great poet.

JONES: I saw Lester across the street in New York one day with one of his children—very young, you know. So I crossed over and asked him how he was doing. Now what he wanted to tell me was he didn't mind if the child wet itself, but he didn't want to clean up any shit. So what he said was, "I don't mind the waterfall, but I can't take the mustard!"

Bobby Scott

The House in the Heart

Bobby Scott's poetic and perceptive tribute to Young appeared in the
Gene Lees *Jazzletter*. Lees has been active in many phases of the music
business and has many close friends among musicians. Among the most
appealing aspects of his monthly publication are the contributions from
some articulate musician-writers.

Bobby Scott led a remarkable career. Born in 1937, he recorded as a
jazz pianist in 1953 (he told me that the "ca. 1954" date usually given is
wrong) and was already touring and recording with the Gene Krupa Trio
in 1955—including the Jazz at the Philharmonic tour described herein.
He also wrote the hit songs "Chain Gang" and "A Taste of Honey,"
recorded as a pop vocalist, wrote big band jazz and classical chamber
music, and—as he hints briefly toward the end of this memorial—was
something of an expert in ecclesiastical matters. In April 1989 he went
into the studios to record a tribute to Nat "King" Cole on the Musicmasters label; he died November 5, 1990.—Ed.

"We the whores, Socks," said the worn-out mouth. The bent shoulders,
old before their time, fought to maintain a balance that the weight of the
tenor saxophone hanging around his neck precariously played with.

Lester always seemed to be leaning like that edifice in Italy, a topple imminent, never to realize itself but seconds away at all times. I swear the crepe soles of his boot-style shoes bore an equalizing agent. Prez *teetered* in those last years.

He was without a sense of the time dimension, like waves lapping one into another on a beach, each so much a part of what was before and will be after that no discernment is possible. You don't count waves unless you are prepared for madness. I do not mean that his playing straddled time and eras, as we've come to catalogue them. No, his mind did. The style of Lester was fashioned within time and imprisoned by it. You knew where he was. But there was so much more to Prez than the notes that crept out of his horn.

"We the whores, Socks."

I was the right proper young fool in the autumn of 1955, when I went on tour with Jazz at the Philharmonic. Full of himself, as the Irish say. But at the time I thought I had a decent reason to make an ass of myself: I was playing with first-class musicians, and I was eighteen years of age. In fact I had been playing with pros since I was twelve, earning a livelihood, and had even recorded my first album, for Savoy, at fifteen. Now I see myself playing then as an exercise in frailing. I still won't listen to any of the records I made in that period of my life.

I had been hired by Gene Krupa (who turned me onto Delius, by the way) to fill the spot vacated by Teddy Napoleon. Krupa had added a bass player to bail out the one-handed piano players of the new generation. I certainly was one of those.

It's not clear to me where we started. I seem to remember Hartford, Connecticut. I came away from the tour with changed opinions and musical values, although this was not obvious in my own playing. Sadly, the experience lowered my estimates of some of the men and their music. But in some cases it raised them. I'd heard very little of Buddy Rich, certainly not enough to make a proper judgment. But his technical prowess alone was mind-boggling. Krupa said to me one night, in an odd matter-of-fact tone, "No one ever played like that before, chappie, and no one will ever play like that again." We were standing in the wings, watching Bud play one of his fabled solos, and Gene—I remember this vividly—didn't share my wide-eyed amazement. I was made to understand that Buddy was Buddy, and that was that. I think the old man envied me my newness of eyes and ears.

All the men on the tour had played too much and too long. I felt the frayed nerves on the plane flights, saw the drawn faces when certain hotels were mentioned, could almost weigh the years of singing for their suppers.

But I think of that time as the fall I met Prez.

"We the whores, Socks."

Lester Young was the first person I had known who was outside my ken. He was a visitor from a small planet. Everything that I'd imagined to be way out and bizarre was living reality in Prez. And he gave me more food for thought than anyone I'd met, excepting my music teacher, Edvard Moritz, and a Lutheran minister named Jacob Wagner. But neither of them had the totality of Prez's person. His was a world, fully constructed with all the loose ends tied up, that created reality could not and did not puncture, not even slightly. Prez reminded me that there was such a state as St. Paul spoke of when he said categorically, "We are *in* this world but not *of* it."

I wondered about his spectral being every second I was in his company. It cut through every tidy notion I had formulated about the meaning of this existence. That he was upsetting to many people is an understatement. His voice did nothing to relieve a searcher's quandary. As it was in him, buried deeply, that to impose himself was somehow not fitting, the converse occurred. St. Anselm says that theology is "faith seeking understanding," the intent of intellectual exercising being the effort to create a "religion" or overt practice, the exercise of one's faith making it into a fortress that can stand up easily to the assaults of Reason. However, faith creates its own brand of counterreason and couches itself in felt words, rather than legalistic scientific terms. That leads me to phrases like "You don't find God. You lose yourself until God finds you." That is the quality of understanding Lester required, if in your search for him you eventually noticed that he had found you.

What struck me most was his openness to younger musical talent. It wasn't patronization, a tip of the hat to the coming generations. It was genuine, and his interest constant.

Norman Granz that year presented every member of the touring party with a battery-operated record player. It could be set on one's knees and gave a decent reproduction, considering the tiny speakers. I ran out and purchased some records, one of which was a wonderful album by Jimmy Giuffre on Capitol, which featured a trumpeter then unknown to me, one Jack Sheldon. Prez didn't cart his own phonograph about with him, for the compelling reason that he could only apply himself to the care of his clothes, his whisky, and his horn. I had no notion then of the virtue of paring down one's duties in life. Prez, unlike myself, knew what he could and could not handle. So my phonograph was shared with him. But only in the measure that he listened, for never once did he ask me to play a recording he knew did not delight me.

Prez fell in love with Jack Sheldon's tone production and melodic invention. Sheldon played a solo on "I Only Have Eyes for You" that Prez found so agreeable—and I, too—that we damn near wore the cut out. Prez tried repeatedly to get one of the trumpeters on the tour to take an interest in this young man's talent, to no avail. As the man was in Lester's age group, Prez used him as a measure of what one should not become: deaf to the newer generations. I became acutely aware of the differences in how Prez and his colleagues looked at life through the microcosm of music. His playing might be imprisoned by the years of his youth, but his hearing was not.

I was looking upon an actuated illumination. Other people perceived that illumination incorrectly. The uninitiated might think that what one saw in Prez was the defeat of the human spirit, or the surrender to alcoholism. Some no doubt thought they were seeing an expression of homosexual dislocation. The puzzle of Lester Young. An alcoholic he might have been; homosexual, no.

I came to think his was the exquisite loneliness that comes of a splendid type of isolation. His heart was an Islandman's heart, the heart of one unhappy on a mainland. It put him outside the temporal stream of life, much like an Aran Islander, judging tides with his eyes before trying twenty-foot waves of the ocean in a curragh made of skins and sticks and spit that no sane boater would take out on a quiet mountain tarn in northern California. And the most shocking thing, in gaining knowledge of where Prez was at, was the wholesale misunderstanding of everyone who crossed his path. He was half to blame for it, to be sure. But it was his dearest, his most precious fault, this almost inherent obfuscation.

Being black in America produces its own survival mechanisms. The most obvious and necessary is a facade. But I am not sure that Lester's behavior can be so easily explained. He was born in a time when "race relations" in the Deep South had indeed formed separate communities— separate worlds, really. To hear him speak of his childhood was to be treated to experiences wherein the outer white community wasn't even mentioned. It is quite possible that in a place such as Woodville, Mississippi, the two never met. Yet he gave no indication of a general condemnation of any group of people. In his words he expressed many attitudes—but never contempt. In fact, his moral posture was refreshing and, surprisingly, rang of a pure Christian view in which offenders are seen as pathetic. It was as if he were more concerned with *how* an offensive person "got that way." But he was pragmatic enough to know that there are junkyard dogs and junkyard dog mentalities. I think what made him almost sympathetic to bigots was his deepest understanding of what they had paid for their hatred and how unrewarding the whole exercise must be.

But he had his own fiction and had transfigured it into the beautiful solos all of us who loved him are familiar with. That some people couldn't exorcise their demons as he did, I'm sure, led him to his sympathetic posture. It wasn't with condescension that he looked upon offensive people. That would have taken him where his heart wouldn't allow him to go. So he pitied, felt bad for such misguided souls. I'd call him Gandhi-like, except that Lester was more perceptive than that overrated ascetic.

If Prez was made to feel he wasn't wanted, he left long before he had to be asked to. I remember him saying wistfully, as he looked down at the passing acres of American heartland from a DC-3, "Sure as hell is enough room for everybody, ain't there, Socks?" Thus he summed up the over-stuffed cities as culprit.

I always felt he was *visiting* pockets of urban discontent, bringing a message. He often looked at the city we had just played and were flying away from with eyes that brought to mind the words of the Carpenter about shaking the dust of a town off one's sandals.

Dusting off one's sandals and blessing the unfriendly congregation was, in his case, initially effected by Scotch and marijuana. As he spoke less than almost anyone I have ever known, I came to read his silences, hoping to see what it was that he wasn't saying. He once said to me, "The best saxophone section I ever heard is the Mills Brothers." That made me laugh, and made me think. The Mills Brothers, a vocal quartet, had a blend one rarely heard in the sax section of a band. This kind of indirect-ness, the very hallmark of his verbal expression, enhanced the misguided ideas about him. Not that he gave a damn. It bothered me, though. Truths become throwaways if life deems that they emanate from an eccentric.

By his late years Prez was more revered than taken seriously. This was to everybody's loss. For his judgments on music had risen from the same source as his unique musical improvising. Oh, I can't say that hearing him live in 1955 was as invigorating as his recordings of the 1930s and 1940s. He had become debilitated and, worse, bored. But not with music. More with his own making of a contribution.

At eighteen I found nothing sacred. I still am not a hero worshipper, believing Admiral Halsey's evaluation that "there are no great men, only little men who do great things." I do lay claim to an understanding, a historical one, of just where Lester fit into jazz, and how tall the shadow he had cast. One had only to listen to Zoot and Stan, or Art Pepper and Paul Desmond, to hear Prez's voice, his heart, hurdle a generation. I leave out the obvious players like Brew Moore who more imitated Prez than were stoked by him. Once, told of a player who "plays exactly like you" and was even called the Something Prez, Lester said, "Then who am I?"

In fact, I think Lester was tickled by my sacrilegious attitude toward giants. He chuckled and chortled at my teenage mind's evaluations. He saw jazz, as I did, as a counterculture, knowing that whatever the critics tried to make of it, it would remain inaccessible to people more disposed to swim in the broad river of Culture than in a streamlet.

Like all good things, jazz is inherently at odds with what is around it. Like philosophy, it contends for ears and hearts and minds. It will never rule, for its nature is to subvert.

One of the great poetic voices of the twentieth century, Padraic Pearse, went to his death relatively unknown and largely unpublished but secure in the knowledge that he had fathered the Irish Republic. (He led the Easter uprising of 1916.) In a poem called "The Fool," he said, "Oh, wise man, riddle me this. What if the dream come true? What if millions shall dwell in the house shaped in my heart?"

When a man is miscast and talented, he of necessity builds a house in his heart to live in. Some men, like Pearse, though dead, build dwellings that others live in. Jazz players are miscasts, too,—my mother quite seriously considered them social mutants—and in their case there are further difficulties in that their houses are not discernible to the casual listener. Their playing then remains—to the large audience—noise from reeds, bent brass, and wind columns. Even noise of course can serve a simple purpose. God forbid that the majority had no noise at all. What then would drown out their own hearts' voices? Mantovani has halted countless important discussions, stayed the dissension in all too many breasts. It is as if Andy Williams typified Voltaire's "best of all possible worlds." (Aaron Copland once bitched about hearing Brahms on Muzak in his bank. The manager said he thought it better than pop music. He didn't understand Copland's reply that he liked to "prepare" himself for Brahms.)

We're all like Pearse. We all try to build houses inside ourselves. Some, like Pearse and Prez, have their houses recognized and the dream becomes a reality that someone can dwell in; and some insinuate the dream and themselves into the main flow of time and culture. They're ofttimes whole communities, as in the cases of Bach and Beethoven. And the most alienated has the greatest need to build a house in his heart, so that he may find a home. From this perspective it is easy to see Kafka's work in an understanding way—or a projectionist like Bradbury. The physical disability of deafness, in the cases of Beethoven and Fauré, might have affected their ordering food in a restaurant, but little else. When told that he was deaf, Beethoven shouted, "Tell them Beethoven hears!" He had long since taken up residence in the house he shaped in his heart.

A talent has a design. The walls are its totality, not its limitation. Within them are color and decor, shades or venetian blinds, tissuelike curtains filtering light. And these houses are filled with other voices, soft compelling ones, abrupt rhetorical ones, often angry voices seeking more than an ear.

The visiting of such a house can impel the guest to go about building his own or, at the very least, cultivating an interest in esoteric architecture. I have always seen my own heart as a door. But it has no knob on the outside. It can be opened only from the inside. If you have been following this rather oblique line of reasoning, you'll know we have arrived at the second phase of the search.

What would make a Lester Young open his door and let us in?

Ten years or so ago a prominent tenor saxophonist with a reputation of giant proportions needed a rhythm section for a gig. Another pianist asked whether I'd do the job. I didn't know the saxophonist personally, so I went to hear him with the players he was using at the moment. I came away confirmed in my mind that the man had no intention of pleasing *any* audience. The evening was a study in antisocial behavior, back-turning included. I am not talking about an off night. We all have those. All this man's nights were "off" nights.

I pondered the reason for his display, knowing I was going to take a pass on the gig, truly wondering why a mature person would be doing something that so obviously pained him. When I remembered Pascal's warning that the brain is a cul-de-sac, I realized that the man was probably trying to open his heart and not succeeding, and I felt sympathy. His heart was locked, from fear of critical judgments. I was made to evaluate the enormous weight of character and balance required for the successfully lived life. Most important of all in his case was the absence of courage. Pure courage. The kind only lovers know of. The kind of giving that opens one's whole person to scrutiny and judgment. And criticism.

Lester had no such problem. He was never touched by such a fear. The point is rather simple. Prez exhibited the bravery of the human spirit. The remarkable aspect of his offering informational aids to my young self was the way he made me absorb them by osmosis. He seemed to be engaging himself in conversation and allowing me to sift through the points made by both sides. He didn't sell me. "It's all in the *way* you look at it, Socks," he'd say, reminding me how powerful were the fictions of life, and how the *way* in which you viewed them altered them for good or ill.

I don't want you to get the idea that Prez was a fountain, gushing forth knowledge. If you had asked Prez a ridiculous question like, "Do you hate Pollacks?" he'd have answered, "I don't know them all." He had an ability to see through many fictions ("Walter Cronkite and the seven o'clock white folks' news," he called it). [I don't think Cronkite was hosting the seven o'clock news until after Young died, so it was probably his predecessor, but the point still holds.—Ed.] And often his own questions ended as answers! He didn't presume to possess intelligence, either. That alone was refreshing, considering that he was forty-five and could have cried out his empiric gatherings. But he didn't even trust himself. He was in every way an outsider, vigilant and artfully suspicious.

That fall of 1955 saw a dream boxing match that made partisans of everyone on the tour. Archie Moore was challenging Rocky Marciano for the championship of the world. Archie was the overwhelming favorite among the musicians. I call him Archie, familiarly, because on several occasions he sat in on bass with my trio. He was no player, of course, but he did thump his way through some blues.

Buddy Rich and Birks, as Dizzy Gillespie was called by friends, led the voices for Moore. All the musicians wanted to lay bets, but they all wanted Moore. Only Prez was for the Rock. So dutifully, he bet "thirteen of my motherfuckin' dollars" with every musician who was hollering for Moore. Lester never did explain to me why he always bet no more and no less than thirteen dollars on anything.

When they had firmed the bets, saying, "You're on, Prez," Lester whispered to me, "Who they think bein' sent in there with Moore? Little Lester?" (He referred to his own son.) "The Rock knocked Joe Louis's ass *through the ropes!*" he chuckled, hearing Buddy and Birks proclaiming Moore's virtues and Marciano's failings. Being a fight fan myself, and having boxed in the amateur, I saw it as a toss-up with a slight edge to Marciano. The Rock had a cast-iron jaw that had been tested and a resilient nature that he had proved against Jersey Joe Walcott. Marciano's fight with Ezzard Charles saw him hit about as hard as a man could be, and still he came away a winner. And he took just a bit better than he could give.

The fight is history. Marciano put the challenger away, but not before Moore provided some first-class moments of his own. He came close to dropping Marciano, but you don't get paid for *close*. Marciano topped off the falling Moore with a hammer blow to the top of the head that would drive someone of my weight through the canvas.

And Prez gloated.

"Give me my motherfuckin' money," he taunted, at the referee's last count, digging into his colleagues' sensibilities in an unkind way, which surprised me. Later he said to me, "*You* should have bet a lot o' money, Socks. They got off too easy." It dawned on me that in laying it into him for his prediction of the outcome, they had offended him. And it seemed that it didn't matter to some of them that they had, as if Prez were not a part of the family, if that's what it was.

Even the respect shown him was often perfunctory, and too many musicians seemed merely to suffer him. (Illinois Jacquet was an outstanding exception.) I was suffered, too, reminded by the musicians in an exquisitely subtle way that at my age I was not entitled to an opinion. I've often thought I came by Lester's friendship as a result. We were both suffered.

In his early years, Prez told me, he'd had trouble at jam sessions. His playing had put more people off than it turned on. He said it was his aversion to gymnastics and the "big" sound. Although he thoroughly enjoyed some of his colleagues—Bean, Byas, and Ben Webster to be sure—he wasn't influenced by them. He mentioned, rather, solos by the Louis Armstrong of the 1920s more than he did his fellow tenor players. Prez didn't arpeggiate in the style of his age. His was a more horizontal linear expression, more in keeping with the approach of a trumpeter, trombonist, or adventurist singer. That distinction is the key to his heavy influence on later players.

It doesn't take a speculative genius to surmise that Getz, Pepper, and Desmond did not like the natural sound of the saxophone. Possibly the enigma of the bastard quality of the instrument—half reed, half brass— nettled them to soften and neutralize it. Prez did the laboratory work for all the successive players and pointed the *way*. Nor do I mean to minimize their accomplishments.

Prez was less harmonic than Coleman Hawkins. His preoccupation with the pentatonic scale sang more of his Mississippi folk roots than it did of his later big-city life. It evoked a country preacher more than a street-wise tart. Zoot often makes me feel Prez is in the room, when he's playing a piece that allows for that brand of proselytizing. Peculiar it is, too, for it makes less use of the blues than it does rural folk elements. That Zoot plays in that manner, coming as he does from a suburb of Los Angeles, can only mean to me that he didn't merely stay in the foyer of the house Prez shaped in his heart. Prez has become a *Tao*, a way, a path. Few artists in the twentieth century have had so many surrogate vicars.

OK, you may say, you've got a point, but I think you're making a mountain out of a molehill. The man played "simple," easily digestible solos. His facility wasn't in a class with the other giants I can name.

I give that argument its due. There's much sense in it and a modicum of truth.

But once I asked Prez why he didn't play certain licks, which everyone I knew did, knocking out a few of them on the piano for him. His face took on a great incredulity, and he fired back, "That's the way Bird played!" He paused, and then he said, "He plays those licks, I play my licks, you play your licks." I nearly fell off the piano bench from the weight of his truth. I had been raised in the high noon of bebop, and wherever I went in those days, I was judged by how well I had adapted myself to the Holy Writ of Bird, Bud, Monk, and Birks.

I am always amazed at how well Prez *wears*. His expression is not one of *immediate* importance, like Charlie Parker's was, nor so energetic in the rhythmical sense. (Bird suffered terribly from rhythm sections that were a decade behind him in understanding.) Bird was subjective and biting, Prez more sedate and objective. Bird's playing was locked into the range and the character of the alto. That is why the bit of tenor playing he did on record is nondescript. In contrast, I am forced to remember how interesting Lester's clarinet playing was. Lester could move into a new setting— export himself, as it were. Was it because his playing was so organic? Was his conception more melodic, of its very nature?

I remember walking into a nightclub where he was performing with a local rhythm section. "Oh, Socks, baby, I'm glad to see you here! This boy playin' piano plays *very well*. But he puts eight changes where there oughta be two! You know me, Socks. Somethin' like "These Foolish Things," I mean, I like the E-flat chord, the C-minor, the F-minor seventh, the B-flat nine. You know. Shit. I can't play when there are eighty-nine motherfuckin' changes in the bar!"

I spoke with the pianist, who wasn't as yet aware what Prez liked to hear behind him. Whether he followed my suggestions or not, I never learned, because for Prez every job ended sooner than later. I mentioned the incident to him at Birdland one night a month or so later, and he was puzzled: it was ancient history by then, and he couldn't raise up a memory. All he remembered of my visit in fact was my outrageous show business silk suit, required by the straight-up singing act I was doing at the time. A stranger he remained, alienated from the moving parts of watches and never noting the differing structures of cities or the many faces he would pass.

For those who became his intimates—alas, a surprising few—he took on a Lewis Carroll dimension. At times his innocence was baffling. Lester could say, "I don't believe it!" and *mean* it. Most of what we see in life is so destructive, so bizarre, that most of us experience a confusion not unlike Prez did. I still have not adjusted to the notion that there are best-selling diet books, going at fifteen or twenty dollars a pop, in a world in which ten thousand human beings are starving to death *each week* in the Horn of Africa. It was only when I realized how hard it was for Prez to commit himself to understanding the unrepentant world out there that I connected a hidden portion of him with the rest of his behavior.

You could call him superstitious, though not to the degree that it froze him. Willie Smith, he once told me, was a "number" person. Prez said that if Willie came up with the wrong numerical position on boarding a plane, he was apt to get off it. Lester felt a huge surge of anxiety if a very ill person—or worse, one in a wheelchair—got onto our flight.

"God damn it, Socks," he'd groan, "it's a Johnny Deathbed!" His eyes would remain fixed on the plane's entrance—until he saw a child, or an infant, board. If it was an infant, he eased immediately, noticeably. Although he never talked about religion, Prez let me know that the Deity was to be taken for granted. He obviously believed in the fair mercy of God, for the presence of the infant on our flight ruled out any chance that God would take out the entire flight to collect the Johnny Deathbed. The implications that vibrated outward from this view amused, and stimulated, me greatly. It was Lester's conviction that people about to take the Big Journey ought to be in their "cribs" waiting, not out here where innocents might have to share their fate. He felt we shared responsibility with the Deity and had to "get our shit together."

I always felt that I must have said something or done something that *signaled* Prez. He was a believer in such things, always open to the unspoken, the unexpected, even to the unwelcome sign. It is told that he had two weeks left of a gig in Europe in 1959 when he upped and flew back home to his almost immediate death. A sign, no doubt, danced before his eyes in Paris.

There was a brilliance to Lester's otherworldliness that made me weigh what is called *educated*. Lincoln defined learning as telling ourselves what we knew all along to be the truth but were afraid to tell ourselves. Prez *sensed* everything. He was somehow aware that the gray matter in the cranium is a first-class deceiver and relied on intuition. Once, when we were looking for a restaurant in a city new to both of us, he said too comfortably, "One more block, Socks, and we'll eat." He was right! I've since credited a good deal of his obliqueness to a preoccupation with inner voices he let lead him. Often people thought they had run up against an alcoholic mist too thick to penetrate. But that was rarely the case. He just wasn't listening, for there were moments when his lucidity was remarkable, although his intake of grass and booze had been his usual.

His day-to-day existence was like a pendulum. Besides, he was a night person. The day for him was a many-houred awakening of a long-toothed spirit. He *entered* the evening. Even the quantity of his words increased as the light of day waned. It was as if he'd climbed a ridge of small hillocks, then settled into a golden period, a span of bewitched time. In a very real sense, his day was ushered in by the pushing of air columns through instruments, the heartbeat of a walking bass, the glistening punctuations of a ride cymbal. His sticklike body, so worn by his utter disregard for its health, straightened to its limit only during those hours of music. And the music turned on his capacity for camaraderie and humor.

For a reason I have never been able to isolate, he shouldered the burden of being resident jester on that 1955 tour. And he was good at it. His brand of storytelling was unique. It was littered with so many "motherfuckers" that it was shushed down, and out, when we found ourselves in the company of the general public. But when we traveled in quarantine, he was allowed to stretch out, and never since then have my sides ached so much.

He would have mock fights with Roy Eldridge and other "shorter" fellows who would grab his arms as if to do him up. "Midget motherfuckers!" he would cry in pretended desperation. "Lawyer Brown, Lady Pete!" he would call to Ray Brown and Oscar Peterson. "Socks! You gotta help me with these midget motherfuckers!" Only Prez could carry it off. For minutes afterwards, he'd mumble to himself, still in his fiction and dramatic mockery, "Those . . . *midget* . . . *motherfuckers!*" And he would say, "Socks, I could take 'em—one at a time! But the midget motherfuckers gang up on me! They gang up on ol' Prez!"

Nobody ever made so much fun so consistently, so hard, so freely. Sometimes, when he was on a roll, it went on for days. Not jokes or one-liners, although he had a few of those. No, it was always situational and personal. As I'm writing this, I can *hear* him again, hear the fake dramatic pauses, the ham acting, the truncated exclamations he was known for and, most of all, the disarming sweetness. The bastard!

It takes a considerable amount of confidence to laugh at one's self. "Dr. Willis Wiggins," as he referred to himself, had it. He knew all about what Rodney Dangerfield has turned into a science. Prez tripped that thin line between self-deprecation and wholesome abandon. To my eye, un-seasoned at the time, there was a truth I couldn't see.

He had the courage that makes for *self.* The quality of bravery that never asks dumb questions or looks for conspiracy in honest words. The great danger of *becoming* your musical expression was one to which Lester never succumbed. It set him apart from other musicians, made less by their inability to be something other than their music. No one who knew him would call him a "regular guy." Not ever. But he *could* be, if he so chose. That in itself broadens his humanity.

Most players of note get used to applause, as they do to the growth of their vanity. Prez acted upon Solomon's assessment that *all* is vanity. He never promoted himself to me, or anyone, in any way. It was odd. Most of the musicians I've spent time with always touch that base, either quietly or with trumpeting.

I got behind the wheel of my car yesterday, and the radio was on with ignition, automatically. The exquisite lyrical tones of Paul Desmond jumped out at me, and my first thought, if sweet Paul will forgive me, was Dr. Willis lives!

A lot of things seem to have changed since 1955. Even memories are refurbished. I find myself reevaluating friends and family, thinking of collisions of Will and Personality, the packets of wrong words we have all let slip at one time or another.

But Prez never changes.

He alone makes me look to my "gate receipts," as he called all bottom lines, and check out the bases of all social comings-together I deemed important over the years.

That he is gone, and has stopped, frozen in time, has only strength-ened the outline of his self in my memory. A handful of people I've known have a near degree of his definition. But no more than a handful.

He never spoke of his lineal roots, but there was no mistaking his being a product of woodpile philanderings. His skin was off-white, a light coffee alabaster, and his hair an obvious auburn that was darkened by a conk. When it was in need of a conk, Roy Eldridge would whisper to me, "Call him a big red motherfucker, Socks. He'll jump up and down."

His clothes draped his frame. I took it that he'd lost weight and simply wouldn't waste money playing at being a fashion plate. There was something rumpled, but not disheveled, about his appearance. His walk, which was more a shuffle than an honest walk, had something Asiatic about it, a reticence to barge in. He sidled. It was in keeping with the side-door quality of his nature. He was punctual. He started early and left later than most of us, maintaining his cool and living rhythm, but his pace was that of a sleepwalker. I think that Prez thought there was nothing worth hustling for.

The two of us, like old Pick and young Pat, shilly-shallied most of the time, rapping. He liked to draw on the romantic liaisons that littered his youth, hoping I'd learn something from the retelling. While he was living with one aggressive and hostile lady, he said, he took to putting his horn, in its case, into a garbage can outside her house before he entered, never knowing how she'd react to his absences, catting. So he took no chances with the "Green Horn-et," as he called the case.

One night, though, he'd had enough of her "beatin' up my ass." So he decided to do a little number himself. "You oughta've seen the bitch . . . drop t' her knees, Socks. Bitch hollerin', 'Don't make a fist, Prez, please don' make a fist!' Shit, I tol' the bitch, 'You been using your goddamn nails on ol' Prez for a year now!'" He'd pause, the light that made the bloodshot eyes seem so alive going down, and he'd look me square in the face. "You *gotta* be a man 'bout some things, Socks."

There was, of course, a lot of comic bravado in his kiss-and-tell stories. But I took away from them an idea of what I might expect if I continued being a gypsy with a song that had to come out.

He was too gentle to have kicked ass. I couldn't imagine him doing it. I might get into a fight, but not Prez. Yet he harped on taking a stand. The late Jack Dempsey said to me, "Don't ever let people use the name you had to fight for, kid. Never." He said it in a restaurant called Jack Dempsey's, which he did not own. And he echoed Prez.

Lester was inclined to remind me that music was a universe and that I ought not to sit only in a corner of it. His own attitude was one of discovery. I once asked him what would most knock him out, and he answered, "My own big band, with Jo Stafford and Frankie-boy as my singers." The few feet between us became a revelation ground as he touched on things no interviewer ever asked him about. His tastes were catholic, and when he liked something, you couldn't run it down to him.

He forced me to think of *music,* not just jazz, and I thank him for it. In fact I had to watch out for his underselling, or I might have come to the conclusion that jazz was no more than an aberration. It's not that he downgraded it. He just took the edge off my idolatry. I thought of jazz as my life's breath; he thought of it as second nature.

It wouldn't have surprised him that a man like Leonard Bernstein would have liked to play jazz. Lester would have encouraged him, regardless of the fact that Bernstein wasn't a first-class jazz talent. For Prez it was unthinkable that the joy he had known would not be of interest to a fellow countryman with musical ability. I suspect that Lester believed no one owned music. Not even a part of it. I welcomed that openness. Few players have earned a niche like his, but there he was, sundering the very notion of the proprietorial.

"You can't own . . . what ain't, Socks."

How could someone "own" what those still unborn might say on a horn twenty years hence? Once I mentioned a talented bass player of real stature who was a rabid racist. A despairing look came into that quiet-eyed face as I told him a story of a man's unkindness, saying that none of us is responsible for the tone of his skin. Prez then told me a story about a man who thought he had lost something valuable, only to remember in his panic that he'd left it at home. "Ain't no truth there, Socks. That's the only good thing about mirrors. They make you look at yourself."

And then he said that a fool makes the other man pay for his inadequacies. And because he doesn't take the loss himself, "he loses the chance to find out who the fuck he is." Prez said that such people hungered for something they had never given themselves. Trouble was, he sighed, "nobody else *can* give it to them."

He was dying then.

I knew he was. I dreamed, and I rationalized. But there were moments when our eyes met and the weariness in his told me. Like an old maid, I counseled him to take better care of his health. It occurs to me now how I bored the shit out of him by doing that.

Prez had come to me, to life, from out of nowhere, really, and it seemed he'd always been around, like the wind in October and the weeping clouds of March. Where would he go, in any case? A person such as Prez *is.* But there were signs. A few shallow-sounding laughs. Twice, quite remarkably, he referred to himself in the past tense and didn't seek to rectify the mistake.

The bottle of Scotch he carried in a red plaid bag was always in his lap. It took priority over his horn and clothing. I began to see that his juicing had gone through the worst form of transubstantiation. Booze was medicine now, and I wasn't fooled by his excuses, good as they were. I remember the sadness that came from that lonely face—that of a kid whose candy had fallen into the dirt. He's been dealt a low blow, his greatest pleasure having been turned into an anesthetic imperative.

Two "sanctified" old ladies lived behind Prez on Long Island, their yards abutting his. They had never conversed with him, indeed did not know him or anyone else who didn't belong to their church congregation. As Lester dressed rather zoot-suity, drank, and played jazz, they had reached their own opinion of him.

One summer afternoon, while the ladies were back-porching and gossiping, Mr. Young and his son, Little Lester, sauntered into the yard and commenced to toss a ball around. The ladies couldn't but start revising their opinion of their neighbor. "Isn't that nice?" they chirped, watching father and son.

They were still watching when Prez decided he'd had enough ball tossing. He and Little Lester walked to the back door. Prez tried the knob. He turned his face down toward Little Lester and said, "*There*, you dumb motherfucker, you done locked us both out the house!"

The ladies never recovered.

Prez used profanity—and *all* language—creatively. And he had the oddest gentle way of saying *motherfucker*.

In a Texas airport he came under the scrutiny of some Texas Rangers. They looked at him as if he were a Martian, in his crepe-soled boots and porkpie hat with the wide brim, forgetting of course their own western headgear. Prez elbowed me and whispered, "Go tell them I'm a cowboy, Socks."

In the winter of 1956, I made a vocal recording that became number one on the hit parade. The "success" it brought ruined the quality of my life and sent me off doing an "act" in nightclubs that, thank God, I never did carry off well enough to be marketed like a bar of soap.

During that time I ran into Lester. After the greetings and questions about immediate family, he said, pointedly, "They say your hat don't fit no more, Socks." I was taken aback. I told him, "That ain't the story, mornin' glory."

He smiled and said, "Letter A, then, Socks," meaning of course, back to the top.

There were entire conversations like that. Countless people said to me, after hearing us talk for a few minutes, "What the hell was he talking about, Bobby?" In the 1980s his behavior would be regarded as mild. So, too, Lenny Bruce's. But being inaccessible didn't help Prez.

Lester was very aware of how people broke hearts with their tongues. A man misjudged as often as Prez was, and offended so easily, would know about that. Accordingly, his own observations were couched in "unknown" terms, that he might not give offense. I saw it as very responsible behavior. In any case, Prez wasn't a presumptuous man and considered his judgments no more important than anyone else's. He was sensitive but not touchy. He took the ribbings of his colleagues well. For instance, every few nights, with much aplomb and mock assurance, Oscar Peterson would lay in those "extra" chord changes during Lester's solo in the Ballad Medley. During a concert in the Montreal Forum, Prez sidled back to the nine-foot grand piano, unaware that just below him and inside the instrument was an open microphone. Turning to Oscar his puzzled, pleading face, he said, "Where are you motherfuckers at?"

The audience's laughter sounded like Niagara Falls.

Norman Granz told Lester to stay after the concert. I found him sitting cross-legged, his face as forlorn as the head of a cracked porcelain doll.

"What are you waiting for, Prez?" said his worshipping eighteen-year-old friend.

His eyebrows raised, in acknowledgment of his faux pas. "Lady Norman's gonna give me a reading." He winked. "I bought it, Socks," he said, as I walked slowly off the stage, looking back and thinking how much he seemed like a kid kept after school.

He never said he thought Norman was wrong about the incident, and he credited Granz with bailing him out of many predicaments.

He had names for everyone, or almost everyone. For some reason he never invented one for Herb Ellis, who, like Lester himself, is a very gentle man. But Lester hung "Sweets" on Harry Edison, and now everyone knows him by that name. And he gave the title Lady to men—Lady Pete, Lady Norman, Lady Stitt, Lady Krupa. And he gave me my name. Because I was the youngest member of the troupe, Bobby Scott became Bobby Socks, and then just Socks.

As a vehicle for his high humor, he conjured up a conspiracy against the two of us. Often, if we boarded a flight at the last minute, the seats we got were served dinner last. Too often we were just digging into our food when the plane began its descent. Lester trotted out his paranoia, blaming everyone from the midget motherfuckers to the White House. I couldn't eat for laughing. He'd squinch up his face in a deviltry that could bring me near to wetting myself, and mumble, "You see this shit, Socks? You see *this?*" He would shake his head, glancing furtively toward the back of the plane where "the enemy" sat. His voice, still softly clandestine, would push out. "They're tryin' to *get* us, Socks." And I of course had to go along with him or let the splendid humor of it die.

The quiet that surrounded and covered Lester was of a contemplative nature and origin. If he allowed me to "divert" him, he did it out of an interest in, and a love for, me. He didn't need diversion. Small things could and would draw his interest and attention.

Whatever he was in his totality, and no one is privy to such knowledge of another, the one observation I could make about him was that the peace that emanated from him was a glowing proof of a *balanced* personality.

Happiness depends, it has always seemed to me, on the health of one's moral condition. Lester was a happy person, no more besieged than the rest of us. But he had the conviction that gives a fighter staying power. He never gave up what was consistent with his values. He skirmished frequently, as sensitive people do, with becoming a number instead of a name, a figure rather than a living person, a reputation instead of a producer of beautiful music.

He knew what made him happy and what he would have to tolerate, and his baleful puss told you how hard it was sometimes to keep apart the rights and the wrongs in the affray.

At the time, I found his complaints nothing but griping. Now that I am a man and have, as the Indians say, walked a mile in his moccasins, I have become an echo of those gripes. He experienced doubts of tremendous size and often converted them before my eyes into something else.

When I arrived at the airport apron one morning, I made my way through the small group of passengers and found Prez with a perplexed and doom-filled face, eyeing our aircraft. It was a DC-3, slightly worn-looking but otherwise apparently fit.

"Socks baby, it's a *two-lunger!*" Prez felt much safer in a four-engine craft. "We gotta have a *four*-lunger, Socks! Shit! You lose one, you still got *three!* One of *these* motherfuckers goes, an' we only got *one* lung left!"

Moments later, having accepted the inevitable, he was sitting next to me, back in his groove, snapping his fingers at the engines outside the window, and hollering (to the chagrin and embarrassment of the tour members): "Get it! Get . . . *it!* God . . . damn . . . IT!"

He talked to the engines, shouting his encouragement as we barreled down the runway. He was still hollering, to the shushing sounds of

Ella Fitzgerald and Norman Granz, when the creaking weight of metal lifted up out of the uncloroxed clouds into the sunshine.

He smiled then. He had fortified himself with Dewars. He whispered, "It's only gettin' here that bothers me, Socks." I told him I had no inclination to be a bird, either. And yet he trusted the pilots implicitly. "They got their shit together," he said.

I have never enjoyed traveling as much since then.

Nor have I ever met anyone who wore aloneness as forthrightly as Prez.

St. Augustine offers us this: God created man that man might seek God. The implication is that even God cannot escape loneliness. Nietzsche quips, not untruthfully, that crying is the same as laughing, except that it is at the other end of the same rainbow, differing only in intensity, not character. Why is loneliness the major tone quality of large cities, where millions congregate? Is Augustine right? Or is what we call "loneliness" an outgrowth of personal dislocation, inasmuch as we are among the multitude? Are we, as the bishop of Hippo implies, made in the image of our Maker, and marked by the loneliness of His own dispersal?

One can safely say that the groundbreakers in the arts are nearly always testaments, monuments, to loneliness. What the artist seeks to offer to others he must hone by himself. Does he then give us his solitariness? Are not the solitary and the lone one and the same? And why is it most likely the source of all the world's joys?

I trust Augustine and believe that loneliness is the glue and ether of existence. Further, how one handles it marks one's life as successfully lived or as a failure. The friendship I developed with Prez was marked by the reeking exquisiteness of his loneliness. What confounded me, and still does, was what made him confident enough to lower the weir that damned his precious solitariness and allowed me to join with it, in concert.

When music is not pedantry, as in Buxtehude, or gymnastics, as in Varèse, or structure, as in the canons of Bach, it is the transfiguration of the loneliness its creator has come to acknowledge and live with. Lester's sound was profoundly beseeching. It sought out the tired residue of the greatest war a human being wages, the one with and inside himself. Prez echoed his own despair, raising it miraculously until it took on a new aspect. What better way to serve one's brothers in loneliness? To be able to express one's own deepest feelings of limitation and incertitude, breaking the fetters and raising up the specter in others so clearly that they begin to see the silhouette of their own solitariness, is a reward unto itself.

For me the best moment of each evening was Lester's solo in the

Ballad Medley. That year he played "I Didn't Know What Time It Was." I never became bored with it. I realized that it was his sound production and phrasing that seduced me. And there was, to my ears, a reverent quality that he instilled in the notes. Although he couldn't help but sound labored and worn, it was the voice of a sage, and there was no shooting from the hip in it. He had to work harder than the other players. They were healthier. He was deceptive, though. I swore I heard hectic winds when he looked me squarely in the eyes. On those few occasions I did indeed see defeat there. But I could do nothing that would alter the situation. At eighteen I wouldn't take it upon myself to inform the powers that be that he might be unable to perform. But on he'd trudge, miraculously, his crepe-soled shoes scraping . . .

He plays the melody so well that it is a bit of a shock to me. Me, who learned three-quarters of the tunes I know purely harmonically. Prez won't play a tune if he doesn't know the lyric—the entire lyric. Knowing the lyric, he makes the shape of his offering more organic, his phrasing elegant. Ultimately Lester shows me *who* and *what* I am; he makes it come to life in his playing. In among the notes I find my recognizable shape and identity.

The tired figure of a man who befriended a boy walks on and points the bell of his horn upward in a strange supplication.

Then come the tones of wonder.

Ralph Gleason

Pres: Lester Young

When Young died, a flood of memorial articles appeared in every language. Ralph Gleason was among the most beloved writers on jazz, as well as the producer of some important jazz series for public television. His sensitive style made him a favorite of the musicians themselves, and this short piece is the one that Lee Young asks everybody to read about his brother. That recommendation alone is enough to secure it a place in this volume.—Ed.

For further reading. Among the more notable memorial tributes from the European press are Maurice Cullaz's reminiscences of Young's visits to Paris in "Mon ami Lester," *Jazz Hot* 143 (May 1959): 13 and 15; a thoughtful piece by Lucien Malson, with photographs of Young's funeral, in the French *Jazz magazine* 48 (May 1959): 20–25, 38; and Dieter Zimmerle's "Der President," *Jazz Podium*, May 1959, 112–13.

Pres died last Sunday morning in a hotel room in New York, and if you don't know who Pres was, you've missed a great part of the native music of America in the past thirty years.

The jazz fans knew him, all right. Everywhere in the world. And last

Originally published in a 1959 newspaper article; reprinted, with revisions, in *Celebrating the Duke and Louis, Bessie, Billie, Bird, Carmen, Miles, Dizzy, and Other Heroes* (New York: Dell Publishing, 1975), 83–85. Copyright © 1959 by Ralph Gleason. Reprinted by permission of Mrs. Jean Gleason.

Sunday night when Ed Walker made the sad announcement at the Sands Ballroom, the audience went "Ooooooooh!" in shock.

For Pres was the President, Lester Young, one of the real giants of jazz music, whose tenor saxophone playing created sounds and phrases and melodies that are inextricably wound up in almost all of jazz music today. He was one of the three great instrumental soloists of jazz who changed the course of this music—the other two, Louis Armstrong and Charlie Parker.

If they built statues to jazz musicians in this country instead of to politicians, there would be one of Pres in Kansas City, for Lester Young of New Orleans and Count Basie of Red Bank, New Jersey, put Kansas City on the musical map. They did it together in the 1930s when the slight, limp figure of Pres, his horn held out sideways, his eyes shut, and his head back, was a familiar sight to the thousands of jazz fans all over the country.

Pres was Kansas City jazz incarnate.

He was only a tenor saxophone player, you say. Oh, no, he was much more than that. Much more. To begin with, he was a poet, sad-eyed and mystical, hurt that the world was not in actuality as beautiful as he dreamed of it. So he made it the way he wanted it with his art—his own beautiful world into which all the paradox and misery of the real one could not enter except to be cleansed. He let us share it with him, and when he died, every jazz fan in the world and every jazz musician lost a member of his family.

Had his natural inclination been painting or sculpture, his master-pieces would be hung on the walls of the great galleries of the world and mounted in the courtyards of palaces. As it was, he etched a tiny portion of his art into the grooves of phonograph records, where it will remain, a treasure for the listener, as long as we can play them. The rest of his precious music he gave away as freely as the wind, in countless jam sessions in after-hours clubs and hotel rooms and basements all over the world, in thousands of choruses of the blues with Count Basie, in ball-rooms and theaters, and in years of nightclubs working with his own band and on countless stages with Jazz at the Philharmonic. That is the music we'll never hear again. That is the lost art of Lester Young.

But there are memories of those times. I never knew him, except most casually, but I have vivid memories. Let me tell you of two. One night in a basement club that used to be a Chinese restaurant in downtown Oakland, Pres gave me a cigarette out of a case that was a foot long and then went on the stand and blew the most beautiful, light, and feathery blues I ever heard. Another night, twenty years ago in the Famous Door on Fifty-second Street, the Basie band was stacked up at the rear of the room with the trumpets knocking on the ceiling. The sound was so great, so intense, that it became almost solid enough to walk through. Out of this acoustical wave Pres, with long and wavy hair and a thin wisp of mustache, rose and whispered, "How d'you do there!" It cut through the brass like a bullet, soft as it was, and hit me right in the pit of my stomach. I almost cried. I can almost cry now thinking of it and the fact that in reality his recognition is still only from a few.

Yes, Pres's memory will outlast sports heroes, scientists, and generals who have been *Time*'s Men of the Year. Because his music set up the ringing of chords in the minds of men that will last as long as the human race.

Frank Büchmann-Møller

The Last Years of Lester Young

Büchmann-Møller has been mentioned several times already as the author of two important recent volumes about Young. The present article contains material that he researched after his books went to print. Thinking back upon several stories about Young's health in later years, he began to suspect that Young's problems were more than psychological. This led him to medical research similar to the sort of work that physicians have done on Mozart—looking back over reports of the symptoms in hopes of finding a logical diagnosis.

Because Büchmann-Møller is an experienced and levelheaded researcher, his conclusions deserve to be heard. If he is in fact correct that Young had serious physical problems, this changes our picture of Young's late years considerably. It also helps to reconcile the disparate portraits of Young, on the one hand as a happy and warm person, and on the other hand as a strange and depressed individual. Perhaps Young was a well-adjusted human being after all, and very happy with his delightful family in New York. Perhaps the deep sadness he carried around with him was not about fame or plagiarism or insecurities—or at least not only about these things. Perhaps his secret was that he was dying from a physical ailment that could not be treated. If so, his life and death no longer seem pathetic—they become tragic.—Ed.

Originally published, in slightly different form, in *Jazz Times*, September 1990, 9.

Among the most interesting and fascinating jazz musicians—but also among the most misunderstood—is the black tenor saxophone player Lester Young (1909–59). Practically alone he created a musical language that influenced a whole generation of musicians of all instruments. Many players adopted his mannerisms as well, such as wearing porkpie hats or dark sunglasses, and some even tried to copy his way of talking. His playing up to about 1950 was consistent, imbued with logic and beauty and in up-tempo numbers also with plenty of drive. After this time the quality of his solos varied, and some critics even condemned what they perceived as his constant decline.

Young was popular among his fellow musicians, always in good spirits, and gifted with a wonderful sense of humor. But like his music, his behavior after the war changed to a certain extent, and he withdrew more and more socially. On tours with Jazz at the Philharmonic, for example, he always checked in at a different hotel from the one originally booked. Actions such as this made him an enigma and led to many hypotheses as to how one of the most brilliant musical minds could change so drastically within ten years.

Of course Lester Young changed—we all do—but when listening to all his issued and unissued recordings, you will find both ups and downs through the 1950s. He was declining, but slowly, because of a disease that gradually affected him mentally and physically, resulting in performances of varying quality. To his death he still could produce superb solos presented with wit and beauty, but along with these came performances where his playing showed no enthusiasm at all.

New information about his disease helps us to arrive at a fairer judgment and understanding of his playing and behavior during his last years. He was restrictive with information about himself, especially concerning his private life. Although he had many friends, only a few were taken into his confidence, and even his closest friends were not told the secret that had such a profound effect on him. On September 30, 1944, this secret was officially detected at his induction into the army in Los Angeles. Young's medical examination revealed that he had contracted syphilis and that he occasionally suffered from epileptic fits, one of the complications of the disease.

It is not known where or when Young caught his syphilis, but in

1944 he must have suffered from it for at least seven years, because as early as 1937 he and three other members of the Basie band had been diagnosed with the disease. All four musicians were asked to undergo treatment, which in those years meant several injections with an arsenic-based compound like Salvarsan alternating with compounds of bismuth. The treatment had only limited effect on the early stages of syphilis, and in Young's case the disease might have been more advanced at that time. In any event the treatment apparently had no effect, because his syphilis remained latent for the following fifteen years. For blacks in those days it was more the rule than the exception to go untreated for syphilis, especially with traveling musicians like Lester Young, since treatment could take weeks or even months to complete.

In 1943 penicillin was tested on syphilis, and it proved effective in curing all stages of the disease. But even after that time Young showed no interest in a cure, maybe because he never really understood—or refused to realize—the seriousness of his disease and therefore never allowed himself to be helped.

We can only guess why Young didn't want to be treated, but several musicians including Bobby Scott, Gil Evans, and Thad Jones noticed a self-destructive trait in Young. Furthermore, several times during his last five years he talked about a wish to die, probably brought on by an awareness of his deterioration.

Based upon the fact that a couple of Young's complications resemble tabes dorsalis and paresis, he must have acquired the form of syphilis called neurosyphilis. Tabes dorsalis usually appears after a lapse of fifteen to twenty-five years, and its most common effect is a series of degenerative changes in the spinal cord or spinal nerves. One result is loss of sensory perception and reflexes, which certainly would have affected his dexterity and ability to execute his musical ideas in fast numbers. Thus he avoided fast tempos, a fact that can be noticed especially in live recordings from 1958 to 1959. A visible symptom of tabes dorsalis is an unsteadiness of gait that becomes more pronounced in the dark, and this accords well with Young's characteristic broad and slow walk; it might also explain why he at times entered the stage sidestepping.

Paresis usually affects patients in their forties or fifties, and in Young's case it caused him insomnia, depressions, and emotional in-stability that sometimes made him cry, all conditions described by col-leagues like Willie Jones, Gil Evans, Jo Jones, and Buddy Tate. Luckily for Young his paresis seemed to be mild, so he avoided some of its worst complications like grandiose visions, loss of bladder sensation, and impotence (his last child was born about two years before he died). More serious for his health was that the syphilis caused him a lot of physical pain, which increased over the years. He tried to allay his pains with different forms of strong alcoholic drinks, and his daily consumption grew to such proportions that already by 1940 he could be described as an alcoholic. Of course his body could not stand this strain, and he developed cirrhosis of the liver and portal hypertension, which in the end led to his untimely death by esophageal varices, that is, internal bleedings caused by varicose veins attached to the esophagus.

It is remarkable that Lester Young, despite all his ailments, was still able to retain his marvelous sense of humor. In 1957 Thad Jones, then a member of the Basie band, took part in a tour that also featured Young. Jones roomed with Young and also sat next to him on the backseat of the bus. He recalls, "You could feel pain in the man, I could, but he was still one of the most humorous. He had the greatest sense of humor you'd ever seen in a man in your life. It was a beautiful sense of humor. He was able to laugh at life. In the midst of all of the pain of it, he was able to laugh at it. That's probably the greatest tribute I can pay the man."

Sources

Balliett, Whitney. "Pres." *New Yorker,* February 23, 1981, 90–100.
Benedek, Thomas G. "The 'Tuskegee Study' of Syphilis: Analysis of Moral versus Methodolic Aspects." *Journal of Chronic Diseases* 31, no. 1 (1978): 35–50.
Büchmann-Møller, Frank. *You Got to Be Original, Man! The Music of Lester Young.* New York: Greenwood Press, 1990.
———. *You Just Fight for Your Life: The Story of Lester Young.* New York: Greenwood Press, 1990.
Davies, Russell. "You Just Fight for Your Life, till Death Do'ee Part." *Listener,* August 13, 1981, 138–39.
Jones, Jo. Interview by Milt Hinton, January 15, 1973. Jazz Oral History Project, Institute of Jazz Studies, Rutgers University, Newark, N.J.
Jones, Thad. Interview with author. Knapstrup, Denmark, December 31, 1984.
Jones, Willie. Interview with author. New York, November 16, 1985.
Kampmeier, R. H. "Syphilis Therapy, an Historical Perspective." *Journal of the American Venereal Diseases Association* 3, no. 2, pt. 2 (1976): 99–108.
McGrew, Roderick E. *Encyclopedia of Medical History.* London: Macmillan, 1985, 329–35.
The Merck Manual of Diagnosis and Therapy. 13th ed. Rahway, N.J.: Merck & Co., 1977.

Scott, Bobby. "The House in the Heart." *Jazzletter* 3, no. 2 (1983): 1–8.

Tate, Buddy. Interview by Gary Giddins, March 1980. Jazz Oral History Project, Institute of Jazz Studies, Rutgers University, Newark, N.J.

United States Army Reserve Personnel Center, St. Louis, Mo. Military file, Private 39729502 Young.

Part Two
Young in His Own Words

Naturally, in putting together the history of an artist, the most important witness is the artist himself or herself. Young told his life story several times to the press beginning in the late 1940s—his period of greatest fame and success—and one might well think that the following chapters should have been in Part One instead of the various secondary accounts represented there. But that's not the way oral history works. Young's interviews are the starting point for every researcher, and many of the pieces in Part One included some of his words, but the final results include many details that Young could not possibly have remembered, and others that he chose not to remember. Besides, like anyone else, Young could remember things he had done but not necessarily with the exact dates.

So I present Young's own words in this section, not as testimony to his "real" life story but for exactly what they are—Young's words. It is fascinating to hear the way Young talks, even though he was heavily edited in the earlier interviews. I transcribed the last two interviews directly from tape. The same stories come up in each interview but are told a bit differently. Young is consistent about the details of his life and is an honest storyteller. Even debatable details sometimes turn out to be our problem in understanding him, and not his fault; for example, he said he toured with King Oliver for "about a year," which at first glance seems impossible, until one realizes, as Laurie Wright pointed out in his King Oliver book, that Young probably meant "on and off for about a year."

It is equally interesting to notice that there are some details about which Young is not so candid, the most notorious being his birthplace. In the first few interviews he says he was born in New Orleans, but in the later ones he clarifies that he was born in Woodville, Mississippi, and later moved to New Orleans.

But those readers who have already read Part One know Young's life story. The point here is to enjoy "hearing" his voice. For that reason I have not corrected Young's words at all, even when there are obvious factual errors such as the birthplace. On the other hand, when the interviewer's narration contains errors, I have emended them as I have throughout this anthology.

The Billy Young band (Minneapolis, 1927), in one of two posed publicity shots taken the same day. According to Leonard Phillips, the personnel from left to right should be Otto "Pete" Jones; Phillips; Ben Wilkerson; Lester's father, Billy Young (in his mid-forties, waving his violin bow as a baton); Ray Jones; Arthur Williams (a trumpeter posing with what was probably Young's tuba); Gurvis Oliver; probably Clyde Turrentine; and Lester Young at the far right, aged about eighteen. Notice that Young is holding an alto saxophone and has a baritone and straight soprano (on which he doubled) in front of him. Photograph courtesy of Alvin Tolbert. (Tolbert, a nephew of Lester and older brother of Jimmy Tolbert, is a retired engineer in Washington, D.C.)

Lester Young (left) and Benny Goodman (right), WNEW radio studio, New
York City, mid-1938. Goodman—who loved Young's style—is seen playing
together with Young while in the studio to appear on Martin Block's "Make
Believe Ballroom" radio show. Young angles his saxophone out to his right, his
characteristic stance until the mid-1940s. One title from the broadcast survives
and was issued on IAJRC record 14. The exact date of the broadcast is
unknown; Russell Connor guesses that it was July (see his Goodman
discography). Photograph courtesy Loren Schoenberg Collection.

The Count Basie orchestra, World's Fair, Treasure Island, San Francisco, California, October 1939. Young is quite a sight, in his sunglasses and fashionable attire of the day—wide pants and all—as he angles his saxophone toward the microphone for his solo. Notice also the hat mutes for the brass. *Left to right:* Buddy Tate (with the end of Freddie Green's guitar showing behind his head), Benny Morton, Earle Warren, Harry Edison (playing trumpet, with sunglasses), Dickie Wells, Jack Washington (holding an alto saxophone, his baritone beside him), and Dan Minor. Photograph courtesy Institute of Jazz Studies, Rutgers University.

Lester Young in Savoy Ballroom, New York City, December 1940. This picture was taken just before Young's big split with Basie. The band was at the Savoy from November 30 through December 12, and Young left before the recording session on December 13. The photograph is by the late Otto Hess. Courtesy Loren Schoenberg.

Young's first group after leaving Basie, at Kelly's Stable, New York City, February or March 1941. This is the rarest of three shots of the group and has not been published before. *Left to right:* Shad Collins, Young, Hal "Doc" West (at the drums), John Collins (no relation to Shad), Nick Fenton (bass), and Clyde Hart. Photograph by Ray Levitt. Courtesy Institute of Jazz Studies, Rutgers University.

Lester Young posing with band members outside the Capri Club on the
afternoon of a rehearsal, February, March, or April 1942. Lee and Lester
Young played in a band with "Slim and Slam" at Billy Berg's Capri Club
beginning February 24, 1942. Within a few months the Capri had closed, and
the group moved to Berg's new Trouville Club. *Left to right:* Slim Gaillard,
Jimmy Rowles, Bumps Myers, Jake Porter, Lester Young, and Slam Stewart.
Photograph courtesy Jimmy Rowles.

Lester Young at Café Society Downtown, New York City, September or October 1942. This beautiful photograph, taken during the engagement with Lee Young, is a little-known companion to the famous one shot from below. The other tenor saxophonist, Bumps Myers, is partially visible in the background. Photograph courtesy Institute of Jazz Studies, Rutgers University.

Lester Young with the Al Sears Band, February, March, or April 1943. During
this period Young played with the big band of fellow tenorist Al Sears at the
Renaissance Casino and Ballroom in Harlem, where this photograph was
probably taken, before they went on a USO tour of American service bases.
The bassist on the left is Wellman Braud, and Sears is at the far right, standing.
Note that Young, seated second from the right among the saxophones, sports
the mustache typical for him of this period, and he is still using a metal
mouthpiece. By 1944 he switched to a hard black rubber mouthpiece.
Photograph courtesy Harry Swisher.

Lester Young with Jazz at the Philharmonic tour, 1952. The troupe is seen here arriving at Amsterdam's airport, April 12 or 13, 1952. *Left to right:* Hank Jones, Roy Eldridge, Flip Phillips, unknown (facing Norman Granz), Norman Granz (with hat on, surrounded by several unknown people without hats), Max Roach, Young (with his saxophone case), Oscar Peterson (partly hidden), and Irving Ashby. Ray Brown and Ella Fitzgerald, who were married at the time, were also on the tour but are not in this photograph. Photograph courtesy Harry Swisher.

Lester Young (left) and fellow saxophonist Flip Phillips (right) in the midst of an animated conversation, backstage at the Jazz at the Philharmonic concert at the Colosseum in Oslo, Norway, February 21 or 22, 1953. Photograph courtesy Harry Swisher.

Allan Morrison

"You Got to Be Original, Man"

As seen in Part One, Young had been newsworthy before he ever made records. But this 1946 article was probably the first to be devoted entirely to Young ("Lester Young," a French essay by Eric Guillod, appeared in the *Hot Club Magazine* [Brussels], March 1947, 10–11) and almost certainly the first anywhere to include interview excerpts. The innovative *Jazz Record* magazine was coedited by pianist Art Hodes, who is still playing and writing today in his eighties, and other musicians were contributors as well. Young was not a writer, and his portrait was prepared by Allan Morrison, one of the few black writers on jazz, who later wrote for *Ebony* (and is quoted in Hentoff's article, above). Young must have been more comfortable with a black author than with a white one.

Young reviews his basic life history but also talks about the importance of originality—hence the title—and discusses the overwhelming influence that Hawkins had on other saxophonists when he was growing up. The reason for Young's leaving Basie that is given by Morrison, and by most of the other authors in this section, is the story about Young not showing up for a recording on Friday the thirteenth.—Ed.

Lester Young, whose many adherents will tell you is far and away the greatest contemporary jazz tenor saxophonist, passionately believes orig-

Originally published in *Jazz Record,* July 1946, 7–9; reprinted in *Selections from the Gutter,* ed. Art Hodes and Chadwick Hansen (Berkeley: University of California Press, 1977), 225–28. Copyright © 1977 by The Regents of the University of California. Reprinted by permission.

inality should be the highest goal of art and life. Without it, he says, art or anything else worthwhile, stagnates, eventually degenerates. He maintains, furthermore, that musicians wishing to say something really vital must learn to express their inner feelings with a minimum of outside influence.

These views were expressed just the other day by the famous tenor artist during an informal conversation between jazz musicians that was held under the best possible circumstances for such talk—a smoky hotel room lighted by a single pale-green bulb.

Outside the skies were gray and a fine rain sprayed gently through the open window. From a disc spinning on a tiny turntable on the floor, the husky, sensuous voice of Billie Holiday flowed all around the room and did soothing things to the ears of the men who listened.

Lester lay across the bed, his belt unbuckled, his half-closed eyes looking up at the ceiling. Every so often he would follow the solos on the records by making funny little humming sounds always in perfect tempo with the music. Sometimes Vic Dickenson's bold trombone choruses shook him out of a luxurious lethargy and made him write crazy patterns in space with his forefingers. No one else moved. No one else spoke. Billie Holiday was insinuatingly saying, "You Go to My Head."

Finally someone broke the long silence and asked Lester wasn't he born in California? Lester said no, and there was a pause. "I was born in Mississippi," he confessed, and there was a tinge of embarrassment in the way he said it.

"But I was raised in the carnivals," he went on. There was real pride in his tone this time.

"The carnivals?" someone asked.

"Yeah, travelin' carnivals, minstrel shows, y'know." The words now began to tumble easily out of Lester's mouth. He was reaching back into the past and remembering things he seldom talked about. His eyes opened wider as he spoke, and he gestured slightly with his hands. He spoke of one-night stands in southern towns and of the peculiar impermanence that characterizes the life of the itinerant musician.

He spoke, too, of the musical prowess of his father, Billie Young, a very remarkable man, who "played all instruments" and gave him the only music lessons he ever received.

Papa Young led a family band that toured with minstrel shows. Lester started playing with the band as a drummer when he was ten. Then he shifted to alto sax.

What made him change instruments? someone wanted to know.

"Bein' lazy, y'know," he replied. "Carryin' all them drums got to be a real grind. I decided I'd better get me a lighter instrument. That's all there was to it, man."

An alto saxophone having been duly obtained, he set about mastering that instrument with the aid of his father. But Papa Young was too busy a man, and after a few weeks the lessons stopped.

He hates to talk in terms of influences because he feels that a real musician doesn't need influence outside of his own imagination and responsiveness to life. So when someone asked who was the biggest single influence in his career, Lester arched his brows and said, "Nobody, really."

Frankie Trumbauer, a white alto player who gained some fame during the twenties, impressed him quite a lot, he said. One record in particular left a mark on his musical mind, "Singin' the Blues," on which was also featured the great Bix Beiderbecke, the poetic trumpeter of jazz's golden age, who died in 1931. Lester carried a copy of "Singin' the Blues" around with him and played it over and over again.

Bix, he remembers, sounded "just like a colored boy sometimes. He was fine." Beiderbecke's lyrical beauty of line and tone moved him. Trumbauer's startling technique made him conscious of how little he knew. He plugged away at alto for five years, covering a lot of territory but always managing to come back to Kansas City, where he did a considerable amount of free-lance jobbing.

In 1931 [actually 1928] he ran away from the family band. "I just wanted to be grown," he said in explanation. That left but seven playing Youngs. Lester drifted into a barnstorming life, starved a little but learned a lot.

While playing with an aggregation styling themselves Art Bronson's Bostonians, he changed instruments again, this time taking up the tenor saxophone. The Bronson band had its headquarters in Salina, Kansas, but got around a lot of the Southwest area.

"What made you change this time?" the bass player, who had been standing in the corner, asked.

"Well, it was a funny deal. There was a tenor player in the band, but he'd get high and never show up for dates. He just kept messin' up till one day the leader got mad and said he'd buy me a tenor if I would play it. I said I'd play it. When I saw the beat-up tenor he bought, though, I almost changed my mind. It was an old Pan-American job. But I played it and liked it, what's more."

He went on to say that he experienced no difficulty transferring his easy fluency on the alto to the heavier-toned tenor. His approach to tenor playing was essentially an alto approach, he said. Before he knew it he was playing tenor, alto style. It was unique, new, exciting to musicians who heard it.

"What about Hawkins?" someone asked him.

Lester looked up without changing expression and said, "What about Hawkins?"

"Didn't he give you any ideas?"

"There you go again," Lester said, showing some slight impatience. "Must a musician always get his ideas from another musician? I don't think so. I never did have a favorite tenor. I never heard much of Hawk except an occasional record. Everybody was copyin' him. The whole jazz world was on a Hawkins kick."

He lay back on the bed and closed his eyes. He continued talking about Coleman Hawkins, of his importance to jazz and the tremendous influence he has exerted on tenor players the world over. One got the impression very quickly that Lester is no devotee of the Hawk's, that the two greatest tenor men in jazz are worlds apart temperamentally and musically. Noticeable, too, in his voice was a slight trace of contempt for tenor players who slavishly followed the Coleman Hawkins pattern.

"I couldn't see copyin' the Hawk or any of the others," he said, shaking his head from side to side. "You got to have a style that's all your own. A man can only be a stylist if he makes up his mind not to copy anybody."

Lester made up his mind a long time ago that he was going to play music the way he felt it and not the way other musicians played it.

He started experimenting with tone colors and eccentricities of line and rhythm while he was with Walter Page's Thirteen Original Oklahoma Blue Devils, one of the most exciting combinations in jazz history. Apart from Page, now Count Basie's bassist, the Blue Devils's other distinguished alumnus is Hot Lips Page, the gutty trumpet man.

"We got around everywhere," Lester recalled, "but we starved to death, you know what I mean. We had no capital, no bookings, no nothing. But it was one great band that played some fine music."

For two years, 1934–35 [actually 1932–33], Lester "scuffled" with the Blue Devils. Musically there were kicks in abundance. Financially, he was broke most of the time. When the band finally broke up, Lester hung around Kansas City earning a thin living from one-night jobs.

"Life in K.C. in them days was hard, man. We were all scufflin' like mad. Saturday and Sunday we'd get a gig or two, but Monday, Tuesday, Wednesday, Thursday, Friday there was nothin' much to be had."

A brief period in Minneapolis was followed by his joining the original Count Basie band that opened in the Reno Club in Kansas City and wound up as one of the top money-makers in the orchestra industry.

"I had a lot of fun with the Basie band," he said slowly, staring out of the window. "There were plenty kicks." The coming to the band of Herschel Evans, the brilliant, deep-toned tenor star whom death cut down in 1939, brought him a new kind of thrill, he admitted. He "dug" him hard, but it wasn't until Hersch died that he realized what a stimulating force he had been not only to himself but the whole band. He quickly qualified this appraisal by saying that Herschel was at heart and in style essentially a Hawkins man.

"Most of the time Hersch sounded just like Hawk to me," he said. There was no softness in his voice as he said it. It was a coldly critical statement. A Hawkins man. There were Hawkins men in the room, and one of them asked why had he resisted the Hawkins trend so vigorously.

"'Cause I wanted to be original. Originality's the thing. You can have tone and technique and a lot of other things but without originality you ain't really nowhere. Gotta be original."

In 1941 he parted company with the Basie group when the Count dropped him for failing to make a recording session. That closed an era. Reverses followed. For a time he found himself drifting downward, his morale sagging, his inspiration ebbing. The small combination he formed with his brother Lee gave him kicks but played unevenly at the outset and suffered ups and downs right out to the coast. By the time of his induction, the band had begun to play with the old fire of the Young family band. [Lee Young's band broke up in 1943, and Lester was drafted while on tour with Basie in September 1944.—Ed.]

"What was the army like?" asked the drummer, who had just come in.

"A nightmare, man, one mad nightmare," Lester murmured, shaking his head sadly. "They sent me down South, Georgia. That was enough to make me blow my top. It was a drag, Jack."

He found it hard to reconstruct the nightmare. All he remembers was hating the army with a furious intensity, hating the brass, reveille, injustice to Negroes, and the caste system in the South. He ended up in a disciplinary center in Savannah [actually near Augusta]. That was sheer hell, he said.

Someone shut the window. Lester sat down on the bed, looked up at the drummer who had just changed the record, and smiled.

The record was "D. B. Blues," a Lester original.

Pat Harris

Pres Talks about Himself, Copycats

Pat Harris's name appeared after many interviews in *Down Beat*. In fact, much of the material in the widely admired compilation of oral histories, *Hear Me Talkin' to Ya*, ed. Nat Shapiro and Nat Hentoff (1955; repr. New York, Dover Publications, 1966), comes from her pieces. She wrote me a letter, dated March 6, 1985, describing her experience interviewing Young:

> Charlie Carpenter [Young's manager] set up the interview for me, and we spent about an hour and a half in Carpenter's hotel room [in Chicago] doing it. Lester had his gin bottle by his side. I was 25 or maybe 24 at the time and sort of an anomaly in the field—a total innocent—in spite of work on the daily papers, etc. As I remember it, Lester didn't use any "questionable" language, because I usually took down everything everyone said. I think most people I interviewed might have done this because of the peculiarities of the interviewer [being a woman]. . . .
>
> Incidentally, I was excited about getting a chance to interview Young. I had researched the literature and found a gap of nothing for years and years. When I gave the interview to my editor, Ned Williams (praise his memory!), I told him, this is a guy who no one has done anything on in recent memory. I felt miffed that he put it on page 15.

The interview begins with another statement about the need to be an original. It continues with Young's life history again, but with some fascinating details. He tells why he first became disenchanted with the Basie band. There are a few factual slips—the birthplace of New Orleans and the exaggerated recollection of spending six months each with Henderson and Andy Kirk. The ending is priceless: Harris evidently asks him about his personal life, and he responds, "You mean like the Condon book?" (In *We Called It Music: A Generation of Jazz* [New York: Holt, Rinehart & Winston, 1947; repr. Westport, Conn.: Greenwood Press, 1970], Condon tells stories from his life.) "No, it was all music; that's all there was."—Ed.

"The trouble with most musicians today is that they are copycats. Of course you have to start out playing like someone else. You have a model, or a teacher, and you learn all that he can show you. But then you start playing for yourself. Show them that you're an individual. And I can count those who are doing that today on the fingers of one hand."

It was the Pres talking. Lester Young, a pioneer of the "new" jazz, whose friends find themselves in the peculiar position of trying to persuade him to tolerate the majority of musicians who can't meet his standards and, on the other hand, getting others to try and understand the Pres.

"Lester Young has been so misunderstood, underestimated, and generally shoved around," one of them said, "that he almost was pushed out of the field of top active jazz musicians." The tendency is to relegate him to the position of a historical "influence."

Not Ready to Settle

"I'm not quite ready to settle down yet," Lester said. "When I do, I'll stay in California. I have a house there, and I like the weather. My mother, brother, and sister live there, too. I like traveling, though. There's always something new."

The tenor saxist was almost something new himself in Chicago, his four weeks at the Blue Note opposite Sarah Vaughan being the first time in several years that the town really had had a chance to hear him.

Rarer than hearing Lester play, however, is getting him to talk about himself. He has the well-deserved reputation of being uncomfortably shy and would be content to gaze silently at his pigeon-turned feet rather than talk. Shy about everything except playing that horn.

"My father, William H. Young, was a carnival musician. He could play all the instruments, although he liked the trumpet best. He taught voice, too, and kept up traveling with carnival minstrel shows and teaching music until he died, in the forties.

"I was born in New Orleans, August 27, 1909. My mother, Lizetta Gray, lives in Los Angeles now. I stayed in New Orleans until I was ten, when my sister Irma, brother Lee, and I went to live with my father. He took us to Minneapolis, where we went to school. During the carnival season we all traveled with the minstrel show, through Kansas, Nebraska, South Dakota, all through there."

Plays Drums

"I played drums from the time I was ten to about thirteen. Quit them because I got tired of packing them up. I'd take a look at the girls after the show, and before I'd get the drums packed, they'd all be gone.

"For a good five or six years after that" (Editor's note: Don't try to make Lester's time estimates jibe; they don't), "I played the alto, and then the baritone when I joined Art Bronson's band.

"Ran away from my father when I was about eighteen. We were in Salina, Kansas, and he had a string of dates down through Texas and the South. I told him how it would be down there, and that we could have some fine jobs back through Nebraska, Kansas, and Iowa, but he didn't have eyes for that. He was set to go.

"Art Bronson and his Bostonians—Played with him two or three or four years. He lives in Denver now, and all the men in the band've got families, like to stay close to home—all except me. Anyway, I was playing the baritone and it was weighing me down.

"I'm real lazy, you know. So when the tenor man left, I took over his instrument. But we stuck to Nebraska and North Dakota. Only time I went through the South was with Basie, and it was different then.

"I worked at the Nest Club in Minneapolis when I first heard Basie's band. Band at the Nest wasn't anyone's, really; they gave it to different people every week.

"Used to hear the Basie band all the time on the radio and figured they needed a tenor player. They were at the Reno Club in Kansas City. It was crazy, the whole band was gone, but just this tenor player. I figured it was about time, so I sent Basie a telegram.

"He had heard me before. We used to go back and forth between

Minneapolis and Kansas City. When I joined the band, he had three brass, three reeds, and three rhythm. I'd sit up all night and wait to go to work.

"But Basie was like school. I used to fall asleep in school, because I had my lesson, and there was nothing else to do. The teacher would be teaching those who hadn't studied at home, but I had, so I'd go to sleep. Then the teacher would go home and tell my mother. So I put that down.

"In Basie's band there always would be someone who didn't know his part. Seems to me that if a musician can't read, he should say so, and then you help him. Or you give him his part before. But Basie wouldn't. I used to talk to him about it, but he had no eyes for it. You had to sit there and play it over and over and over again. Just sit in that chair . . ."

And Then Henderson

"I joined Fletcher Henderson in Detroit in 1934. Basie was in Little Rock then, and Henderson offered me more money. Basie said I could go.

"Was with Henderson only about six months. The band wasn't working very much. Was with Andy Kirk for six months about that time, too. Kirk was wonderful to work for. Then back to Basie until 1944 and the army.

"What else happened during that time? You mean like the Condon book? No, it was all music; that's all there was."

Leonard Feather

Here's Pres!

For fifty years Leonard Feather, born in 1914 in London, has been one of the foremost contributors to the literature about jazz. His encyclopedias of jazz (three separately titled volumes, reissued by Da Capo Press) are the starting point for most jazz biographies (although one must beware of erroneous data provided by the musicians themselves), and their indexes and appendixes are still invaluable. Feather's *Book of Jazz: From Then till Now* (New York: Horizon Press, 1957; 2d ed. 1965; rev. ed. 1976) provides a useful introduction to the field for laypersons as well as musicians (there is a chapter of musical analysis with many transcribed solos). An accomplished pianist and composer, Feather wrote "Evil Gal Blues" for Dinah Washington (an early hit for her) and such harmonically sophisticated pieces as "I Remember Bird" and "Twelve Tone Blues," two variations on the blues form. He has produced unusual recording sessions that included all-female sessions in the 1940s and 1950s, and international groups in the 1950s and 1960s. Today, he continues to write regularly for the *Los Angeles Times*.

Feather has interviewed virtually all the major names in jazz and has had the opportunity to spend time with these people and get to know them. His profiles and essays are collected in several books. But this interview with Young has never been reprinted, even though it is often quoted without being credited. In it Young fills in some details not found in the earlier portraits. He talks about the family band and tells for the first time about his father forcing him to read and not just to play by ear.

Originally published in *Melody Maker* (London), July 15, 1950, 3. Copyright © 1950 by Leonard Feather. Reprinted by permission.

He talks about sitting in with the Henderson band one night when Hawkins was absent (he'd gone to visit his family in St. Joseph, Missouri), and at the end he discusses the younger players, who by this time were emulating him in droves.

It is unfortunate but entirely understandable that, as Feather tells us at the outset, he has not attempted "the impossible task of quoting Lester verbatim."—Ed.

For further reading. See Feather's essay "Prez," in *From Satchmo to Miles* (New York: Stein and Day, 1972), 115–27, which includes a brief quote from Young's mother.

A sleepy, disheveled figure poked a head around the door of the Forty-fourth Street hotel room.

"Hey, come on in," said the President.

The room was large, bare, but littered with a fantastic assortment of odds and ends. On the long mantelpiece were innumerable figurines, many of them religious. A table nearby housed several soiled plates, a bottle of gin, and another of sherry. I refused the former but agreed to a glass of wine, as Lester Young tried to wake up with a stiff shot of juniper juice.

"Got to take this in to be fixed," said President, as he fooled with a beat-looking, all-metal clarinet. "It's half a tone off."

I thought back to the Kansas City Six records featuring Lester on clarinet, the ones he cut for Commodore back in the late 1940s. "Why don't you play clarinet on the job?" I'd listened to him until four that morning.

"Maybe I will when I get this horn fixed. I use a wooden reed for this—always have a plastic reed on my tenor."

Lester blew a few cadenzas, put the horn down abruptly, and sat by the window looking out on Forty-fourth Street. It was a sad, gray afternoon. He reached out to set the phonograph in motion. Kay Kyser's "Slow Boat to China" was the incumbent item, and with the automatic changer working, but with no other records on the machine, our entire interview was accompanied by the incessant repetition of the Harry Babbitt vocal, until Pres finally decided to make a change by putting on some of his favorite Dick Haymes records.

I leafed through the three boxes of records, found many popular

singers, little jazz, and only one section of old Basie sides, while Lester
began to unfold the story of his life in the laconic manner that can only be
understood by those who have met him.

Jazz Jargon

He is one of the few musicians whose vocabulary corresponds with the
popular magazine and radio conception of a jazz musician's jargon. Such
terms as "dig," "cool," and "hip" are key words with him. A person is not a
person but a "cat" or a "stud." I have not attempted the impossible task of
quoting Lester verbatim.

"Lester Willis Young, that's right. New Orleans, 1909. Father played
violin, was a teacher with choirs. Musicians in the family? Well, my sister
Irma, she was musical, but she's not a professional musician."

He started playing drums at the age of ten in his father's carnival
band, doubling as a handbill carrier. "Pretty soon I was tired of packing
and carrying and unpacking drums, so I got my dad to get me an alto. He
wrote out the scales for me, but I'd get to listening to a lot of music, and I'd
goof off and play everything but the scales. My sister was a better reader
than I was. She played saxophone, too, and so did my brother Lee."

Baritone to Tenor

"I always played by ear, until one day my father just told me to get out.
That hurt me real bad, so I started reading, and pretty soon I could cut
everybody and I was teaching other people to read. I was about thirteen. I
really appreciated what my father did for me. He'd been a blacksmith, but
he studied at Tuskegee and he knew so much. He tried to teach me
everything.

"I got to the third or fourth grade at school, but I've been earning
my own living since I was five, shining shoes, selling papers. And I was a
good kid; I would *never* steal. Mother was a seamstress and a school-
teacher.

"Finally, when I was about eighteen I ran away from home. My
father wanted to go to Texas, and I didn't. I ran away and went to a cop,
who asked me whether I could take care of myself. I had nothing but the
clothes on my back. But this fellow Art Bronson, from Salina, Kansas, who
had the Bostonians, accommodated me. The only horn he could get me

was a baritone, so I joined the Bostonians and later on, when the tenor man goofed off, they switched me and got me a Pan-American horn."

Lester also worked for several months with the late King Oliver, from his home town.

Tough Times

Lester spent several years, both with his family and with various bands, in and around Minneapolis. Once when he was there he heard Walter Page and his Thirteen Original Blue Devils on the air, with a tenor man who sounded pretty sad to the future president. Wiring Page an offer of his services, he got the job. Most of the men in the band were from Oklahoma City. [You will recognize from Part One that this is actually the story of Young's joining Basie, not the Blue Devils.—Ed.]

Buster Smith, a saxophonist who wrote a lot of the arrangements, was the originator of what later became famous as the "One O'Clock Jump."

"Those were tough times. The band was getting bruised, I mean really bruised, playing to audiences of three people. One time all our instruments were impounded, in West Virginia I think it was, and they took us right to the railroad track and told us to get out of town.

"There we were sitting around with these hobos, and they showed us how to grab the train. We made it—with bruises. We got to Cincinnati, no loot, no horns, all raggedy and dirty, and we were trying to make it to St. Louis or Kansas City.

"I found a man who had an alto, and he loaned it out for gigs, so I managed to play a couple of dates. Finally we all had a meeting—Walter and the boys—and we decided it was 'every tub'—every man for himself."

Meeting Hawk

"Well, I got to Kansas City, got hold of a tenor, borrowed some clothes from Herschel Evans—he was playing with Bennie Moten. Moten was stranded, too, and all the men put him down; Count [Basie] had been playing piano with him, but they'd been squabbling, so Count cut out and took over most of the band while Bennie Moten and George Lee formed another group, and I went with them.

"That was the time I first heard Hawkins. I'd always heard so much

about Hawk—he was from St. Joseph, Missouri—and while I was working at the Paseo Club in K.C., Fletcher Henderson was in town. I ran over
to dig him between sets; I hadn't any loot, so I stayed outside listening.
Herschel was out there, too.

"Then one night Fletcher said his tenor man hadn't showed up, and
wanted to know if there was someone around that could blow. I went in,
read the book—clarinet part and all—blew Hawk's horns, then ran back
to my own job at the Paseo."

The incident had a sequel long afterwards, when Lester was at the
Reno Club working from 10:00 P.M. to 5:00 A.M. for $1.50 a night with
Basie. Fletcher wired Lester from Little Rock, Arkansas. [This happened
about three months after sitting in with Henderson, and it was Lester who
was in Little Rock.—Ed.] Count, though reluctant to lose Lester, said he
didn't want to hold him back. As it turned out, it might have been better if
he had.

"They expected me to sound like Hawk," recalls Pres. "But why
should I blow like someone else? We got to New York in 1934—feeling the
draught all the way—and they rang the bell on me. Fletcher's wife gave
me this 'Why don't you blow like Hawk?' line and took me down in the
basement to listen to Hawkins's records. I asked Fletcher to give me a
letter of release saying that he hadn't fired me, and that was it.

"I went back to K.C., played with Andy Kirk, then after a while went
back with Count at the Reno."

This is the summer of 1936, when the money at the Reno was up to
$2.50 a night. The late Dick Wilson, Kirk's great silken-toned tenor man,
would join forces with Herschel and Lester after hours for some historic
tenor battles. Then one night Count asked Lester how he would feel
about it if Herschel were to rejoin the band.

Lester said he didn't care, so from then on there were two tenors
with Basie—the beginning, as Pres recalls it, of the two-tenor-battle idea
that was to become almost standard operation procedure in big jazz
bands.

Then Basie went to the Grand Terrace in Chicago, and Lester cut his
first records, making "Shoe Shine Boy," "Lady Be Good," "Boogie Woogie," and "Evenin'" with Count, Tatti Smith on trumpet, Walter Page, and
Jo Jones.

Hot to Cool

It was the beginning of something much more important than anyone
realized. Lester, more than anyone else at the time, augured the slow

changeover from hot jazz to cool jazz. His relaxed, infectious beat and seemingly listless sound constituted a radical departure from the accepted standards of those times for jazz extemporization.

From this point on it was comparatively easygoing. In New York, Lester became the darling of the recording studios, making innumerable house dates with Billie Holiday, Teddy Wilson, and others, as well as the matchless series of Decca, Vocalion, Columbia, and OKeh dates with Basie, until the memorable day in 1940 when he refused to make a session allegedly because he didn't want to record on Friday the thirteenth and was rewarded with the axe.

Call-up

"Remember the little band I had at Kelly's after that? Shad on trumpet, Clyde Hart on piano, Johnny Collins guitar, Hal West drums, Nick Fenton bass. We didn't get a date on our own, but we made some sides for Bluebird accompanying Una Mae Carlisle, and I had solos on 'Blitzkrieg Baby' and 'Beautiful Eyes.'

"It was a good band, but the boss was a crow; he didn't like mixing. I got a lot of kicks sitting in at other places—Minton's, the Village Vanguard, Nick's—and toured for the USO with Al Sears's band. Then I had to go back to Kansas City; my father and stepmother both died.

"I made it out to the [West] Coast, and my brother Lee and I started a band together; we brought it east to Café Society, but we never did make records. After that I was back with Count again out on the coast, at the Plantation; but they wanted me. The army wanted me so bad they took me right off the bandstand."

The following fifteen months, as Lester recalls them, were the most miserable of his life. Adjustment to the rigors of military discipline did not jell too well with Lester's laissez-faire nature, a nature that is reflected vividly in his style of playing.

Lag-Along Style

After his discharge came the series of tours with Norman Granz, record dates for him on Philo/Aladdin, and an abrupt end to the Granz relationship, followed by the formation of his own group, with ex-songsmith Charlie Carpenter holding the managerial reins. Lester is cautious when he talks about bop and boppers. Some bop, he points out, is "just chromatics—no heart, no soul. I like to express feeling; I play from *here*," with a gesture to the heart. "Anybody can flat a fifth. And I play a *swing* tenor."

Lester was no stranger to the work of the bop pioneers. He knew Charlie Parker when Bird was a schoolboy; knew Charlie Christian, too, around Oklahoma and Minnesota, as all of them were developing what Pres describes as "that lag-along style where you relax instead of hitting everything on the nose."

Lester's Choice

The old troupers are reluctant to accept new ideas, Lester concedes. "We all love to be young and new. These guys love to come in, but they hate to go out. They'll ring the bell on me for talking like that, but it's the truth. Sure, bop can be pretty—but my music is swing!"

Of his hundreds of recordings, Lester picks Basie's "Taxi War Dance" [and] Billie Holiday's "Sailboat in the Moonlight" and "Back in Your Own Backyard" as his personal favorites. His reason for the first selection is the strange one that at one point in his solo he sounds "like a foghorn," a description that has been applied indiscriminately to all his work by some of the less Pres-minded critics. [I wonder what Young means by a "foghorn"—perhaps his soft low playing at the beginning, or his high F-sharp during the breaks near the end?—Ed.]

And of his own compositions, he selects the delightful "Tickle Toe," which Columbia would be well advised to reissue.

"Gray Boys"

Lester is playing differently today from the Lester who set a new trend in jazz tenor. There are those who say that many of the youngsters who started out by copying him now excel him at his own game. But Pres is a strange and complex character, who at any time is liable to scare the wits out of anyone who believes he's washed up.

As he prepared to leave the hotel, I tried to pin him down on a question he's always reluctant to answer—who are his favorite tenor men in the new school?

After much hemming and hawing and requests not to be quoted, Lester finally came out with a blanket endorsement of Wardell Gray. Then he added, "If you're talking about the gray boys, Allen Eager can blow."

I wasn't talking about any particular race of boys and was surprised to hear Lester draw the racial distinction, since in these times a difference in complexion has no bearing whatever on individual styles.

Not that it matters much whom Lester wants to elect as vice president or to succeed him as chief tenor executive.

To judge by the opinions of innumerable tenor saxophonists all over the United States, one of the few stable things in jazz today is the presidency of Lester Willis Young.

Leonard Feather

The Blindfold Test:
Pres Digs Every Kind of Music

"The Blindfold Test" is Feather's most famous innovation, and it continues in *Down Beat* today, with other authors. (Feather has recently gone on to a related feature called "Before and After" in *Jazz Times*.) The idea is to get musicians to sit down and listen to records without any introduction or any information about whom or what they are hearing. The advantages of this approach are that one gets spontaneous discussion about musical likes and dislikes, influences and favorites. The blindfold test approach is perfect for musicians who don't usually talk much, because one thing musicians do love to talk about is music. It gives them a specific focus and task rather than vague questions about their life that they may have answered dozens of times before.

This procedure does get Young talking—about his love for a "great big strong voice" (record no. 2), his appreciation for the classics but lack of experience with them (no. 9), his predictable preference for saxophones. He has nice things to say about virtually everything. But if you read closely, you'll realize that he disliked number 7. With characteristic wit, he says, "It's kinda over my head." Of course it's not—this is his polite way of saying he doesn't like it. The final sentences are filled with Young's lovely verbal poetry.—Ed.

Lester Young is a doubly unique personality. That he has been the chief influence among tenor sax men in the last fifteen years is well known; less known is the fact that his speech, in some respects, has been no less influential.

Pres sometimes talks in a jargon sometimes comprehensible only to Pres, but at his most lucid he sprinkles his talk with words and phrases that have been used by countless musicians after him. He was probably the first to use "cool" and "no eyes" in their current colloquial sense. Also he addresses everybody else as "Pres," the nickname by which he himself is known.

The following blindfold test is taken almost verbatim from a tape recording of the interview. Because I had often noticed Lester's tendency to like everything, the music for this session included pop stuff as well as jazz of all kinds, plus one straight classical item.

Records Played for Pres

Lester Young was given no information whatever about the records played for him.

1. Les Brown, "Blue Moon" (Coral). Ray Sims, trombone.
2. Bob Eberly, "But Not Like You" (Capitol).
3. Boyd Raeburn, "Hip Boyds" (Savoy), arr. Ralph Flanagan. Lucky Thompson, tenor; Dodo Marmarosa, piano.
4. The Ink Spots, "I Don't Stand a Ghost of a Chance with You" (Decca). Featuring Bill Kenny.
5. Woody Herman, "Four Brothers" (Columbia). Stan Getz, Zoot Sims, [and] Herb Steward, tenors; Serge Chaloff, baritone.
6. James Moody, "Two Fathers" (Prestige). Moody, Lars Gullin, tenors (recorded in Sweden).
7. Mr. Google-Eyes with Billy Ford's V-Eights, "No Wine, No Women" (OKeh).
8. Bud Freeman, "Tia Juana" (Decca). Freeman, tenor; Pee Wee Russell, clarinet.

9. Milhaud, *Corcovado,* arr. Hershey Kay (Columbia). Artie Shaw, with orchestra conducted by Walter Hendl.
10. Jazz at the Philharmonic, "Mordido" (Mercury). Illinois Jacquet, Flip Phillips, tenors; Howard McGhee, trumpet; Bill Harris, trombone; Hank Jones, piano; Ray Brown, bass; Jo Jones, drums.
11. Count Basie, "Little Pony" (Columbia), arr. Neal Hefti. Wardell Gray, tenor.

1. Very nice record—everything is so beautiful about it. Trombone is sort of a Bill Harris tip. I don't think I can dig the band, since playing in small combos makes it kind of difficult for me to dig the big bands, but I know it was very smooth and clean and clear. I thought it was crazy. Three stars.

2. Was that the man that used to be up to Bop City? Either Bill Farrell or that Ray what's-his-name—with the big band, out in California, he's got a great big strong voice—Gordon MacRae. I thought this was pretty, the lyric, too. Rating? Well, comme ci, comme ça. Three stars?

3. That's the kind of music that I like. Swingin' eyes. Tenor sounds like Paul Gonsalves, as of today, and then, Ben Websterini, lot of times he sounds like that. I wouldn't be too sure of the band 'cause Duke has changed—his band sounds different—but he plays very nice piano. Piano tricked me; sounded like Stan Kenton, then like Duke. So you dig? I'm kinda lost. Nice eyes for that one. Four stars.

4. I thought that was very nice. It's been quite a while since I heard any records that they made, what's his name, Kenny something isn't it? They've been fine for years, you know. Reminds me of the way Pha Terrell used to sing this with Andy Kirk. Three.

5. I don't think I could tell the different voices, but I think the record is real great. I don't think I ever heard any saxophones sound like that. I remember when Coleman Hawkins went to Europe, way back, you know, he made some records that had four saxes—"Crazy Rhythm"—and I thought they were great, too. Well I'm just weak for saxophones anyway, but I don't think they can cap that, as far as a section. I can just hear that over and over and over. Nothing but eyes—great big eyes. Give 'em all the stars. Can you give 'em eight?

6. You know really how it sounded to me, Pres? Sounded like Sonny Stitt and Gene Ammons. Anyway, there's two different tenor players. One always plays faster than the other one, the other one mostly swingerini. I always like to hear two tenors play, on account of Herschel Evans and I used to battle. All the time fours for the saxophones.

7. It's kinda over my head, but it's—I can't get with that rhythm that goes like that (shuffle rhythm)—if it were straight rhythm I could make it. Just give them a number. Two, I guess.

8. I'll go for that style, too. We played in Chicago with Muggsy Spanier, and they was wailin' with the Dixielanderini, you know? So, people like things like that. Bet you a dollar I know who's playing clarinet. Pee Wee Russell. That's that Chicago style on tenor; Bud Freeman? All the time I used to hear him with Tommy Dorsey—nobody *ever* played like him, and I like a stylist. Stars? On account of the Dixieland, I think three.

9. All the way! I don't know the band, but it's beautiful music. I never dig into the classicals, you know, I've heard very few records—I've never dug that deep. I'd give them four, whoever it is. I'm going to practice my clarinet. I'd like to hear that again. (Later, when informed it was Shaw: "Artie is so underrated it's a shame. People play him so cheap.")

10. King Cole? . . . It might be Kersey . . . and there was a gray boy out in California who used to play a lot of dates with Norman. Bill Harris can blow; he's a wailin' man. Drums gave himself away—that's Buddy Rich. Bass must be Ray Brown or that other stud that sounds like him—Al McKibbon? Or Pettiford? He was wailin', whoever it was, making them smears and things. That's Flip now. It might not be Buddy Rich—Krupa? Trumpet—I'd say Al Killian. Well, I have to like this. That's my people. Great big eyes. Four stars.

11. That's real crazy! I think I heard it once in Chicago. Onliest thing I would say would be Woody Herman or either Stan Kenton. I don't know the tenor, but it sure is crazy, the way the arrangement goes. I'm going to get the name from you so I can get the record. Four stars.

Afterthoughts by Pres

Favorite records? I like variety. I don't like to get hung up with one thing. Anything they play over the radio that I like, I'll get it. Just all music, all day and all night music. Just any kind of music you play for me, I melt with all of it.

Derek Young

He Holds His Office Graciously

A few words by Lester Young appear in this brief piece written during the 1953 Jazz at the Philharmonic (JATP) tour of Europe. The counterpart to this piece was a negative review of Young's performance by Mike Nevard, which you will find in Part One. Both reviews were given the overall heading "Is Lester Still the President?"—Ed.

Between concerts at the State Theatre, Kilburn, I hurried backstage and found the President—Lester Young in dressing room number 4 with his horn and his little tankard.

Aided by his own particular brand of humor and a gentle drawl, Pres holds his office graciously. In replying to a compliment he is warm and sincere, making one feel pleased to have made it.

A fan, miraculously having penetrated the stage-door defenses, entered diffidently, requesting his autograph, and having achieved his object, immediately disappeared again, not hearing Lester telling him that he didn't have to rush away.

"How's Billie Holiday these days?"

"Lady Day? Many moons, no see. Still nice!"

The next to enter was a tall colored guy who shook hands and sat down. After a while he picked up Ray Brown's bass and began to play.

"Say, who are you, anyway?" asked Lester as an afterthought.

Reprinted from *Melody Maker,* March 21, 1953, 4.

"Major Holley, with Rose Murphy. I used to be with Oscar Peterson."
Enter Ray Brown.

"I thought I could hear my baby crying," quipped Ray. Then Pres produced a bottle of 100 percent proof whisky. The dressing room became crowded, so I decided it was time to leave.

After the second show, we discussed JATP.

"I'm tired of all this noise. I like to play cool," said Pres.

"I hope you'll be back soon."

"I don't think so. I've nothing against this country, but all this rushing around . . . I'm losing my weight. . . ."

"Man, I'm so tired!"

"I'll say good-bye, then. It's been a pleasure meeting you."

"Ah, that's nice. Keep happy!"

"Stay cool, Pres!"

Bill Coss

Lester Young

Bill Coss, then editor of *Metronome,* captures an attractive informality in this short piece. His puzzlement about Young's fondness for Dorsey and Trumbauer is typical of the 1950s, during which time few people knew their records, and the general reputation was that they were bland pop performers. Knowledgeable listeners today know that Dorsey and Trumbauer were both leaders in 1920s jazz saxophone playing and were so regarded at the time by blacks as well as whites.—Ed.

The solemn, slow, slouching enigma of jazz, Lester Young, who, more than anyone else, bridged the gap from "our music" to Bird, still stands astride the jazz world today—one foot in New Orleans, the other on Broadway, at Fifty-first or Fifty-second Street. In either place, in all places, he presents the swinging, light, fluent, smoky sound, his almost tiptoe walk, his colorful expressions, his phlegmatic exterior. This mask that covers him is a product of the particular price he paid for his own bid for individuality: "I won't call names, but they [the Hendersons] used to take me down to the cellar and play Hawk's records for me—you dig?—and asked me couldn't I play like that. But I hardly even listened most of the time, 'cause I knew I wasn't goin' that way."

The way he did go was filled with rebuffs: "The critics used to call me the honk man. Mike Levin said I had a cardboard sound and that I couldn't play my horn. You dig? That made it harder to play my horn. That's why I don't put the kids down. They're all playing. It depends on whether you dig them."

Along with all the other things that hurt Prez were the always prevalent rumors; things like people saying that he couldn't read: "I sure hate to read. When I was twelve years old, I tried to get by in my daddy's band just on my ear, but he threw me out when he dug. So I got mad and practiced and came back and cut everyone else on the band. And I read Mundy's scores on Basie's band."

In these early years, Prez had the oddest kind of musical heroes— Jimmy Dorsey and Frankie Trumbauer: "I finally decided on Trumbauer as the one who floored me the most. But, you see, he was playing alto or C-melody sax and, in copying all his records, that's how I developed my sound."

Now that he's served his sentence he seems still to pay more; the sensitivity has deepened, the mask has become more firmly himself. Not so much so that he won't tip it from time to time, revealing sudden warmth, humor, shrewdness. As a rabid Giants fan, for example, now "waiting for next year," he is an incessant, though modest, gambler: "I will bet you thirteen dollars of my money," is his usual expression. Or his happiness in playing: "Still kicks." Or about his imitators: "I listen to records I made, only I'm not sure they're mine, and I don't even know if it's me." Or about being booked with his friend Paul Quinichette on the same Birdland show—this to his manager Charlie Carpenter: "Lady Carp, if I go up there and play me, I'm playing him, and if I play something else, that isn't what the people came to hear." (Incidentally, he feels that Paul and "maybe Eager" come closest to him.) But sometimes the mask tilts instead of tipping and reveals confusion and hurt: "That singing that everybody talks about—I'm just being funny. But I sing lyrics with my horn, and I'd like to play those slow ballads—but the people make so much noise. By the time you play a chorus and a half you wish it was long over. Not like that everywhere. Funny, they come in to hear, but I guess they get goin' on the drinks . . ." Or about imitators: "So many guys doing Bird—just running chromatics, just running chromatics." But he goes on what seems to be his tired way, enlivening life for many of us, shrouding his inner self from the probes of the world around him, occasionally indulging in the bizarre (his eyes glow with secret humor at the mention of water-pistol fights at Birdland), enjoying his lovely wife and sprouting son, his modest brick home, his midafternoon nap (he sleeps very few hours at a time), and the constant and sometimes simultaneous din of television set and record player. The coolness disappeared for just a moment during the afternoon of this interview. Bob Crosby's show was over, and Prez, a jazz immortal, paid instant, enthusiastic tribute: "That Bob Crosby—he's still wailing." And so, of course, is Prez.

Nat Hentoff

Pres

For over thirty years Nat Hentoff has contributed some of the most perceptive writings on jazz; more recently he writes on politics for the *Village Voice* in New York City. In this lengthy interview (subtitled "In Which One of Jazzdom's Greats Reminisces, Evaluates, and Chats"), Young explains for the first time that he was not born in New Orleans but rather moved there while a child. He tells us what he liked about Trumbauer and describes King Oliver's playing in 1932 and 1933, when Oliver had ceased making records. The last half of the interview captures Young talking in greater detail than anywhere else about musical matters—the role of a good pianist, bassist, and drummer, opinions of other saxophonists, advice to younger musicians, his own listening habits. There is an interesting connection here with the blindfold test of 1951: At that session Feather introduced him to the Woody Herman band's recording of "Four Brothers" (see above, "The Blindfold Test"). Here, Young cites that as his favorite recording by younger tenors.

It is particularly fascinating to hear Young's advice on learning jazz. He describes a time-honored process that is still the model for jazz education—playing along with records, repeating passages as much as necessary, and slowing them down to try out different keys and to learn the fast runs more easily.—Ed.

On a recent Saturday afternoon at his home in St. Albans, [Queens,] Lester Young was alternately watching television and answering questions. Eight-year-old Lester Young, Jr., had gone to the movies. The pet of the house, a seven-year-old spitz named Concert ("We got him on the day of a concert"), was in quizzical attendance. Making coffee was Mary, Lester's wife; also present was the astute, outspoken Charlie Carpenter, Lester's longtime friend who has been with him since 1946 and has been his manager since 1948.

Lester had recently recovered from an illness. He looked to be in good health, was much more relaxed than he usually is in interviews, and his answers were lucid and carefully thought out before they were delivered. A few days after this interview, Lester made a record session for Norman Granz [on January 12, 1956] with Vic Dickenson, Roy Eldridge, Teddy Wilson, Gene Ramey, Freddie Green, and Jo Jones. He played so well that Granz delayed his departure from New York so that he could record Pres again, this time with Wilson, Ramey, and Jones. In both his current conversation and music, then, Lester indicates that he is finding some of the inner peace and confidence for which he's been searching a long time. Below are some of the subjects Lester talked about.

Autobiography. "I was born in Woodville, Mississippi, not New Orleans. The family moved to New Orleans after I was born and stayed there until I was ten. I remember I liked to hear the music in New Orleans. I remember there were trucks advertising dances, and I'd follow them all around. I don't remember the names of all the musicians I heard then.

"I was raised up in a carnival, a week in each town. I liked it, but in the wintertimes my father, who was in charge of the band, wanted to go down South. I didn't like the idea, and I'd run away.

"I've been playing music ever since I was ten. I started on the drums, but it was too much trouble to carry the traps. So I switched to alto. Frankie Trumbauer and Jimmy Dorsey were battling for honors in those days, and I finally found out that I liked Trumbauer. Trumbauer was my idol. When I had just started to play, I used to buy all his records. I imagine I can still play all those solos off the record. He played the C-melody saxophone. I tried to get the sound of a C-melody on a tenor. That's why I don't sound like other people. Trumbauer always told a little story. And I liked the way he slurred the notes. He'd play the melody first and then after that, he'd play around the melody. I did like Bud Freeman very much. Nobody played like him. That's what knocked me out. I remember when he was with Benny Goodman.

"I played in my father's band until I joined the Bostonians, an outfit from Salina, Kansas. My father could swing. He liked to play. He taught and could play all the instruments. I was with the Bostonians for about two or three years when I was around sixteen and seventeen. We played through North and South Dakota and Minnesota. Sometimes I used to go back to my father's band.

"The first instrument I played was alto. The way I switched to tenor is that when I was with the Bostonians, the tenor player kept grandstanding all the time. So I told the leader, if you buy a tenor for me, I'll play it. You see, the regular tenor was a boy from a well-to-do family. He didn't have to play. I remember we'd go by his house sometimes and beg him to play. I got sick of it.

"After the Bostonians, I played with King Oliver. He had a very nice band, and I worked regularly with him for one or two years around Kansas and Missouri mostly. He had three brass, three reeds, and four rhythm. He was playing well. He was old then and didn't play all night, but his tone was full when he played. He was the star of the show and played one or two songs each set. The blues. He could play some nice blues. He was a very nice fellow, a gay old fellow. He was crazy about all the boys, and it wasn't a drag playing for him at all.

"As for how I went with Basie, I was playing at the Cotton Club in Minneapolis. I used to hear the Count on his broadcasts when I was off from work. I used to hear his tenor, and I knew they needed a tenor player. Everything was fine with the band but the tenor player. I sent Basie a telegram and asked him if he could use a tenor player. I was in my twenties by this time. He'd heard of me because people had gone up to Minneapolis for various shows, and Minneapolis was the winter quarters for the band I was with.

"So I joined Basie. It was very nice. Just like I thought it was going to be. Jo Jones came into the band after I did. I've always liked his drumming. He did a lot of things then that the modern drummers do now. Would I compare the Basie band then with the way it is now? It was different from today's, a different style, so I wouldn't compare them. But the band he has now is very nice.

"I remember Buster Smith. I played with him in the Thirteen Original Blue Devils led by Walter Page. They came to Minneapolis while I was there, and they had a sad tenor, too, so I joined them. Buster used to write all the arrangements, and he could play crazy alto and clarinet. Oh, he could blow.

"I played with Fletcher Henderson for a short time when Coleman Hawkins left. I had a lot of trouble there. The whole band was buzzing on me because I had taken Hawk's place. I didn't have the same kind of sound he had. I was rooming at the Henderson's house, and Leora Henderson would wake me early in the morning and play Hawkins's records for me so I could play like he did. I wanted to play my own way, but I just listened. I didn't want to hurt her feelings. Finally I left and went to Kansas City. I had in my mind what I wanted to play, and I was going to play that way. That's the only time that ever happened, someone telling me to play differently from the way I wanted to."

Tenors, etc. "Herschel Evans was a Hawk man. That was the difference between the way we played. He played well, but his man was Hawk, like my man at the beginning was Trumbauer. As for Coleman Hawkins, I used to ride in Hawk's car. He plays fine. He was the first to really start playing tenor. I thought Chu Berry played nice, too. He was on a Coleman Hawkins style. I think he got the job with Henderson after I left. Ben Webster had a taste of it, too. I think Ben plays fine, too.

"Of the newer tenors, I like all them little youngsters. I like to hear them play. About the finest I heard them play is on that "Four Brothers" record. Do I hear my influence in what they play? Yes, I hear a lot of little things from what I play, but I never say anything. I mean I hear a lot of little riffs and things that I've done. But I don't want it to sound like I think I influenced everybody."

(At this point Charlie Carpenter told the story of the night Lester and Paul Quinichette, who are good friends, were leading units on alternate sets at Birdland: "Lester came off the bandstand and said, 'I don't know whether to play like me or like Lady Q, because he's playing so much like me.' He wasn't putting Paul down. Why, Paul is the only man I've ever known him lend a tenor to. But that night, Paul sounded so much like Lester that Lester was at loose ends as to what to do.")

"Have any of the younger tenors," Lester echoed a question, "come up to me and said anything about my having influenced them? No, none have.

"I like a lot of the younger hornmen. I've heard more of Miles than most, and I like him. And Jesse Drakes, who has been playing trumpet with me since 1949. I like him because he plays his own way and doesn't try to imitate nobody. We've been playing together so long I just call a number and we're gone. Things like that mean a lot.

"I thought Bird was a genius. The way he knew his instrument he'd be a hard man to cap. We did a little jamming mostly when I was out in California in the forties. He was a very nice person, well educated. He loved that instrument. The people woke up very quickly to his playing.

"I like some of the musicians I played with in Europe. In some places I played in two or three places a night after the Jazz at the Philharmonic concerts. I was surprised because you hear funny things over here before you go, but when you get to Europe you find they can play very good, too."

The functions of a rhythm section. "The piano should play little fill-ins. Just nice little full chords behind the horn. I don't get in his way, and I let him play, and he shouldn't get in mine. Otherwise your mind gets twisted. That's why I always let my little kiddies play solos. That way they don't bother me when I solo. In fact, sometimes I get bawled out by people who want to hear me play more, but I believe if you're paying a man to play, and if that man is on the bandstand and can play, he should get a chance to tell his story.

"An example of the kind of pianist I like is Gildo Mahones, who plays with me a lot. He never gets in your way. Some pianists just run all over the piano when you're playing, and that's a drag. I like John Lewis's playing very much. The Modern Jazz Quartet I think is very nice, but they have to play someplace where it's quiet so you can hear them. The little things they play are their own. It's something new. I've never heard anybody like that but them.

"A bass should play nice, four-beat rhythm that can be heard, but no slapping. I can't stand bass players when they slap the strings. I love bowed work. It's very nice on ballads. But not all bass players can play good with a bow, and yet it's so nice to have one who can in a small group. I like Johnny Ore, who has worked with me a lot.

"On drumming I don't go for the bombs. I want the drummer to be straight with the section. He's messing with the rhythm when he drops those bombs. In small groups I like the drummer to play a little tinkety-boom on that one cymbal, four beats on the pedal. Just little simple things, but no bombs.

"The Basie rhythm section was good because they played together and everybody in it was playing rhythm. They played for you to play when you were taking a solo. They weren't playing solos behind you.

"On a date I play a variety of tempos. I set my own tempos, and I take my time. I wish jazz were played more often for dancing. I have a lot of fun playing for dances because I like to dance, too. The rhythm of the dancers comes back to you when you're playing. When you're playing for dancing, it all adds up to playing the right tempo. After three or four tempos, you find the tempos they like. What they like changes from dance date to dance date."

The clarinet. "I never could find the one I wanted. I used a metal clarinet on those Kansas City Six records for Commodore, but I never could find one like that one afterwards. I got a tone on that metal one like I wanted. I'd like to pick up on it this year if I could find one. Of the newer clarinetists, I'm going to pick up on Jimmy Giuffre's records. I think he was the one I heard being played on the radio. He sure plays me, especially in the low tones. About clarinetists I have to put it right on Benny Goodman always, him and Artie Shaw."

Honking tenors. "Those tenors who stay on one note, I don't go for that. I like to see a person stand flat-footed and play the instrument. When I'm on the stage with honking going on, I never pay it no mind. I don't buy that no kind of way when a person gets on one note for an hour. But they sell it like hotcakes. Yet it's dying out, if you notice. I wouldn't go to see nothing like that."

Advice to young musicians. "A musician should know the lyrics of the songs he plays, too. That completes it. Then you can go for yourself and you know what you're doing. A lot of musicians that play nowadays don't know the lyrics of the songs. That way they're just playing the changes. That's why I like records by singers when I'm listening at home. I pick up the words right from there.

"Every musician should be a stylist. I played like Trumbauer when I was starting out. But then there's a time when you have to go out for yourself and tell your story. Your influence has already told his.

"You have to have a nice rhythm section. When you get with a rhythm section that doesn't swing, you can't do what you want to do.

"A good way to learn is jamming with records. Find somebody you like and play with his records. That's the way I started. That way you can stop the record and repeat it. If it isn't in the key you like, you can slow it down. Some of the records I used to play with were 'Singin' the Blues,' 'A Good Man Is Hard to Find,' and 'Way Down Yonder in New Orleans.' I have great big eyes for Bix. I used to be confused between him and Red Nichols but finally had to put Bix on top."

Dreams. "If I could put together exactly the kind of band I wanted, it wouldn't be a great big band. I'd have a guitar that just played rhythm— like Freddie Green. I'd have three more rhythm, a trumpet, trombone, baritone, and myself. Frank Sinatra would be the singer. But that's kind of way out. That'll never happen. As for arrangements, there are a lot of people I'd like, but I'd have to think about it.

"I'd also like to make some records with strings, some soft ballads. And if we did jump tunes with strings, the strings would play some whole tones in the background. I was supposed to make some records with strings in California. It still might happen. I'd maybe also like to make some more records with Billie, but that would be left up to her. Those records we made with Billie and Teddy Wilson were mostly heads, you know. He'd always have some little guide to go by, just a little sketch. I remember them well—like '[A] Sailboat in the Moonlight,' 'Mean to Me,' and 'This Year's Kisses.'"

Records. "I usually hear records over the radio and the TV, but I also collect some. I like to get records with singing. Really my man is Frank Sinatra. And I like Lady Day, Ella, Sarah, and others like that. I forgot Al Hibbler. He registers on me very greatly. He sure did break through, didn't he? Most of the time I spend in listening to records is listening to singers and getting the lyrics to different songs.

"I feel funny listening to my own records. I think I enjoy them too well. I might repeat them when I play, so I don't like to listen to them over and over. If I listened to them too much, I'd be thinking about them when I'm playing or recording new ones instead of creating. Among those of mine I like the best are 'Lester Leaps In,' 'Clap Hands, Here Comes Charlie,' 'Every Tub,' 'Swinging the Blues,' 'One O'Clock Jump,' and 'Shoe Shine Boy,' the first record I made."

Conclusions. "I think they'll all be finally coming back to swinging and to dancing to music again. A lot of the things now are just novelties. For me the music has to swing first.

"I'd like to hear nice big bands with a variety of music that people can dance to and good soloists. I myself, though, wouldn't like to play in a big band. You don't get a chance to play. You walk to the mike for your eight bars of sixteen bars, and then you sit down. You're just sitting there and reading the music. There are no kicks for me that way.

"After all these years there's still kicks for me in music. I don't practice because I think I've been playing long enough. But I love to play.

"Let me ask *you* something," Lester said at the door. "Do you like Dixieland?"

"Yes, if it's good," I said.

"Same with me," said Lester.

"The only thing in music he can't stand," Charlie Carpenter pointed to Lester, "is hillbilly music."

Lester nodded.

"And radio and TV jingles?" I added.

"Yes, indeed," Lester laughed. "Those and hillbilly music."

Chris Albertson

Interview with Lester Young

On August 24, 1958 (see Büchmann-Møller's biography, pp. 211 and 269, on this probable date), during an engagement in Philadelphia, Young got together with jazz journalist and researcher Chris Albertson and taped an interview. Albertson has written many articles on jazz in the *Saturday Review* and elsewhere and today is active in the Macintosh computer world, reviewing software among other things. But he is best known for his book on Bessie Smith (*Bessie* [Briarcliff Manor, N.Y.: Stein and Day, 1972]), which was one of the first biographies of a black musician to be carefully researched.

The rough tape of Young's interview, which runs under fifteen minutes, was not meant to be heard or published in whole. In Albertson's own words, "It is unstructured, and the questions are often simple and seemingly pointless, because my sole purpose was to get quotes from Lester that could be extracted for insertion in a series of radio documentaries." Because of its historic importance, Albertson allowed a transcript of the unedited tape to be published in *The World of Count Basie*. What follows is my own transcription, which corrects numerous errors and omissions in the original publication. Because Young's quotes were to be used in several shows, devoted to a variety of topics, Albertson gets Young to talk not only about his own background but also about his feelings toward Coleman Hawkins, the day's young players, various singers, and "modern" recording techniques. Young is impressive in his ability to stick

Originally published in *The World of Count Basie,* ed. Stanley Dance (New York: Charles Scribner's Sons, 1980), 28–33. New transcription by the editor, published by permission of Chris Albertson.

to his guns and maintain his own opinions when challenged—no shy flower here!—Ed.

CHRIS ALBERTSON: OK, we're ready to start. First, I'd like you, if you can, [to] talk about the old days, about—You played with King Oliver for a year, didn't you?

LESTER YOUNG: Yes, about a year.

ALBERTSON: That was after Louis Armstrong moved away from the band, wasn't it?

YOUNG: Oh, many moons after, you know, because that was a older tribe than me, you know.

ALBERTSON: Right.

YOUNG: I came like in the middle of that.

ALBERTSON: But then you played with—let's see, from there where did you go?

YOUNG: From King Oliver? Then I played with a band called the Bostonians. They were out of Salina, Kansas. And it was a nice little group, 'bout eight or ten pieces.

ALBERTSON: Anybody that we might know in the band?

YOUNG: Oh, I'm sure you wouldn't. The boss man's name was Art Bronson, so I know you never heard of him. He played piano.

ALBERTSON: Did you make your first records with Basie?

YOUNG: Wh—yes. My first records—I made 'em in Chicago.

ALBERTSON: With—was it the old Basie band?

YOUNG: Right. During the time we was playing at the Grand Terrace.

ALBERTSON: Did you always play the way you did, or did your—I mean, Coleman Hawkins was the tenor sax man then in those days.

YOUNG: Yeah, well, I had a lot of trouble along those days, because people couldn't understand the way I sound, and they wanted me to play like Coleman Hawkins, you know. Well, to each his own, you know? Things like that. So I played in a band [Fletcher Henderson's], and there was—there was about three boys from the West. They fired the trombone player—great big envelope [i.e., severance pay]. Then they fired the trumpet player. He was gone. Well, I'm the third party. I know they're gonna fire me too, you dig? We were all from Kansas City, you know? We came to New York, so we wasn't in the New York clique, you know? So that made the difference. So I went to him [Henderson] and asked him could I get a recommendation so I could split and go back home, you know? So he did, and I went back, then I start playing with Andy Kirk.

ALBERTSON: But you replaced Hawkins, didn't you, in the Fletcher Henderson band?

YOUNG: Yes, I did.

ALBERTSON: Wasn't it pretty tough for you to replace him, when everybody was so used to the Hawkins style—

YOUNG: Oh, yeah. I caught all kind of troubles, you know, like that, because most of the people would come out to hear *him* and see me up there and listen to the way I sound, you know. And they looking for him. I think he was in Switzerland or Sweden or something like that.

ALBERTSON: And then you—when did you first meet Billie Holiday?

YOUNG: When I came to New York, in 1934 [with Henderson]. I used to live at her house, with her mother, you know, 'cause I didn't know my way around. And she taught me a lot of things, you know, and got me little record dates, you know, playing behind her, little solos and things like that.

ALBERTSON: Well, you're her favorite soloist.

YOUNG: Well, she's mine, too. [*They both chuckle.*] So that's a draw.

ALBERTSON: I understand she gave you the name Pres, didn't she?

YOUNG: Yeah, she did, and I gave her the name of Lady Day. So, that was even.

ALBERTSON: But—I think she has said that she sort of—her style of singing is formed after your style on tenor sax.

YOUNG: Well, I think you *can* hear that on some of the old records, you know. Some time I'd sit down and listen to 'em myself, and it sound like two of the same voices, if you don't be careful, you know, or the same mind, or something like that.

ALBERTSON: Tell me, did you ever make records with Hawkins?

YOUNG: With Hawkins? No, I never did.

ALBERTSON: Never did.

YOUNG: Uh, uh.

ALBERTSON: You probably will some day. [*They both chuckle.*] [Actually they did appear together on concert recordings from JATP, Jubilee, and elsewhere.—Ed.] Now, is there anything you can tell us about Billie Holiday, or any funny incidents when you were on the road with the Basie band, or something like that—might be of interest?

YOUNG: Oh, no, I couldn't think of nothing like that. I just know we were all happy, you know, always waiting to go to work, and things like that.

ALBERTSON: I was talking to Basie the other day, on this same show—

YOUNG [*evidently preoccupied*]: I'm listening.

ALBERTSON: and he was telling me that he preferred recording in the old days, when you had just one microphone. And now, he said, you have the rhythm section around the corner and (it's) so confusing, and the feeling isn't there. Do you feel that way?

YOUNG [*after a pause*]: One microphone?

ALBERTSON: Yes, in the old days when they had just one microphone. Now it's become so technical, you know, there are microphones all over the studio, and you're so split up. You're not together, I mean in a big band.

YOUNG: Um, I don't think I'd go for that. Because I mean, if—if you only have one mike, you got to run over to the mike and play and then come and sit down, it's only one mike. Now they make it convenient, there's a mike here and a mike there and a mike everywhere, you know?

ALBERTSON: But didn't you have just one mike when you recorded with Basie?

YOUNG [*unconvinced*]: Yeah, that's true.

ALBERTSON: And—well, several musicians that I've interviewed have said the same thing, that they felt the spirit was more there in the old days, when you were recording. There were clinkers, but there was more feeling in the music because it wasn't so technical. And nowadays everything is very technical, with high fidelity and everything. They feel they just can't get into the right feeling.

YOUNG: Um, I still don't buy that—

ALBERTSON: You don't? That's good. [*Chuckles.*]

YOUNG: Uh, uh. To each his own. No, I don't think like that.

ALBERTSON: What other bands have you played with?

YOUNG: Bands?

ALBERTSON: Mostly recording groups, I take it.

YOUNG: Well, like Teddy Wilson, records and things like that. I never played with him regular.

ALBERTSON: Do you have any favorite records of your own?

YOUNG: You know, I really couldn't say this offhand. I just, you know, when I get by myself, I just play 'em and enjoy 'em all, you know. [*Chuckles.*]

ALBERTSON: What about—did you ever hear Bessie Smith? I'm sure you did.

YOUNG: Yeah. I thought *she* was a wild lady with her blues. Um hm.

ALBERTSON: Do you think there's anybody nowadays who can sing like her?

YOUNG: Yeah—

ALBERTSON: Whom—of the vocalists today, whom do you like?

YOUNG: Oh, you left the Bessie Smith, huh? [*Albertson laughs.*] You don't want me to say that.

ALBERTSON: Well—no, I mean, you liked Bessie Smith, didn't you?

YOUNG: Yeah, well, some time you pick up on Kay Starr and listen to her voice and play one of Bessie Smith's records. See if you hear anything.

ALBERTSON: You feel there is a similarity there.

YOUNG: Yeah, very much.

ALBERTSON: Well, we have played Kay Starr records on this show—

YOUNG: Um hm.

ALBERTSON: and she definitely does have a good voice for jazz. How about some of the new singers popping up, like Dakota Staton and all these singers that are coming out nowadays?

YOUNG: (You) know, I can tell you this really—my favorite singer is Kay Starr. No, that's the wrong name. What's that other lady's name? Her husband has a band—

ALBERTSON: It's not Jo Stafford?

YOUNG: There you are! Yeah, I'll go there.

ALBERTSON [*incredulous*]: Jo Stafford is your favorite singer?

YOUNG: Yeah. And Lady Day. And I'm through.

ALBERTSON: But Jo Stafford doesn't sing jazz, does she?

YOUNG: No, but I hear her voice and the *sound* and the way she puts her songs on.

ALBERTSON: You like them, huh. That's amazing.

YOUNG: Um hm.

ALBERTSON: What about—how do you feel now when you hear your old records? Do you feel that you—

YOUNG: I think it was nice during those days, you know. See, like, I have a lot of trouble on the bandstand, they all come up and ask me, "How come you don't play like you played when you played with Count Basie?" Well, that's not progressive, you know. If I'm going to stay there and play that same stuff year after year, well, Jesus, I'll be a *old* man, you know? So I don't think like that, so I have to try to think of little new tricks and little new sounds and things like that—that's the way *I* live.

ALBERTSON: Are there any tenor sax men nowadays, newcomers, that you like particularly?

YOUNG: Well, I imagine I'll just say I like 'em all. They all sound the same to me. [*Albertson chuckles.*] Y' dig? Because most of 'em all went to Juilliard, you dig, and whoever that teacher was, he taught 'em all the same thing. This one will start playing it, this one will pick it up and play the same thing ( ). In my mind, where's the individual who's gonna come out and play for himself? Like, if you have thirteen people and the teacher teach all thirteen of them, you mean to tell me out of thirteen he can't get *one* individual? So that's the way I think.

ALBERTSON: Well—so you don't have any favorites?

YOUNG: Oh, no; I like them all.

ALBERTSON: You like them all?

YOUNG: Oh, I like modern—

ALBERTSON: You just feel they should be more individual—

YOUNG: Um hm.

ALBERTSON: More individual styles?

YOUNG: That's all.

ALBERTSON: Well, how do you feel about Coleman Hawkins's style?

YOUNG [*after a pause*]: Well, the way I look at him, he's the first person who played the tenor saxophone, you know, who woke you up and let you know there *was* a tenor saxophone, and things like that. And so now I see all the kiddies, you know, is copying his style and things like that—that's about all I can say on that. [*They both chuckle.*]

ALBERTSON: I take it you don't think very highly of his style, huh? It's not your type of music?

YOUNG: Well, that's incomplete. [*They both chuckle.*]

ALBERTSON: Now, when you travel with the Jazz at the Philharmonic—you've done a lot of traveling with them—

YOUNG: Right.

ALBERTSON: all over Europe. How do you feel the Europeans—how do they react? Do you feel any difference—

YOUNG: No.

ALBERTSON: in the audience in Europe?

YOUNG: No, audiences are very nice over there. I've been over twice.

ALBERTSON: Like, Dizzy Gillespie, he feels that they appreciate the music more than American audiences. How do you feel about that?

YOUNG: I don't think I'll buy that.

ALBERTSON: Think it's about the same, huh?

YOUNG: It's just if, if a person likes you, they like you, and if they don't, they don't like you, that's all. [*Laughs.*]

ALBERTSON: Do you ever play the clarinet anymore?

YOUNG: Yeah, I just made some records for Norman Granz, 'bout four or five or six months ago, on my clarinet. [It was February 8, 1958.—Ed.]

ALBERTSON: I heard some records with—was it Walter Page and his Blue Devils?—that you made—

YOUNG: Yeah, many moons ago.

ALBERTSON: "Way Down Yonder in New Orleans"? [Actually the Kansas City Six.—Ed.]

YOUNG: Right.

ALBERTSON: Yes.

YOUNG: Um hm.

ALBERTSON: Are these the latest records you made—have you made any since—the ones with Norman Granz I mean?

YOUNG: Well, the way we make records for Norman, him and I— pardon me. [*Coughs.*] You'll make so many records, and then he'd keep 'em and put 'em like in a vault, and he stash 'em, and when he wants to go and get 'em, you know, then he bring 'em out. So you can never tell when you'll *hear* one, 'cause that's his business, you know?

ALBERTSON: I see.

YOUNG: So that's the way it is.

ALBERTSON: What do you feel about the reissues of the old Basie records? Do you ever go back and listen to the old records?

YOUNG: Um hm. I have some in my room. I listen at 'em, you know, and try to dig little mistakes, little things that you could have, you know, did a little better, or something like that.

ALBERTSON: We did a show on Coleman Hawkins the other day, about two weeks ago—

YOUNG: Um hm.

ALBERTSON: And we played one of your—we explained the difference between your style(s), and we played one of your records, "Lester Leaps In," with Count Basie's Kansas City Seven.

YOUNG: Um hm.

ALBERTSON: That was a long time ago.

YOUNG: Right.

ALBERTSON: Do you still play that number?

YOUNG: I must have made about three or four different [*laughing*], you know, records of that. Yeah, that's—it's like a crib. ["Crib" meant one's personal bag of musical tricks.—Ed.] I used to play it all night long.

ALBERTSON: It's like, well, Hawkins—they're always asking him to play "Body and Soul."

YOUNG: Same difference. Um hm.

ALBERTSON: So what are you doing now, you're just touring the States and playing various spots?

YOUNG: No, I've been off. I was a little sick, you know, and had to go to the hospital and all that. I haven't worked since the fifth of August—I mean July. This is my first week that I've had, you know. It take you a (little) time to build your chops up, you know?

ALBERTSON: Yeah.

YOUNG: Dig?

ALBERTSON: Before we close, I just want to ask what do you think of Mahalia Jackson, her voice?

YOUNG: I think that's great.

ALBERTSON: She has been compared with Bessie Smith. Do you think that's—think she could sing like Bessie Smith if she sang the blues?

YOUNG [*after a pause*]: That's a little deep for me there, you know? 'Cause she's religious, right?

ALBERTSON: Yes, very religious.

YOUNG: Um hm.

ALBERTSON: She won't sing anything but religious songs, but she has this tremendous voice.

YOUNG: Yeah.

ALBERTSON: Very strong voice and powerful.

YOUNG: Yeah, I heard that record, what does she play?—"Hold My Hand," or something like that.

ALBERTSON: Ah, yes, she's got so many of them, I can't remember them, all—"He's Got the Whole World in His Hand"—

YOUNG: Yeah, something like that.

ALBERTSON: Right.

YOUNG: Um hm.

ALBERTSON: Well, thank you very much, and now we'll take the tape and we'll edit it, and we'll use it—

YOUNG: All right. Pleasure meeting you, Chris.

ALBERTSON: Pleasure meeting you. Thank you.

François Postif

Interview with Lester Young

The longest surviving interview with Young was conducted under very informal circumstances, in his hotel room in Paris with other people coming in and out. François Postif, a much published writer on jazz in France, was at that time a young man with a portable reel-to-reel tape recorder. He brought with him an accomplished photographer, Jean-Pierre Leloir. The tape of Young's freewheeling and uninhibited discourse runs about forty-five minutes.

Perhaps "freewheeling" is putting it lightly. Young was clearly drunk at the time, and early on—when he begins to tell the story of how he started on tenor saxophone with Basie because he hated Basie's current tenor player—he asks Postif if it's all right for him to talk "nasty." "Can you cut the nasty talk out?" he asks. Obviously any nasty talk was cut out of earlier interviews by Harris, Feather, and Hentoff, although Young may have been on better behavior in those more formal settings. The Postif interview was printed in a heavily edited form in the important French magazine *Jazz Hot,* then in English in *Jazz Review,* and this was reprinted in *Kultur.* Parts of the interview, unexpurgated, appeared in the liner notes to the *Lester Young Story,* a series of five albums on Columbia Records. Most of the interview appeared uncensored in *Jazz Hot* 362 (June 1979): 18–22, and 363 (Summer 1979): 34–37, in English and French, and later in *Wire* (England), April 1986, but there were numerous small errors and

Originally published in *Jazz Hot* (Paris) 142 (April 1959): 11–13. Copyright © 1959 by François Postif. New transcription by Postif and Porter, published by permission.

omissions in those. In my previous book (*Lester Young* [Boston: Twayne Publishers, 1985]), I used large portions of the interview, corrected and unedited, but this is the first American publication of the entire interview.

The date of the interview has been a mystery for a long time. One version placed it in March 1959, two weeks before Young died, another said only a few days before; one claimed it took place late at night, another said late afternoon. Phil Schaap pointed out to me that there is a clue in the interview. Toward the end Young asks Kansas Fields, his drummer friend who was present, when the Basie band was to be in Paris. Fields says the twenty-eighth, and Young says angrily that he thought they'd be there in ten days. Since the Basie band played in Paris on February 28, 1959, the interview could not have taken place in March, and I asked Postif to check his notes to see what the date might have been. He found that he had not recorded the exact date, but his photographer, Jean-Pierre Leloir, had—it was Friday, February 6, 1959, at six in the afternoon, in Young's room at the Hôtel d'Angleterre. So Young's response to Fields meant, "I thought they'd be here in only ten days, but it will be more than ten days." That's why he was disappointed.

Postif wrote me in May 1986 to say that Leloir did not take any photos "because Lester was lying quite nude on his bed, unshaved and ill-looking. He was drinking port wine, and I think he was not quite in his normal attitude. Otherwise, he wouldn't have been so free and 'nasty'— and the interview would have been more conventional." He added in October 1989 that "Lester used to mix port wine and gin, mezzo-mezzo, and called the mixture 'up and down.' Leloir thinks that Lester was 'high' when I began my interview."

Part of the reason the interview is so difficult to transcribe is that Postif used what he describes as "a very heavy English tape recorder, which had a noisy motor." Postif sent me his draft transcription of the interview, and I made numerous corrections and returned it to him. Early in 1989 Postif published that transcription in French in a volume of his collected interviews (Paris: Editions de l'Instant). By his kind permission I am including my own transcription here, which incorporates still more corrections from jazz writer Peter Pullman. Postif reviewed it and added some commentary, which I have incorporated into my notes.

NOTE: Blank parentheses—( )—indicate words not audible on the tape or partially cut off. If barely audible the words appear inside parentheses. In a few places I have added information to clarify the conversation. These notes are enclosed in square brackets.—Ed.

FRANÇOIS POSTIF: OK. Oh, Lester, some people say you're born in New Orleans. You're not born in New Orleans?

LESTER YOUNG: Uh, uh.

POSTIF: Where were you born?

YOUNG: Should I really tell you?

POSTIF: Why? (Come,) tell me.

YOUNG: [*Laughs.*] I could tell you a lie. Is this pickin' up now? [*Indicating the recorder.*]

POSTIF: Yeah.

YOUNG: It is?

POSTIF: Yeah.

YOUNG: OK—I was born in Woodville, Mississippi.

POSTIF: Oh, it's very close to New Orleans.

YOUNG: I was born there, then they *take* me to New Orleans. That's where I was raised.

POSTIF: But you were very young—

YOUNG: In Algiers. [There is an Algiers section of New Orleans, across the river from the main part of the city.—Ed.]

POSTIF: Uh—how many years?

YOUNG: New Orleans?

POSTIF: Yeah.

YOUNG: I stayed there ten years.

POSTIF: At ten years old, you've gone back to New Orleans. But you've been—

YOUNG: No, I was born in Woodville, Mississippi.

POSTIF: Yeah.

YOUNG: And my mother was scared, you know. [*Whispering*] "Baby"—that type. So she wanted to go back home to the family in case something happened, that type. So, after I was straight, and she made it, and everything was cool, *then* she take me to New Orleans, and we lived in Algiers, which is a river across from New Orleans.

POSTIF: Uh-huh. Algiers.

YOUNG: Uh-huh.

POSTIF: Do you remember something about your youth in New Orleans?

YOUNG: In New Orleans? Yes.

POSTIF: When did you leave New Orleans?

YOUNG: When I was ten.

POSTIF: Ten. You remember going to some places and hearing some—you're born in nineteen—

YOUNG: O-nine. [Postif joins in on "nine."]

POSTIF: Nineteen-nine.

YOUNG: Yeah, I used to go around and—I loved this music so well—

POSTIF: Even when you were ( )?

YOUNG: ( ) meet my father until ten years old. I didn't know I had one.

POSTIF: Oh.

YOUNG: Just me and my mother, my sister, and my brother, that's all. That type of stuff, but the music got me. See, like in New Orleans they had them trucks that go round and advertise for a dance this night, you giving a dance, and there were all these trucks and things, and this excited me, you know? So I'd be the handbill boy; they give me some handbills, I'll be running around and giving (motherfuckers) handbills—[*laughs*] you know, like that—and I just loved that music. I'd be just running till my tongue was hanging out like this. *Still* I didn't know my father was the musician, you dig?

POSTIF: Yeah.

YOUNG: This was in me, I reckon. So every time they'd start to play, anything I was doing, they start playing some music—Boom! I'd run there, you know, until it's like this. [*Probably hangs his tongue out. Laughs.*] And I knew the stops, you know, they made like certain stops on corners, and things like that, to let the people know they advertising a dance that night you giving, that type of thing. So, that's about it. Then my father came, and he takin' us away from the family, and all . . .

POSTIF: He was a musician?

YOUNG: He played all instruments.

POSTIF: He was a drummer, and he got a band.

YOUNG: Uh, uh.

POSTIF: No?

YOUNG: Trumpet.

POSTIF: Trumpet, yeah.

YOUNG: That's what he liked best.

POSTIF: Um hm. And he was a bandleader.

[*Drummer Kansas Fields knocks at the door.*]

YOUNG: That's Kansas.

KANSAS FIELDS: Hey.

YOUNG: I should knock you down!

FIELDS: Phew—you feeling (gay that night).

YOUNG: Well, fuck it, I'm ( ) myself, I'm forty— [*Tape recorder is shut off.*]

POSTIF: So you moved to New York after—

YOUNG: No.

POSTIF: From New Orleans?

YOUNG: From New Orleans, I went to Memphis.

POSTIF: Memphis, Tennessee.

YOUNG: There you are—right. Then from Memphis to Minneapolis, Minnesota. So I was raised mostly in Minneapolis, Minnesota, than I was in all those places.

POSTIF: And after that, you go to New York—after Minneapolis?

YOUNG: No, I came back to Kansas City.

POSTIF: Aha.

YOUNG: That's when I got with Count [Basie] and them.

POSTIF: Oh, yeah. (You mean—)

YOUNG: He used to have a tenor player, and I hear him playing every night in Minneapolis, you know, and I said—I don't know, I talk nasty, you know? Can you cut the nasty talk out?

POSTIF: Oh, yeah. [*Laughs.*]

YOUNG: You'll cut that? So I went to Minneapolis, right, trying to go to school and all that bullshit—I wasn't interested. So, Count Basie had a tenor player that played, and every night I'd get off, you know—like the time was different like in Minneapolis, maybe it's 1:00 o'clock, maybe it's 1:30 in Kansas, that type of shit. So, *I* sent him [Basie] a telegram saying: "Man, I can't stand to hear this motherfucker blowing that shit. Do you accept me for a job?" During that time Earl Hines had eyes for me, and everybody was hitting on me, but I just hear this motherfucker, turn my radio, and (hear this) thing: [*he sings*] "Hmmm." So they sent me a ticket, and I left my madam, you know, there, then I went on that way. And things like that.

POSTIF: But you were first playing drums, before going to—

YOUNG: Right.

POSTIF: Yeah.

YOUNG: Um hm.

POSTIF: Why did you choice drums the first?

YOUNG: Because, like I was telling you about them trucks that was playing when I sent out the handbills—he was the onliest person I liked up there was the drums, you dig? [*Laughs.*] So I'd be running . . .

POSTIF: Do you enjoy playing drums, still now? You—

YOUNG: Uh, uh. No eyes! [*Disgusted*] Ooohh! I don't want to see those motherfuckers!

POSTIF: Some people told me that you changed, you switched to alto, you know, because the drums was too loud to, you know, to carry and to—

YOUNG: Every time I'd be in a nice little place and meet me a nice little bitch, dig, her mother say(s) [*mimicking*]: "Hurry up, Mary, come on, let's go." Goddamn, I'm trying to pack these motherfuckers fast, and shit like this, 'cause I want this little bitch, you dig? And all this jumped off. So, well, she call her once, and twice, and I'm trying to get this shit straight. So I just said, fuck it! I'm through with drums, motherfuck some drums. All the other boys got little clarinet cases, trombone cases, trumpet cases, and here I am wiggling around with all this shit! (So have to hire another move . . .) Fuck these motherfuckers! And I really played them, Lady Kansas!

FIELDS: Yes.

YOUNG: I could play my ass off—I'm playing for a year.

FIELDS: Um hm.

YOUNG: You know, with that strap around you up there. Shit [*mimics drum sounds*]—"ivey, divey, oobie, doobie" [*gets excited*] "ivey, shitty, rootie, pootie!"

FIELDS: Like military drums.

YOUNG: No. Everything but that.

POSTIF: And you switched to alto after that. When did you switch to alto?

YOUNG: Oh, I switched to tenor. I was playing the alto, and they had a old evil ass motherfucker [in the Bronson band]. He had a nice beautiful background—you know, mother and father with whole lot of bread, and all that shit like that. So every time we'd get a job—this was in Salina, Kansas, [*to Fields*] you must know something about that city—so, every time we'd go to see this motherfucker, we'd all be ready, we're waiting for ninety years to get us a gig, you know, and he'd go [*mimicking*]: "Oh, wait for me while I put my shirt on and get my tie on." [*Makes high sound of frustration.*] Oh, yeah, everybody was waiting, disgusted. So I told the boss man—his name was Art Bronson—I said, "Listen, let's don't go through this shit." I said, "You buy me a tenor saxophone, and I'll play this motherfucker, and we'll be straight then."

And he worked at a music store, so all he had to do was go and get me a tenor saxophone, and we split—fuck that motherfucker! So, that's how I started playing it. Soon as I heard this bitch, I knew it was for me. That alto was a little too high for me, you know.

POSTIF: But you—some people tell that, when playing tenor, you know, you just blow with the high notes of the tenor, like an alto.

YOUNG: Uh-huh.

POSTIF: You think so?

YOUNG: I *know* so. I want it to be like that [referring to his tone— Ed.]. If you want it to be like a tenor, I can play it like that, too.

POSTIF: But—you play on the high notes of the tenor, you know, just—[*Young is apparently shaking his head in disagreement.*] You don't think so?

YOUNG [*realizing that Postif thinks his tone is achieved by avoiding low notes*]: Uh, uh. Not *that* much.

POSTIF: (No.) Can you tell me the personnel of the King Oliver band when you were playing there?

YOUNG: Shit, that's too long ago.

POSTIF: It was in 1930, or something like that.

YOUNG: You see, that's where the people get fucked at, you dig? They want me to come up—I get all kind of insults about, "You don't play like you played when you were with Count Basie." Here's a man getting older and things, and he's got to look for young things (and shit, the) young boys fucking with him, shit like that. I say, "No, I don't remember no shit with Count Basie," you know, unless I have eyes—right? So I've developed my saxophone to play it, make it sound just like a alto, make it sound like a tenor, make it sound like a *bass*, and everything, and I'm not through working on it yet. That's why they get all trapped up, they go, "Goddamn, I never heard him play like this!" That's the way I *want* (things), that's *modern*, dig? Fuck what you played back in forty-nine, what the fuck you gonna play today, you dig? So a lot of them get lost, a lot of them walk out, you know. They say, "Shit, he ain't playing like he used to play." Well, what the fuck—do you play the same thing every day?

POSTIF: No, it's impossible.

YOUNG: [*Laughs.*] Unless you want to be, you know, on a henpecked tip.

POSTIF: But you think you are playing quite modern "saxotenor" right now?

YOUNG: Yeah.

POSTIF: Modern, yeah?

YOUNG: Um hm.

POSTIF: Definitely?

YOUNG: In my heart, I'm sure of it.

POSTIF: Uh-huh. And, uh, what about Herschel Evans?

YOUNG: About him?

POSTIF: Yeah.

YOUNG: We were nice friends and things, but I mean there wasn't no bullshit or nothing. When we got up on the bandstand to play, like a duel [*laughs*]—you know? And then other nights we'd get along nice. You know what I mean. But I mean it's coming through these instruments, you dig? He was a nice person. I was the last one to see him die—in fact, I paid the doctor for his bill and everything. [*Pause.*] So, it was just like that. I don't blame him—he loved his instrument, and I loved mine, too, so, fuck you, fuck me, boom! That's all I did.

POSTIF: But you—were you considered like the star of the band when you were in the Count Basie band?

YOUNG: What was that?

POSTIF: The star of the band—when you were in the Count Basie band, in 1939 or something like that.

YOUNG: Oh, after I came down to Kansas City?

POSTIF: Yeah . . . no, not the first time you went with Count Basie, in 1933, but in 1939 or something like that, you know? You were the star of the band?

YOUNG: Yes. Oh, I see what you're saying.

POSTIF: Yeah. You were starring every night, you know, people go for you *and* the Count Basie band, or—Did you get a big name over in the States in 1939?

YOUNG: Well, I'll tell you about that. Like all the little shit out west round Kansas City and all that shit like that, you know, I made that for myself.

POSTIF: Yeah.

YOUNG: You know?

POSTIF: Oh, yeah. And, some people say you are very independent.

YOUNG: Who?

POSTIF: Independent. Some people, you know.

YOUNG: Independent? Very much so.

POSTIF: Very much, yeah.

YOUNG: Yeah.

POSTIF: Yeah. You're doing every—Can you tell some anecdotes, you know, about your independent mind?

YOUNG: That's true. I'd have left here the other night if I had five hundred dollars.

POSTIF: Yeah.

YOUNG: Um hm. I just can't take that bull*shit*, you dig, it's all bull*shit*. And they want everybody who is a Negro to be a Uncle Tom or Uncle Remus or Uncle Sam, and I can't make it.

POSTIF: Not here, you know, not in France.

YOUNG: Shi-i-it! [This repeats due to an awkward splice in the tape.—Ed.] Are you kidding? I've been here two weeks, I've been pickin' up on that!

POSTIF: [*Pause.*] (I) don't think so.

YOUNG: No? Well, I won't tell you what I know what jumped off.

POSTIF: Yeah.

YOUNG: Right here. Seeing is believing, and hearin' is a bitch—that's a sound. Right here in Gay Paree. Maybe it wouldn't happen to you, you dig—you're not a colored person like I am, you dig? They'll take advantage of me. But all I can do is tell you what happened. And I'm not gonna tell you that part of it—but it did happen. By somebody you wouldn't believe, too—great person. But it's the same way all over, you dig? It's fight for your life, that's all. Until death do we part, you got it made. But it's the same way . . .

POSTIF: Who was the tenor player who made an influence on you?

YOUNG: Oh . . . hmm . . . he died. Frankie Trumbauer. I had to make a decision between Frankie Trumbauer and—what's the name—Tommy Dorsey, Jimmy, Jimmy Dorsey?

POSTIF: Jimmy Dorsey.

YOUNG: You dig? I wasn't sure which way I wanted to go, you dig? And I had these motherfucking records, and I'd play one of Jimmy's, I'd play one of Trumbauer's, and all that shit. I don't know nothin' about Hawk then, you dig? But I can see the only people that was telling stories that *I* liked to hear were them. So I'd play one of his, one of them, you dig? So I had both of 'em made, you dig?

POSTIF: But do you think your sound is close to the Trumbauer sound?

YOUNG: Yes.

POSTIF: (   ).

YOUNG: That's right.

POSTIF: Some people told me about Bud Freeman doing an influence on you.

YOUNG [*incredulous*]: Bud *Freeman?*

POSTIF: No, you don't think so. [*Chuckles.*]

YOUNG: Oh, we're nice friends, I saw him in the union the other day, but ivey-divey, in*fluence* on me!

POSTIF: No.

YOUNG: Ooh, [sounds like "mishoo, peshwah"—maybe Monsieur, François? Franchement? or just a sound—Ed.]. Shit!

POSTIF: No.

YOUNG: Uh, uh!

POSTIF: So, it's Trumbauer?

YOUNG: That was my man. I had to pick from two, right?

POSTIF: Did you listen to him on, you know, direct? [He means in person.—Ed.]

YOUNG: Yes. Did you ever hear him play "Singin' the Blues" [a recording of 1927—Ed.]?

POSTIF: Yeah, nice record.

YOUNG: That tricked me right there, that's where I went.

POSTIF: Oh, by the way, what is your—what is your opinion about the blues?

YOUNG: Blues? Great big eyes. Because if you play with a new band like I have, you know, working around, if they don't know no blues, they can't play shit. (Why,) everybody plays the blues, and *have* 'em too!

POSTIF: You play wonderful blues anyway. [*All laugh.*]

YOUNG: (Yeah.)

POSTIF: What was the idea about the "Lester Leaps In"?

YOUNG: The idea?

POSTIF: Yeah, you know, when composing it. When did you compose this tune?

YOUNG [*flippantly*]: Nine years ago.

POSTIF: Nine years ago?

YOUNG: [*Laughs.*] I really don't know. Long time. Uh-huh.

POSTIF: Are you a very easy composer? For example, the ideas, you know, go right down through the sheet of paper?

YOUNG: No, I'll tell you about that, I see what you're saying. You see, when I was coming up playing in the [family] band, I wasn't reading music, I was bullshitting—but I was in the band. And my father got me an alto out of a pawn shop, and I just picked the motherfucker up and just started playing it. And that's the way that went. So he was a musician, he played all the instruments [*laughs*], and all this shit! And my sister, see, she was playing, and I'd get close to her and pick up on the parts, you know?

Playing marches, and all them shit like that. And finally my father said one day, he say [*pointing to Kansas Fields as an example*]: "Kansas, play your part." I knew goddamn well I'd lose my ass; he knew I wasn't reading. "Play *your* part, Kansas." [*Singing*] "Hup, ta ta lup, da da la da la da lup, boom." He said [to the next person], "Now play *your* part—go!" Say, "Now Lester, play *your* part." I couldn't read a motherfuckin' note, not a goddamn note. He say, "Get up"—you know, he don't curse like I do, (different)—"get up and get your fuckin' ass and work you some scales. Get out!" Dig?

The rest of them went rehearsing. Now you know my heart was broke, you dig? I went and cried, and give up my little teardrops and shit, I said, "Well, I'll come back and catch these motherfuckers if that's the way they *want* it." Like that, you know? So I went away and learned how to read the music, *still* by myself, y' dig, and I came back in the band, played this music and shit, and all the time I was copyin' on the records also with the music, so I could fuck these motherfuckers *completely* up. So I went in the band, and they threw the goddamn marches out, and I read the music and shit, and everything was great. But what was in *my* heart, why all the motherfuckers [who] laughed when they put me out, when I *couldn't* read, (and) come up and say, "Won't you show me how this goes? You play like that?" Yeah, sure, I'll show you shit, you rusty motherfucker! So that's the way that went down.

POSTIF: Um hm.

YOUNG: Now, I made that score: I don't like to read music, I don't like to read—

POSTIF: Just play soul?

YOUNG: There you are.

POSTIF: Yeah.

YOUNG: I got a man in New York now [reportedly Gil Evans] writin' some music for me. When I get back, I got bass violin, two cellos and a viola, and a French horn, see what I mean? And the three rhythm, you know what goes with that.

POSTIF: But you know, Pres, your compositions are very easy swing.

YOUNG: Um hm. I'm gonna take my time and gonna just try this, if it don't come out right, fuck it! I'll say no, you know. But this is my first time, and I always wanted to do that. Norman Granz never did let *me* make a record with no strings, you know. Yardbird made millions of records with strings and things.

POSTIF: And they're fine records.

YOUNG: Um hm.

POSTIF: Do you want to get a full band with strings and you playing in front (of it)?

YOUNG: Well, when I was over here before, I played with the—the first winners. I think they must have been Germans. They have a (lot) over here. Anyway, I played with the first one, and the second one. [Evidently first and second prizewinners—perhaps student orchestras.—Ed.] That's all I can say, 'cause I don't understand too much about it. And they treated me nice, and played nice for me, and things like that, you know. There's nothing wrong with that, but I played with the first one, first, number one—then, I played with the second one.

POSTIF: When have you made your last recordings?

YOUNG: Oh, in—I just made some now for Norman [Granz]—

POSTIF: (Norman)

YOUNG: with my clarinet.

POSTIF: Oh!

YOUNG: Um hm.

POSTIF: What was the idea of not playing clarinet for years and years, because, you know, in France—I don't know in the States, but in France you're known as one of the best clarinetist.

YOUNG: Well [sadly], my friend stole it. [Long pause then whispering] That's the way it goes, I mean . . .

POSTIF: You made some recordings on clarinet. When did you made those one?

YOUNG: Um hm, this is fifty-nine—fifty-eight, by the first of it.

POSTIF: Uh-huh.

YOUNG: Uh-huh.

POSTIF: Just in the beginning of the year, or—

YOUNG: Somewhere in there. You know, you've heard about the Hollywood Bowl, and all that shit? Well, during that, that's the time I made the record date.

POSTIF: But I mean, on a concert or—

YOUNG: No, no, in a studio.

POSTIF: Yeah, yeah. And who was playing there?

YOUNG: Oh, Oscar Peterson and his little group.

POSTIF: Herb Ellis and—

YOUNG: Um hm.

POSTIF: Um hm. Did you ever, uh, listen back to them?

YOUNG: No. We fell out—we fell out. [Young recorded on clarinet on July 31, 1957—a few weeks before a Hollywood Bowl concert, which may be the one he means—and also in February 1958, which may be what he means by "the first of" fifty-eight. These recordings were unsuccessful because Young himself was out of practice—his complaints are audible on some of the session tapes, and you may read them in appendix 1—which may be why he says "we fell out."—Ed.]

Postif: Uh-huh. Do you listen a lot of your recordings? (I see)—do you listen to the records? Do you listen back to the recordings?

Young: Of myself?

Postif: Yeah.

Young: Uh, uh.

Postif: No?

Young: Not very much.

Postif: No. Which is the one you prefer (of) all you've done?

Young: No, I could never answer that. Did you ever hear "Clap Hands, Here Comes Charlie" [Basie, 1939]?

Postif: Yeah.

Young: That's a spark in my heart.

Postif: I love this one you made with King Cole, you know, "Back Land Blues" [i.e., "Back to the Land," probably spring 1946, now on Verve—Ed.].

Young: Many moons.

Postif: That's a very fine thing.

Young [*changing the subject*]: Well, it's so rough out here, you know? Everybody's so chicken shit, you know? I'm enjoying myself up here by myself, you know, to get away from all that shit and things, and I ain't got a quarter, you know! [*Laughs.*] But I don't walk around sighing the blues and shit, 'cause my old lady will take care of me, so fuck it.

[*Pause.*]

Postif: Billie gave you the name of "Pres"?

Young: Um hm.

Postif: And you gave her the name of "Lady Day."

Young: (At) her house, see, when I first came to New York in thirty-four [with Henderson], I used to live there for a long time. She was teaching me about the city, you know, which way to go, you know, where everything is shitty. [*Wistfully*] Yes, she's still my Lady Day.

Postif: Oh, yeah, she came here, you know, last fall.

Young: Um hm. [*Long pause, then begins slowly.*] What people do, man, is so obvious, you know. If you want to speak like that, what the fuck I give a fuck what you do. What he do—What he does—what nobody do—is nobody's business!

Postif: No, it's your own business.

YOUNG: So, why you gonna get into it and say: "Oh, he's a old [*mumbles*]." Goddamn, I'd go crazy thinking about that shit. [*Laughs, then puts on a hoarse voice.*] "He's a old junky, he's a old funky, he's a old fucky," and all that shit. That's not nice, you know? Whatever they do, let them do that, and enjoy themselves—and get your kicks yourself. Why you envy them because they enjoyin' themselves? Fuck it, you dig? All I do is smoke some New Orleans cigarettes, that's perfect (arms). [*Shows his arms to prove there are no needle marks.*] No sniff, no shit in my nose, nothing. Still, I drink, and I smoke, and that's all that—

POSTIF: Anyway, it's your business.

YOUNG: Um hm. But a lot of people think I'm this. [*Perhaps makes a gesture of shooting heroin.*] I don't like that. I resent that like a bitch. If I ever find the motherfucker, (I) would . . . ivey-divey, shit, I'd go crazy! Don't put that weight on me; I know what I do.

POSTIF: Anyway, you know, it's your business, it's not my business. My business is the musical thing, you know.

YOUNG: Mine is too—all the way. [*Both laugh.*] *Real* musical thing!

POSTIF: What do you think about what you are playing now?

YOUNG: Hmm?

POSTIF: What do you think about what you are playing now?

YOUNG: My music?

POSTIF: Yeah.

YOUNG: Well, I'll tell you. In my mind, the way I play, I try not to be a repeater pencil, you dig. I'm always loosening spaces, and laying out to somewhere, and something like that. Don't think you'll catch me like that, playing like "Lester Leaps In" or something like that. That's my crib [personal vocabulary], you know—that type of shit, but I'm always reaching (like that).

POSTIF: But do you think you can create something right now, you know, a new sound or a new—or something more that you've done?

YOUNG: Um hm.

POSTIF: You think so?

YOUNG: I can play a bass clarinet.

POSTIF: Um hm.

YOUNG: Wouldn't that upset everything? I'd say that'd kind of upset everything, wouldn't it?

POSTIF: Yeah.

YOUNG: If I bring out a bass clarinet? Pres, I can play all those instruments.

POSTIF: Do you know some new jazzmen, like Coltrane or Sonny Rollins?

YOUNG: I know them both. Um hm.

POSTIF: Oh, yeah. And—are you quite in the new jazz field? You know, when in New York, are you interested in what the other people in the new generation is doing?

YOUNG [*curtly*]: Everybody knows.

POSTIF: What do you think about Coltrane? Did you heard him personally?

YOUNG: No, I haven't heard him.

POSTIF: Do you have his records?

YOUNG: No. No, I haven't.

POSTIF: And Rollins?

YOUNG: Rollins? Him and I played together in Detroit one night, so I've heard him. What's that other one? What's that other alto player, (Kansas)?

POSTIF: Cannonball. Cannonball Adderley.

YOUNG: Cannonball.

FIELDS: Cannonball—

POSTIF: Adderley.

YOUNG: Um hm.

POSTIF: You know, he plays like Bird.

YOUNG: I've heard him. He's got a station wagon over there, taking his group around the country.

POSTIF: You made some sessions with Bird.

YOUNG: Me?

POSTIF: Yeah.

YOUNG: I don't think so.

POSTIF: You played with him.

YOUNG: Yeah?

POSTIF: You played with him.

YOUNG: Oh, yeah, J.A.P.—Jazz at the Philharmonic.

POSTIF: Oh, yeah. Oh, yeah, yeah.

YOUNG: That's right.

POSTIF: Um hm.

[*The sound of a glass being filled. Then, a long pause. Young seems to say, "Bonjour."*]

POSTIF: Um, Lester, why did you leave the Count Basie band?

YOUNG: That's some deep shit you're askin' me now! [*All laugh.*]

POSTIF: Don't answer if you don't want to, (you know).

YOUNG: No, I won't say that. Skip that one. But I sure could tell you why, but I think it's a little (sporty). They're supposed to be here shortly, aren't they?

FIELDS: Twenty-eighth. [The Basie band played in France on February 28, 1959.—Ed.]

YOUNG: Hmm?

FIELDS: Twenty-eighth.

YOUNG: The bitch [the wife of Ben Benjamin, owner of the Blue Note Club in Paris—Ed.] told me [they] should be here in ten days.

[JEAN-PIERRE LELOIR?]: (Well, they comes first in Europe before).

FIELDS: They're in England now.

YOUNG: Hmm?

FIELDS: They're in England.

YOUNG: Yeah?

FIELDS: Um hm.

POSTIF: Did you enjoy your last recording with the Count in, uh, Newport? You know, it's just published—it's just released in France today. [*Pause.*] You know, when you blow "Lester Leaps In"—you blow mad.

YOUNG: I've got it right here, I've been playing it all day. [He had been playing it on his little portable record player while waiting for Postif to arrive.—Ed.] Nice eyes. Oh, I mean I always bust my nuts when I play with them, you know.

POSTIF: Yeah, I know. You were in the twentieth birthday of music, or something like that. [The Verve recording was made at the 1957 Newport Festival celebrating Basie's twentieth anniversary as a recording bandleader.—Ed.]

[*Pause.*]

YOUNG: I still have nice eyes, you know, I can't go around thinking evil and all that shit. Everything is still cool with me, you know, 'cause I don't bother nobody. Things like that—it comes out nice, you know. That's why I say what you do is your business, what I do is my business. So, fuck it!

[*The tape cuts off and back on.*]

POSTIF: Um hm. Have you got some anecdotes to say, you know, something, um—for example, in, you know, *The Jazz Makers*, the book by Nat Hentoff and Nat Shapiro—they said that you were supposed to play in a dance party, or something like that, far from New York, and you take your car, but you get [in] an accident, you know. And after that you take a taxi, and you spent a lot of money for just for being at the right time. [See Hentoff, "Lester Young," above.—Ed.]

YOUNG: Yeah. I don't have a car, so they told a lie that time.

POSTIF: [*Laughs.*] So it's not true.

YOUNG: [*Laughs.*] So that was wrong.

POSTIF: Yeah. They're telling a lot of things, you know, in the saga of Lester Young, and, you know, some people's trying to say things and things and things and—

YOUNG: But you take a person like me, I stay by myself. So how the fuck do you know anything about me? Nothing. A motherfucker walked up and told me, said, "Pres, I thought you were dead," and all that shit. [*Laughs.*] I'm probably more alive than he is! You dig, from that hearsay shit. Hearing aid. Don't go like that, man. Not with me.

POSTIF: Which way would you like better to play—with a trio, with a quartet, or just with a band?

YOUNG: No. Give me my little three rhythm and me—happiness.

POSTIF: Yeah.

YOUNG: That's four, the four Mills Brothers. [Jazz harmonica virtuoso Toots Thielemans told Postif that this was a favorite expression of Young when gambling with dice—a favorite pastime. If he rolled four, he'd say, "Mills Brothers!"—Ed.]

POSTIF: [*Laughs.*] Yeah.

YOUNG: That's me, I can relax better, you dig? ('Cause) I don't like a whole lot of noise no goddamn way. Take them trumpets and trombones and all of them (   ), fuck it!

POSTIF: Just a quiet sound?

YOUNG: I'm looking for something right now—like a little puff that a lady put on her pussy when she cleans up, and shit like that—soft eyes for me. I can't *stand* no loud shit. You dig? And the bitches come in a place in New York, and them trumpets be screaming and shit. The bitches put their fingers in their ears, you know? It's got to be sweetness, man, you dig? Sweetness can be funky, filthy, or anything, but which part do *you* want? The funkies [funky parts] about it or the sweet? [*Laughs.*] Shit, what am I talking about? [*Laughs throughout the next question.*]

POSTIF: That's why I'm—that's why I'm very interested by the new clarinet record you made, just with a trio, you know?

YOUNG [*stops laughing; almost to himself, disregarding Postif's comment*]: OK. Well, I can smile, once in a while.

POSTIF: Oh, yeah. And—in nineteen—well, when did you begin to get this sound, you know?

YOUNG [*finally comes down to earth.*]: Ooooh, shit!

POSTIF: And where did you begin to get this sound? It was quite new in 1935 or something like that. Everybody was playing on the tempo, you know, and you seem floating on (the) tempo.

YOUNG: (I dunno), I think it just came natural. There wasn't no bitches around me or nothing. [*Pause.*] (   ) I just think—oh, yes, I dig what you mean. When I first went to New York, in thirty-four, so I got this job from Coleman Hawkins [replacing Hawkins in Henderson's band—Ed.]. But in Kansas City [in December 1933], I ran a million miles to hear Coleman Hawkins play, and he wasn't there. So Fletcher Henderson ran out the door, saying, "Don't you have no tenor players here in Kansas City? Can any of you motherfuckers play?" You know, that type of shit like that. Herschel was out there, you dig, but he couldn't *read.* Herschel played good, but *he* couldn't read. So them motherfuckers just shoved me and said, "Red"—they called me Red then [after his light complexion]—"Say, Red, go on in there, and blow this goddamn saxophone." And I'm coming to see Coleman Hawkins, they told me how great he was, I wasn't seein' the fuck how great he is! You know? That type of shit.

So they shoved me on in there, and I sat up and grabbed *his* saxophone and played the motherfucker and read the music, and read his clarinet parts, and *everything.* Now I got to run back to my job, where there's thirteen people in it. [*Laughs.*] Run ten blocks back to get to *them.* Because I want[ed] to see Coleman, you know, they was telling me how great he was, shit, I want[ed] to see a *great* motherfucker. So, that's the way that happened. So I don't think he showed at all. And then I went to Little Rock with Count Basie, and I got this telegram, Fletcher Henderson saying [*softly*], "Come with me." So I (wasn't a stinking) motherfucker when I got the telegram, you know, I was all excited, you know, about this big time shit, and I showed him [Count] the telegram, I say, "What you think I should do, Count, about it?" (He) said, "Well, ain't nothin' I can do but say"—you dig?—"ivey-divey," you dig? And I split, went to Detroit first, you know, and I lived at Fletcher Henderson's house, you know, paying bread and things like that. [Young met the band on tour in Detroit and stayed at the Henderson's home when they arrived in New York, perhaps paying them rent.—Ed.] But [*pause*] it wasn't for me. I wasn't happy. The motherfuckers was whispering on me everytime I played—I can't make that! [*Pause.*] I won't say nothing while you playing, nothing like that. You hear a group of motherfuckers whispering—Jesus!

So I split. So I went to Fletcher and asked him, I said, "Will you give me a nice recommendation? I'm going back to Kansas City." This type of shit, you know? He said, "Oh, yeah, right quick!" [*Laughing.*] You dig? I said, "Thank you." (   ) And I went to Andy Kirk's band and had a nice time. Nah, I won't have no shit, fuck it! Don't make no sense. If it's right . . . but if it's stinking, fucking, you a stinking motherfucker trying to put some shit on some people! (No better) for your ass if you have bad luck. But I know I got a good heart, man, and I ain't thinking about no (cunt) or nothing like that. Just trying to get me some money for my family—and it's all clean, believe that.

And this bitch would take me down there—Fletcher Henderson's wife—take me down in the basement and play one of them old windup (vendors) [record players] and shit, and asked me, said [*mimicking*], "Lester, can't you play like this?" Coleman Hawkins playing. [*Young feigns disinterest.*] "Hmm—ivey divey." [Mrs. Henderson again:] "But I mean, don't you hear this? Can't you get with this?" You dig? That's when I split! Every morning that bitch would wake me up at nine o'clock to try to teach *me* to play like Coleman Hawkins! And she played trumpet herself—

POSTIF: She was playing—

YOUNG: circus trumpet! [*Laughs.*] Shit, fuck these motherfuckers, I'm gone! Now that's real shit, that's not no bullshit!

[The following portion is not on Porter's tape:]

POSTIF: Do you think that your style can give birth to new talents?

YOUNG: They play their way, but sometimes I take pleasure to listen to some records where the tenor plays exactly like me.

POSTIF: And what about Coleman Hawkins?

YOUNG: Oh, I know what you mean. As far as I'm concerned, I think Coleman Hawkins was the President first, right? When I first heard him, I thought that was some great jazz I was listening to. As far as myself, I think I am the second one. No braggadocio, you know, I don't talk like that. There's only one way to go. If a guy plays tenor, he's got to sound like Hawk or like Lester. If he plays alto, he's got to be Bird or Johnny Hodges. There's another way, the way I hear all the guys playing in New York, running all over the place.

Part Three
The Music

Because I am a jazz saxophonist, my own writings on jazz have centered on musical issues more than anything else, although I've done my share of biographical research and a great deal of discographical research. I suppose I'm biased, yet it seems to make sense to say that the music is the most important thing about Lester Young, that it is only through his music that we become interested in his life story and personality.

Young's music was controversial even in his youth, as illustrated by his unhappy experience in the Fletcher Henderson band. But today that controversy is long gone. In its place a debate rages around the significance of Young's music after he left Basie in 1940. Some of the debate is clearly ridiculous—for example, the insistence that all of Young's work from 1940 through 1959 is of a piece, and a bad piece at that, is totally absurd. No listener could possibly miss the driving intensity of Young's work with the Basie band after he rejoined at the end of 1943 or the searching beauty of his improvisation around "My Foolish Things" that was recorded just after he came out of the army in 1945. It is equally unlikely that any discerning listener would confuse the Young of these titles with the Young to be heard on the last Paris recordings or with Harry Edison in 1955.

Certainly, Young had his low points, but they were only in the 1950s and even then represented a minority of his output. And even so it is more valuable to try and sort through what was happening with Young's style, how it developed and changed, than to make it a simple question of accepting or rejecting all this work outright. Young maintained, in the Hentoff and Postif interviews and elsewhere, that he did not want to stand still. He was consciously seeking other things—as evidenced, for example, by his change of mouthpiece in 1943, from a metal one to a hard rubber black one. In the late 1940s he told *Ebony* magazine and Leonard Feather that he was experimenting with plastic reeds. (These more permanent reeds still have their advocates, among them Jim Snidero and sometimes Lee Konitz, both altoists.) A musician cannot do these things by accident. Young's sound did change drastically over the years, through his own choosing, and it is our task to try and understand what the master was up to, not to dismiss his mastery out of hand. This was in fact the main thesis of my previous book, and I brought in numerous musical examples to illustrate the differences between Young's work in the 1930s, 1940s, and 1950s and the relative merits of each.

The articles in this section reflect the greatest possible variety of approaches to Young's music. You will find criticism, some of which dismisses the later works, and some of which embraces them. You will find perceptive discussions of Young's style and recordings in nontechnical terms by the critic Martin Williams, saxophonist Loren Schoenberg, and others. You will also find Young's music analyzed with musical illustrations, informally but perceptively in the articles of Dave Gelly and Louis Gottlieb, more formally in the essays of Don Heckman, Bernard Cash, and musicologist Lawrence Gushee.

The organization of these articles was dictated by a sort of flow of consciousness. They are arranged according to their content, as much as possible—those that discuss Young's output in total come first, followed by those that discuss only the early recordings, and then those that focus on the later recordings.

Martin Williams

Lester Young: Style beyond Swing

We begin Part Three with an overview of Young's career written after his death, when all the evidence was available. Martin Williams regularly offers his readers insights into a broad spectrum of jazz recordings. He has the ability to make accurate and perceptive observations about technical matters in nontechnical terms, which makes his writing excellent for the classroom. He is among the most respected jazz critics and is also the author of books on film.

Williams's best-known publication is *The Smithsonian Collection of Classic Jazz,* a boxed set of recordings with an informative booklet. He has also written several other books on jazz, edited *The Art of Jazz: Essays on the Nature and Development of Jazz* (New York: Oxford University Press, 1959) and *Jazz Panorama: From the Pages of Jazz Review* (New York: Crowell-Collier, 1962), and authored scores of articles. He was coeditor with Nat Hentoff of the *Jazz Review,* an important magazine that stimulated a great deal of serious writing by and about jazz musicians from 1958 through 1962. Since that time Williams has continued to be a prominent advocate for critical writing on jazz. The present book and many other books and articles owe their existence to his firm belief in the need for scholarly research in this field.

The present excerpt from his book *The Jazz Tradition*—probably the best introduction to Williams's work—provides some insights into Young's approach by referring the reader to numerous recorded high-

Originally published in *The Jazz Tradition*, 2d ed. (New York: Oxford University Press, 1983). Copyright © 1983 by Martin Williams. Reprinted by permission.

lights. With Williams's permission, I have omitted the opening part of the chapter, which discusses the Basie band without Young.—Ed.

For further reading. Gerhard Kühn, "Jazzporträt: Lester Young," *HiFiStereophonie,* December 1974, 1476–84, provides a balanced assessment (in German) of Young's recorded career.

Gunther Schuller's *Swing Era: The Development of Jazz, 1930–1945* (New York: Oxford University Press, 1989) contains a lengthy chapter on Young and quite a bit of discussion of Young in the Basie section as well. The lucid insights and copious musical examples are what we have come to expect from Schuller. He does miss an opportunity by neglecting to compare the famous recording of "Lester Leaps In" with the more recently uncovered alternate take, where Basie does not play during Young's second chorus but gives him the clean breaks that were obviously supposed to have been there on the master take.

Schuller is one of the few who pays attention to Young's clarinet playing. Jean Tronchot's piece "Lester Young, Clarinettiste," in the French magazine *Jazz Hot* 145 (July–August 1959): 25, is the only article devoted to this aspect of Young's art.

On Basie's records we listen to the group spirit and to the soloists. We hear what a highly personal style Basie made of Waller. We may note that Buck Clayton formed a personal approach within outlines suggested by Armstrong. That Harry Edison built a more complex trumpet style with less obvious use of Armstrong. That Herschel Evans knew the Hawkins of the early thirties. But when we discuss Lester Young we enter his own musical world.

An account of Lester Young's historical importance has often been given, but it is an account always worth giving again. He created a new aesthetic, not only for the tenor saxophone but for all jazz. One compares him usually with Coleman Hawkins, and the comparison is handy and instructive, but one might compare him with everyone who had preceded him.

Like any original talent, Lester Young reinterpreted tradition, and we may hear in him touches of King Oliver, of Armstrong (even of the most advanced Armstrong), of Trumbauer, and Beiderbecke. But in pointing them out, we only acknowledge a part of the foundation on which he built his own airy structures.

There seems to me no question that Lester Young was the most gifted and original improviser between Louis Armstrong and Charlie

Parker. He simply defied the rules and made new ones by example. His sound was light, almost vibratoless. He showed that such a sound could carry the most compelling ideas, that one could swing quietly and with a minimum of notes, and that one could command a whole orchestra by understatement. His style depended on an original and flexible use of the even, four beats that Armstrong's work made the norm. The beats were not inflexibly heavy or light in Young—indeed an occasional accent might even fall a shade ahead of the beat or behind it. And he did not phrase four bars at a time. (If he had any important precursor in the matter of flexible phrasing besides Armstrong, by the way, it was trumpeter Henry "Red" Allen, Jr.)

Lester Young's solo on Count Basie's "Doggin' Around" is a handy example, and one of the best. He begins, actually, by phrasing under the final two bars of Basie's piano chorus (thus does "Lester leap in"). His own chorus starts with a single note in a full bar of music—many a reed player and many a horn player at the time would have used at least four notes. His second musical phrase begins at the second bar and dances gracefully through the seventh, unbroken. His eighth bar is silent—balancing the opening perhaps. In nine he begins his third phrase, which links logically with his second. But the basic impulse here is not breaking through the four- and eight-bar phrases, nor in the daring symmetry of balancing one casual note at the beginning against a silence eight bars later. It is in his accents, in a sort of freely dancing rhythmic impulse, which seem almost to dictate how his melodies shall move. Then in his bridge he consumes the first half with a series of one-bar spurts and the second with a single phrase spun out of them.

With a marvelous ear, and a refusal to allow a literal reading of chords to detain him, he might freely, casually, and tantalizingly phrase several beats ahead of a coming chord change. Similarly, he might phrase behind an already departed chord. His opening chorus on "Taxi War Dance" contains a bold enough use of such horizontal, linear phrases to have captivated a whole generation of players and to seem bold still.

Thus one might say that his originality was not harmonic but a-harmonic. He announced it on his very first recording date in the dense and ultimately self-justifying dissonances of "Shoe Shine Boy," rather different from the simple harmonic ignorance of some of his predecessors. And he affirmed it with a fine harmonic high-handedness in solos like "I Never Knew." In general what he did was hit the tonic chords and read through the others as his ear and sense of melody dictated.[1]

He was an exceptional sketch artist and a master of a kind of melodic ellipsis. As Louis Gottlieb has said, he could make one hear a scale by playing only a couple of notes, as on his introduction to "Every Tub."

Sometimes one even suspects a perverseness perhaps born of a defensive introversion. He leaves out beats other players would accent. He offers an ascending phrase where one expects a descent. He turns a cliché inside out. He uses melodic intervals no one else would use, in places where one would not expect to hear them, even from him.

But he was no mere phrasemonger. However original his phrases might be, his sense of order was sometimes exceptional. We are apt to think that the best of his solos delight us because they are so eventful that they maintain themselves only out of a kind of sustained unexpectedness and energetic surprise that somehow satisfies us. But on "One O'Clock Jump," he begins with a light parody of the brass riff that accompanies him and develops that parody into a melody. His first recording of "Lady Be Good" has a motivic logic that is announced by his opening phrase. And a classic performance like "Lester Leaps In" is full of ideas that link melodically, one to the next. Perhaps the great example of this is his playing on "Jive at Five." Every phrase of that beautiful solo has been imitated and fed back to us a hundred times in other contexts by Lester's followers, but that knowledge only helps us to affirm the commendable decorum and the originality of the master's work, whenever we return to it.

Lester Young could directly reinterpret a simple, traditional idea, as he does in his clarinet solos on "Pagin' the Devil" and "Blues for Helen." And he could play jazz counterpoint—as with Buck Clayton on "Way Down Yonder in New Orleans" and "Them There Eyes," or with Billie Holiday on "Me, Myself and I" and "He's Funny That Way"—in such a way as to make one reassess all New Orleans and Dixieland jazz one has ever heard. He is—or he should be—the despair of his imitators as much as Basie the pianist should be.

We have few examples of Lester Young's slow blues playing from the years with Basie, and almost every one of them makes us wish we had more. Besides "Pagin' the Devil" and "Blues for Helen," there is a beautifully simple chorus on a never rereleased Sammy Price pickup date, "Things 'Bout Coming My Way,"[2] and the accompaniments to Jimmy Rushing on both "Blues in the Dark" (before Ed Lewis takes over to reproduce Armstrong's "Gully Low Blues" solo) and "I Left My Baby." The last is especially remarkable because Lester Young imitates a man in tears almost literally, yet aesthetically.

In 1939 Lester Young contributed a beautiful saxophone theme on the slow blues "Nobody Knows," and under his guidance the sax section plays it, curving and bending its notes with the plaintive depth of Lester himself. And in 1940 he provided the Basie orchestra with an original theme called, with typical innocence, "Tickle Toe," on which he had the group play a melodic line in eighth notes. On this basis one might have hoped for even further changes in style within the large jazz ensemble itself, with Lester Young showing the way.

His temperament was not universal. Indeed one sometimes feels he was gaily gentle to the point of deliberate innocence and innocent to the point of self-delusion. Yet his musical personality is so strong that, while one is in its presence, little else exists. He did create a world in which one can believe fully, but when his personal world came in touch with the real one, we know that the results might be tragic. The Lester Young of 1943, after he left Basie briefly and returned, was a somewhat different player, for some of the leaping energy was gone. And the Lester Young who returned from army service in late 1945 was a very different player and man.

Young once indicated that he spent his early days with Basie exploring the upper range of his horn, "alto tenor," as he put it. His middle days on "tenor tenor." And his last years, on the low notes of "baritone tenor." [This is an interpretation of a statement that appears early in the interview with Postif (q.v.).—Ed.] Beyond question, his creative energy descended as he descended the range of his horn, and his rhythmic sense gradually became that of a tired and finally exhausted man. But there are compensations, as perhaps there were bound to be from a soloist of his brilliance. Slow balladry was seldom allowed him in the years with the Basie orchestra, but his post-Basie years produced the superb musings of "These Foolish Things."[3] And, perhaps inevitably, they also produced a further extension of his blues language with the profoundly ironic, melancholy joy of "Jumpin' with Symphony Sid," with its touches of bebop phrasing, and the resignation of "No Eyes Blues." [All three titles are from the Aladdin sessions.—Ed.]

I suppose that any man who loves Lester's music will have favorite recordings from his later years in which something of his youthful energy was recaptured. Mine are from a 1949 [Savoy] session that produced "Ding Dong" and "Blues 'n' Bells." Incidentally, the "cool" tenor players seem to have liked the latter piece, too, for it contains almost the only phrases from Young's later career that they borrowed.

Lester Young created a new aesthetic for jazz, but whatever one says about his rhythmic originality, about his expansion of the very sound of jazz music, about his elusive sense of solo structure, he was a great original melodist, like all great jazzmen. Great Lester Young solos—"When You're Smiling" with Teddy Wilson, or "You Can Depend on Me," or "Way Down Yonder in New Orleans"—are self-contained. They seem to make their own rules of order and be their own excuse for being.

Notes

1. A recorded rehearsal from 1940 (released on an unauthorized LP in the seventies) with Benny Goodman and guitarist Charlie Christian finds Lester Young being more careful about his chord changes, and a challenging soloist results. [After the unauthorized LP was withdrawn, the session was reissued on Jazz Archives 42.—Ed.]

2. [The entire date was once rereleased in Japan, but in the United States only individual titles have appeared.—Ed.]

3. A 1946 broadcast version of this piece survives with Young accompanied by Nat Cole's trio. It is a fine complement to the studio recorded version and perhaps equally superb. [It was issued in 1989 on Jass CD-18, *Prez Conferences.*—Ed.]

Loren Schoenberg

East of the Sun:
The Changes of Lester Young

Loren Schoenberg, a jazz saxophonist and bandleader in New York City, contributed this overview of Young's work. Schoenberg has recorded several lovely albums of unusual repertory from the 1930s and 1940s (on the Musicmasters and Aviva labels), with big bands as well as small groups. On June 24, 1989, his band performed a tribute to Benny Goodman with Lionel Hampton at the JVC Jazz Festival in Carnegie Hall. Schoenberg was closely associated with Goodman: his big band accompanied Goodman's last recording and TV appearances, and he was Goodman's archivist for several years before that. He continues in the latter capacity as a consultant to the Goodman collection (donated to Yale University) in preparing a series of CDs containing previously unreleased Goodman performances.

Schoenberg has made a lifelong study of Young's music (although his own playing is in no way imitative of Young but reflects a distinctive combination of influences). As a regular commentator on WKCR radio, he was called upon to contribute an essay about Young for the program guide. With a quiet sincerity this piece debunks many of the stereotypes about Young's style.—Ed.

Lester Young made sounds on his instrument never heard before or since. He was one of the most influential instrumentalists the music has had, yet his contributions have remained widely misunderstood and unrecognized. The same clichés about his style are repeated ad nauseam: he didn't use vibrato (if that's not a large and obvious vibrato on his first recording of "Lady Be Good," I don't know what is), he had a small sound (listen to the way he soars over the Basie band on the broadcast version of "Swinging the Blues" to hear how penetrating his tone could be), he was washed up by the early 1950s (at the 1957 reunion with Basie at the Newport Jazz Festival, he is every bit of the magical Pres), and, most ridiculous of all, he was limited in the technique department. If technique is being able to do absolutely anything one wants to on one's instrument, then Lester had all of it that he ever needed, plus more. To be sure, Lester had his antecedents in the jazz tradition, most notably Louis Armstrong, Bix Beiderbecke, and Frank Trumbauer, but it was the way that he took their lessons and melded them into his own conception that made him so special. He could convey the most enticing sense of forward momentum without losing his posture and play way over his head without ever losing it. Every time we listen to his musical poetry it becomes all the more clear that he was one of a kind. He was as abstract an artist as jazz has seen, yet his work remains accessible to anyone with two ears in working order.

To this day many players think Lester Young's playing is just a mixture of pentatonic scales, usually played descending, repeated notes, usually the minor third, and a "wimpy" sound. Why is this? Probably because the subtleties of his music are still beyond most listeners and musicians. Is it any wonder that Lester took refuge in his own world, when during his lifetime very few people had any idea of what he was doing? Many great musicians still thought that his a-harmonic style was due to a lack of harmonic knowledge—or to laziness. He had a sense of humor in his playing that many mistook for either premature senility or weakness. For instance, a hilarious moment occurs on a JATP concert performance in Europe in 1953, when the whole troupe, plus Ella Fitzgerald, all play his theme "Lester Leaps In" and lead up to a huge break for Lester. When the big moment comes, Pres emits a musical Bronx cheer, which should have broken them all up. He then proceeds to blow his brains out [Europa Jazz LP, EJ-1050].

As great as the Basie recordings of the period 1936–40 are, his best moments come on the small group sessions made with Billie Holiday during 1937–38. The material he had to deal with on the big band recordings was either blues, "I Got Rhythm," or some other common chord sequence repeated over and over again. On the Holiday sides he encountered tunes further off the beaten track, with more challenging changes, and in nonstandard keys. And whereas the Basie band became either a background for his solos or his laying out, Billie and Lester repeatedly encouraged each other to greater heights—a good example is the high note Lester plays on the last bridge of "A Sailboat in the Moonlight." Mention should be made of the overtone he achieves on the high F-sharp [on saxophone], an aspect of saxophone playing largely ignored during those years and not fully explored until the late 1940s by Stan Getz (Illinois Jacquet's contributions notwithstanding). His use of space, the length he left between phrases is something to marvel at. One can almost hear him think at times, and he seemed to thrive in contexts where many musicians would not—for example, his dynamic work in the 1939 session with roller-rink organist Glenn Hardman or the exquisite obbligato and solo work on the 1941 date with vocalist Una Mae Carlisle.

Much has been made of the change in his playing that occurred in the middle 1940s. It has been attributed to his awful year and a half in the army, but in reality the change began as far back as early 1942. Undoubtedly, the failure of his career as a bandleader was a blow of great magnitude, as was his eventual return "home" to the Basie band in late 1943. Recently discovered airchecks have made this progression easier to document than previously possible.

In the years 1936–41 he appears to gradually soften his tone and to phrase with increasing subtlety; as Mel Powell said so aptly, his tone seemed to turn into velvet. Earle Warren, who sat next to Lester in the Basie reed section, attributed some of the change to a decreased ability on Lester's part to breathe into the horn as strongly as he had in earlier years; many of his phrases do seem to be shorter than they were earlier. He also switched mouthpieces during the war years, from a metal Otto Link, which he had handcrafted over the years and carried in his pocket at all times, to a stock model rubber mouthpiece, which changed the basic nature of the tone. The recordings made with pianist Nat "King" Cole and bassist Red Callender were once dated as 1943 but are now known to have taken place in July 1942 with the 1943 date being fabricated so not to have interfered with the recording ban that was in effect on commercial recording during 1942–44. Lester's consistency did begin to waver during this period; during the course of one day in March 1944, he recorded two sessions for Savoy Records, and there is a marked difference between his playing on the Johnny Guarnieri small-group date and the Basie big band sides. Given this fluctuation on a daily basis, it would have been very difficult to assign a specific time period to the aforementioned Cole trio sessions [on style alone]. Some recently discovered airchecks of Lee and

Lester Young's band from mid-1942 have Lester playing in a style very close to his work on the 1944 Kansas City Six date for Commodore Records, while the material recorded for the soundtrack of the film *Jammin' the Blues* is very close to the Cole date in its soft tone and exquisite use of space. Also the sense of humor in his music grew more and more sardonic as the years passed. Compare the bridge of his second chorus of Basie's 1939 "Clap Hands, Here Comes Charlie" with the lower register punctuations of "Six Cats and a Prince" from 1944.

The next major rejuvenation in Lester Young's playing occurred in 1949. Throughout 1947 and 1948 a lack of precision had manifested itself on many of his recordings, culminating in his last session for Aladdin Records in late 1948, which produced "East of the Sun" among others. Then, all of a sudden, he came up with some of his best work of all time on the 1949 Savoy session and the Carnegie Hall concert with Roy Eldridge and Charlie Parker in September of that year. He continued in this vein throughout the year, and well into 1950, when he recorded a quartet session with pianist John Lewis that features some uncanny musical telepathy; on several occasions Lewis completes Young's phrases without losing a stitch. Throughout the 1950s there were frequent returns to this level of inspiration, most notably the *Jazz Giants '56* date for Norman Granz, some live recordings from Germany the same year, and the reunion with Basie at Newport in 1957. I think that his physical condition influenced his output during the later stages of his career, and at times he had to conserve energy—something he did with great ingenuity. When he was feeling strong, however, there was no stopping him. On the aforementioned club performances recorded in Germany in late 1956, and issued on the unfortunately out-of-print Onyx LP *Prez in Europe,* he plays his longest recorded solos on "Lester Leaps In" and on "Lester's [European] Blues." He mixes the different components of his style in such a way that he sustains interest for solos that, by his standards, were extremely long.

Lester Young said many times that he was preoccupied with the *sound* possible on the tenor saxophone, and he does some real stretching out in this regard on these items.

Lester's clarinet work is intriguing, since he tended to play a little "hotter" on it than on the tenor sax. This is readily apparent on the 1939 "I Ain't Got Nobody," for which he solos on both instruments. His tenor solo floats along, implying passion rather than acting it out, while his clarinet solo has much more bite. And it's interesting to observe the resultant change in his "story" on the different instruments. He recorded

on the clarinet between summer 1938 and spring 1939 and never picked
it up again, with the exception of a faltering attempt about a year before
his death. Artie Shaw has said that the more prominent clarinetists of the
1930s played the clarinet better than Lester, but that Lester played better
clarinet. His work is a mixture of the New Orleans and Southwestern
approaches to the instrument. In 1948 Ross Russell noted that there was a
similarity between Lester's clarinet style and that of Eddie Barefield, both
of whom knew each other as early as 1927. They shared a "lemony" tone
and a fondness for correlative phrasing, playing in questions and answers.
The ensemble interplay between Lester and trumpeter Buck Clayton on
the 1938 Commodore Kansas City Six date shows Lester's mastery of
contrapuntal playing, and it's a shame that he didn't get to showcase more
often. It is prominent, however, in a few places, most notably the duo with
trumpeter Harry "Sweets" Edison on the slow blues that opens the film
Jammin' the Blues and on a recently issued JATP item from 1946, with
trumpeter Joe Guy on "Tea for Two" [Verve LP 825.101-1].

When people talk about the influence that Lester had on Charlie
Parker, it is usually limited to finding some Pres phrases in Bird's solos, as
on the Wichita transcriptions from 1940. But I submit that the influence
went way beyond that, since Parker surely grasped the more abstract and
more subtle effects Lester achieved, and this certainly played a large role
in opening up Parker's conception to the point where he was able to
express himself completely.

It is certain that Lester has had a much greater effect on the music
that followed his career than we know about. This is a relatively unex-
plored area of research.

Dave Gelly

Review of *Prez: Lester Young Solos* by Bernard Cash

Dave Gelly's review is a good introduction to some of the musical details of Young's solos from the 1930s. Gelly writes regularly for *Jazz Journal* and other English publications and is a saxophonist as well. His ninety-six-page book on Lester Young (Tunbridge Wells: Spellmount Ltd., 1984) consists of a review of Young's life and musical career, with commentary on important recording sessions and a selective discography.

There are no musical examples in his book, but Gelly's musical training comes to the fore in this review of a collection of Young's transcribed solos (which I believe is no longer available) issued by Bernard Cash, another English musician whose work is included later in Part Three. In this brief essay Gelly manages to elucidate many of the unique aspects of Young's playing in clear and witty prose, and he touches upon the problems inherent in transcribing from recordings. The reader will notice, in comparing music examples for the articles in this collection, that the same examples are transcribed a little differently by each author. Please note that in England a quarter note is called a "crotchet."—Ed.

Rudolf Nureyev once said that a great dancer is not one who makes a difficult step look easy but one who makes an easy step look interesting. Further to which, exhibit A:

—which is Lester's two-bar break into his solo on "Clap Hands, Here Comes Charlie." You can't get much easier than eight even crotchets on the tonic note, can you? And yet, when you hear it, it's not just interesting, it's electrifying.

Of course, it doesn't *sound* like eight even crotchets, and I never thought of it as such until spending several instructive hours with this most welcome book. There are twenty-five solos, all drawn from Lester's recordings between 1936 and 1942—the years when his imagination was at its most fluent.

"No transcription can exactly communicate the actuality of performance," says Bernard Cash in his introduction, and that's putting it mildly. Eight dots on a page can't tell you how Prez announces his arrival and smacks into the break, chewing the notes like gum. Each one of those E-flats is slightly, magically different; each has force, life, exact weight, and texture. If you haven't got the record to hand, the dots aren't much use to you, but if you have they focus your attention wonderfully and help you to hear the music better.

The first thing you notice is how simple Lester's phrases are. Take "Taxi War Dance," his own favorite solo. The middle eight is in C minor, and his opening phrase is:

Eh? Can't be! But it is. Half of Lester's phraseology is made up of scales and arpeggios as basic as that. The secret lies in the way they are put together, the unerring confidence of delivery, the strategy, the design, the unity of line and tone.

Written music is diagrammatic. A quick glance at the page will quickly reveal patterns that, on closer inspection, turn out to be characteristic parts of a player's style. In Lester's case, one of these is the kind of across-the-barline phrase [from "Way Down Yonder in New Orleans," master take, 1938—Ed.] that probably attracted the young Charlie Parker's attention:

The same glance will also show you that there are very few accidentals, and hence very little in the way of chromatic elaboration. By contrast, a page of Bird is a veritable forest of sharps and flats. So much for those helpful writers who still earnestly tell us that Lester Young "paved the way" for Charlie Parker's harmonic thinking.

To say that Lester was a simple player is not to make light of his technique however. Try playing this when you've had a few [i.e., the beginning of Young's solo on "Ad-Lib Blues" (October 28, 1940)—Ed.]:

Transcribing this kind of music is murder because there are so many indefinite things. Is that lazy little flick an upper mordent

or just a slight exaggeration of the vibrato? If you write it all out it looks unnaturally complicated, but if you just put a wiggly line over the first note it could mean anything. Even notes themselves are maddeningly uncertain because one of the characteristics of the jazz line is variable density. Half a phrase can disappear in a kind of sotto voce shrug. It is interesting to compare Bernard Cash's version of "Lester Leaps In" with the one in the recent *Front Line Jazz Solos*. As early as the fifth bar there is serious disagreement, not just about time, which is slippery in any case, but about actual notes—the pitch and even the *number* of them. This is easier to understand when you remember that an extra push on the vibrato can bisect a note, and when that note is sliding up or down, who is to say whether it's two separate notes or one note bent?

If Bernard Cash intends to produce more of these books, and I hope he does (including a few more Lester ones), I humbly offer two constructive suggestions. First, please put the chords over or under the notes. It doesn't matter when it's a blues or "Rhythm," but not everybody knows the changes to "Taxi War Dance." I had to sort them out and write them in—which was good practice, I suppose. Secondly, why not mark off the choruses with double barlines? The "Tickle Toe" solo starts before the chorus, so does "Clap Hands," so does the first take of "Way Down Yonder," but not the second, which could be confusing.

Louis Gottlieb

Why So Sad, Pres?

This article basically concerns itself with Young's Basie days. There is a little discussion of the later years at the end, but, as Gottlieb notes, there were not enough recordings available at that time to make a proper study. Gottlieb is a musicologist trained at the University of California, Berkeley, who clearly knows Young's work well. In this article he illustrates many important and subtle details about Young's work with a deceptive informality. For example, he mentions in a footnote toward the end that most of Young's faster ornaments used the concert pitches F and G, regardless of what key he was playing in. This little comment must have resulted from endless hours of careful listening with saxophone in hand (if not in Gottlieb's hand, then one of the musician friends he thanks at the end!). It happens to be corroborated by my own research, which began with "hunches" like these but eventually ended up with computerized analysis of transcribed solos. One of the computer's results agreed fairly well with Gottlieb's claim.

Gottlieb touches on Young's treatment of harmony and his approach to rhythm, and he illustrates some of Young's standard formulas. He also discusses Young's sense of form (during most of section IV) but, I think, grossly underestimates how motivic Young's playing could be. In fact his choice of "Jive at Five" as an example of free playing without "any identifiable patterns" is strange, since that is a particularly motivic passage. On the other hand his discussion offers many original observations about such things as Young's way of beginning his solos.

Originally published in *Jazz: A Quarterly of American Music*, ed. Ralph Gleason, no. 3 (Summer 1959): 185–96. Copyright © 1959 by Ralph Gleason. Reprinted by permission of Mrs. Jean Gleason.

211

Perhaps Gottlieb's most amazing statement appears at the end of section IV. He suggests a number of ideas for dissertations in musicology based on the study of Young's music and points out that such dissertations would be far more valuable than some of the topics usually pursued. Gottlieb was a prophet, because today it is increasingly believed that we need more American dissertations about American music, and especially jazz, and it is specifically in musicology—only infrequently in ethnomusicology or in music theory—that this is happening. I am in touch with graduate students across the United States and Europe, and I have seen works completed or in progress on John Coltrane, Charlie Parker, interaction in jazz, and many other subjects. It used to be outrageous for a musicologist to study jazz, but it is now accepted and even encouraged in many graduate programs.—Ed.

Jazz musicians are the most vital fraction of the "jazz people," that element within the population of the United States whose members, perhaps because they are the least self-consciously interracial, synthesize American national character so accurately. Lester Young gave musical expression to what was widely felt by jazz people but ne'er so well played. That his music truthfully expressed and shaped the ideas of our time may be seen by the size of the "school" that operates where Lester cleared the land. His antenna was more sensitive to the "vibrations" of our time; he burned hotter and felt more deeply than others.

When a great jazz musician dies, we all have different reasons for feeling sad but a common impulse to reflect a moment on our loss. What follows is a sort of systematic recollection of some of the things Lester Young used to do that delighted this one of his many fans.

II

Composition and performance in a jazz solo constitute a single process; *what* is played is the same as *how* it's played.[1] To facilitate the discussion of a personal style in jazz playing, however, it's a good idea to abstract the composition from the performance by writing out the solos to be studied. The two aspects of personal style may then be considered separately, as objective and subjective sets of data. The objective data are the compositional aspects—those elements of a jazz solo that *can* be written down. Every solo, of course, contains much that cannot be adequately expressed in musical notation: tone quality, pitch deviations for expressive purposes, the precise measurements of the long-short subdivision of the quarter note, between-the-beat placement of rhythmic figures, and so on, in short, the main features of performance by which a personality is identified. These constitute the subjective data in the study of personal style in jazz playing.[2]

It is impossible to say which elements are more decisive in the definition of personal style. It would be kicks to prepare "blindfold tests" that included recordings of transcribed solos played on instruments other than the ones on which they were conceived.

One thing is certain: It is comparatively easy to handle the objective compositional elements of personal style and admittedly difficult to be specific in the discussion of the subjective aspects of personal style. How, for example, does one explain even to a good musician who has never heard Lester Young or Coleman Hawkins the difference between Young's tone and that of Hawkins? The use of metaphor in the discussion of the subjective aspects is justified for lack of something more concrete, but even the discussion of the objective aspects of personal style has, alas, been the occasion for much use of language that is excessively vague and rhapsodic.

III

Pres mentioned more than once that his playing had been influenced by that of Frank Trumbauer and Bud Freeman. [Actually, Young regarded Freeman as a peer rather than an influence. See the Postif interview above.—Ed.] It's useless to try to trace these influences in the available recorded performances. By [November] 9, 1936—the date of his first recording session—Lester Young was a completely mature artist capable of inventing jazz melodies of striking originality and great "density"—to borrow one of Malraux's bons mots. He was twenty-seven years old at the "Jones-Smith, Inc." date, and, as one might expect, all influences had been thoroughly assimilated into his own highly individual style.

If recordings of Lester in his eighteenth or twentieth year existed, perhaps the influences of Trumbauer and Freeman might be easier to spot. At any rate, it is clear that no one influenced Lester Young to the extent that he overwhelmed the development of others.[3]

IV

All jazz soloists evolve a stock of melodic formulas that they use as spring-boards for invention. Since they as a rule vary quite a bit with each appearance, by comparing the specific forms in which these "licks" appear, one gains a certain insight into the musical thought of the player.

Lester had some great ones. My favorite may be called the "doh-mi" formula. The first two pitches of numerous solos are the first and third degrees of the tonic scale. The first "doh" invariably appears on the first beat of the chorus and may be repeated any number of times before "mi" enters. The classic formulation can be seen in example 1a; other variations are shown in examples 1b–1d.

a. "Lester Leaps In" (September 5, 1939)

b. "I Never Knew" (March 19, 1940)

c. "Swinging the Blues" (February 16, 1938)

d. "Pound Cake" (May 19, 1939)

EXAMPLE 1

The rhythmic variety in these four appearances of the "doh-mi" formula is considerable. Each of the "dohs" receives a slightly different accent and attack, and the "mi" is often approached from a grace note a half step below. It is invariably an exciting kickoff that imparts a great swing to the whole solo.

Certain subjective aspects in Lester's use of this lick are also noteworthy. For example, the first note of his solo on "Swinging the Blues" (ex. 1c) is played quite flat, and this invests the whole solo with a raucous, "let-the-good-times-roll" quality.

Another favored melodic gesture is what I call the "sigh," and Lester usually employed it in pairs (see ex. 2). The position of the descending fourth, C–G, in example 2a is worthy of note. It's a pretty advanced way to begin the blues in B-flat for twenty years ago. In phrases like these Lester always seems to be riding the crest of the beat.

a. "Riff Interlude" (November 6, 1939), mm. 1–5

b. "Lester Leaps In" (September 5, 1939), mm. 9–12 of Lester's second chorus

EXAMPLE 2

In examples 2a and 2b there is another characteristic feature of Lester's style: the varied repetition of an idea that shifts its metrical position. A somewhat clearer instance of this procedure in a typical ascending line is shown in example 3, where the figure is shifted from the strong beat to the weak beat on repetition.

EXAMPLE 3. "Riff Interlude," mm. 5–8 of Lester's second blues chorus

Lester Young was *the* master of metric shifting. There are countless instances in his solos where he obliterates the difference between strong and weak beats, and strong and weak *halves* of the beat. I will never forget the first time I heard "I Never Knew" in a record store in Washington, D.C. I thought the record had slipped a groove at the spot marked by an asterisk in example 4. With the exception of the little embellishing note, F (marked with a double asterisk in ex. 4), the first six and a half measures of this bridge use only five pitches. Should any philologist of the twenty-first

EXAMPLE 4. "I Never Knew" (December 28, 1943), bridge of Lester's third chorus

century seek a definition of the expression "gone!" or "gone again!" this bridge would do quite well.

The harmonic implications of Lester's lines are frequently amazing. He was able to invent apparently simple melodies that bear a complex chromatic relationship to their harmonic context. The opening measures of one of his most famous solos, a solo that Charlie Parker apparently knew from memory,[4] are worthy of a close look (see ex. 5). One might well imagine that Lester simply "didn't know the chords" until the specific "heat" of each of the dissonances is recognized, and the line understood to possess a suprahuman jazz-melodic logic.

EXAMPLE 5. "Shoe Shine Boy" ([November] 9, 1936)

Lester was fond of elaborating the submediant harmony in major keys, the chord based upon the sixth degree, superimposing it upon various other chords, mainly the tonic. In the last four measures of his solo on "Blow Top" (ex. 6), Lester sets off the fixed tones of the C-minor triad [C–E♭–G] against a shifting harmonic background. I've always been partial to the passage from "Lester Leaps Again" shown in example 7; it

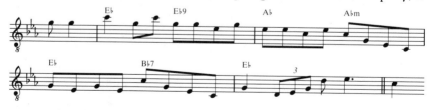

EXAMPLE 6. "Blow Top" (March 31, 1940), last four measures of Lester's solo

EXAMPLE 7. "Lester Leaps Again" (March 22, 1944)

seems such a perfect "goin' home" riff. [Here the tones of an E-minor triad are used: E–G–B.—Ed.]

The sixth itself had an attraction for Pres. One of his best-known solos stays on the sixth [B-flat, sixth note in the key of D-flat] for a full three and one-half measures (see ex. 8). In example 8, of course, Pres is using his well-known technique of alternative fingerings to produce changes in the sonorities on the same pitch. I sometimes wonder if this device didn't originate on trumpet.

EXAMPLE 8. "One O'Clock Jump" (July 7, 1937)

The augmented triad held a special fascination for Lester. The four-measure break in "Easy Does It" (ex. 9) within which he modulates from F major to D-flat major is unorthodox but completely convincing. Oh, yes, and the use of the lowest note on the horn (see the asterisk) with a characteristic BAWP was a real Lester Young trademark. In this connection his brilliant introduction to "Every Tub" (see ex. 10) must be mentioned. Notice especially the restrained way in which the two whole-tone scales are implied in the second four measures. Some players these days

EXAMPLE 9. "Easy Does It" (March 19, 1939)

EXAMPLE 10. "Every Tub" (February 16, 1938)

run up and down the whole-tone scales until the listener is positively punchy.

Even the greatest jazz solo consists to some extent of a more-or-less spontaneous reshuffling of generalizable melodic procedures such as have been discussed so far. The "challenge of thematic improvisation"[5] is new in jazz, and although evidences of motivic construction could be shown in Lester's work, it was not really an important feature of his musical thought. In this sense Pres was a folk artist and used his best licks wherever they did the most good depending upon the tempo and key.

Occasionally this could mean the use of an identical phrase in solos on completely different pieces in the same key and roughly the same tempo. Examples 11a and 11b are cases in point: Both solos are in E-flat major, up tempo, and—incidentally—cut within six months of each other.

a. "Clap Hands, Here Comes Charlie" (August 4, 1939), last four measures of the solo

b. "Twelfth Street Rag" (April 5, 1939), mm. 18–21 of Lester's second chorus

EXAMPLE 11

After this nosy peak into Pres's workshop, we should include at least one example of a solo that is a burst of pure lyricism and doesn't particularly rely on any identifiable patterns. I have selected with difficulty from many possible choices and perhaps for reasons of pure nostalgia one of my favorite moments in the entire world of music (see ex. 12). The

EXAMPLE 12. "Jive at Five" (February 2, 1939), mm. 1–16

second eight measures begin with a repetition of the preceding phrase (see m. 7)—a classic device for spinning out a melodic line—and going as it does into the delightful bouncing around of measures 9–10, this section is positively magic.

There are so many facets of Lester Young's style that await methodical investigation: his ability to "play the melody"—that is, paraphrase it; his clarinet playing; his use of quotations (the solo on "Taxi War Dance" begins with "Ol' Man River"); the extent of his influence on Count Basie's band, Charlie Parker, the "brothers" [of Woody Herman's band], and other instrumentalists; the whole question of "development" within the compositional aspects as he grew older; and so on. Any one of these topics properly handled could be fine for a master's or even a doctoral dissertation in musicology and would constitute a far more valuable contribution to scholarship than some of the subjects that American graduate students in musicology are developing eyestrain over right now.

V

What of the subjective aspects of Lester Young's style? As with so many other jazz greats, his playing gives the impression of inexhaustible energy that manifests itself in many ways: for example, the "drive-to-get-started." Very rarely does Lester wait until after his solo space has begun to start blowing. He often "leaps in" a measure or so before it or else comes on strong with the first beat.

This characteristic of boundless, almost surplus energy produces figures like the one shown in example 13.[6] One frequently gets the impression that Pres, like other jazz greats, is rushing the eighth notes. He really "stays after it" in a passage like that in example 14.

EXAMPLE 13. "When You're Smiling" (January 6, 1938), Teddy Wilson's Orchestra

EXAMPLE 14. "Lester Leaps In," second eight measures

VI

Obviously this isn't the place to discuss the subjective aspects of Lester Young's style thoroughly, but one final question may perhaps be best treated from the subjective point of view. The reader may have noticed that most of the examples selected date from before World War II. This is partly for sentimental reasons and partly because these are the solos I know best. But jazz criticism is much concerned these days, as it rightly should be, with the problem of development in the careers of jazz artists. Do they grow in artistic stature or do they, like athletes, set records only to have them broken by subsequent generations? It is safe to assume that the life work of each artist will provide a different specific answer to this question, but this does not invalidate the overall question.

It is my impression that major developments in the compositional elements—the objective side—of Lester Young's personal style will not be found. With Pres it is as if we have no "early, middle, and late periods" of creative activity but rather only an extended middle period.[7]

It is true that in some of the early recordings we find certain procedures that he eliminated from his later works, especially sequential patterns like those in "Lady Be Good" (ex. 15a) and "Taxi War Dance" (ex. 15b, a type of which I was rather fond). It is clear that in analogous situations Pres found that the same kinds of ideas were in his fingers.

On the whole, though, it is difficult to point out concrete developments in the compositional elements of his style. [Over the years] the line

a. "Lady Be Good" ([November] 9, 1936), beginning seven measures from the end of Lester's second chorus

b. "Taxi War Dance" (March 19, 1939), beginning seven measures—coincidentally—from the end of Lester's only chorus

EXAMPLE 15

becomes somewhat more disjunct—the individual motives seem to stand out more prominently.

The situation is quite different in the development of the subjective elements. For one thing, it is much harder to transcribe a Lester Young solo of 1956 than one of 1936, because the use of between-the-beat figures is so much more in evidence. But most of all there is the change in tone.

In the last records I hear an unspeakable sadness—an actual pessimism that is rarely to be found in the art of the American Negro up to now. The existence of this quality is not susceptible of rigorous demonstration in prose, but it's there for anyone who can hear. Why so sad, Pres?

The personal tragedy in the subjective aspect of Lester Young's late records is related to but not entirely explained by the impeditive social situation that he as an American Negro faced every day of his life. This personal tragedy in the subjective aspects is, I feel, specifically of the jazz world and his craft, and it demands some attempt at explanation, however speculative.

Starting out in the music business, the beginner of Lester's generation was for a while the "worst man in the band"—perhaps even the "fall guy." Everyone takes it upon himself to instruct, criticize, tease, and occasionally praise the novice—he LEARNS DAILY about his craft from everyone. Later he becomes one of the "regular guys" in the band, and most of us stay about there.

Real conflicts are only encountered by the "best man in the band." There is no one to teach him. He has no "pappy." Since his relationship with his coworkers is not that of teacher-pupil, he is open to the charge of egotism. He is not afraid of anyone "stealing his stuff" but rather is concerned because there is no longer anyone's "stuff" for him to "steal." A strange loneliness. Remember, jazz is collective music.

Pres was the "best man in the band" for a long time. A personality as unique as this is at once tormented and pleased to hear the by-products of his self-assertion become fads. Pres had to smile when others "had bulging eyes" and others "felt a draft." But how then to continue the definition of Lester Young? That requires a bootstrap that is not available in jazz. Jacques Hadamard is quoted as saying that the more vigorous creative minds among the scientists are often inclined to drop a project when the less inventive begin to swarm upon it and to go on to something fresh.[8] In jazz for Lester Young there was not much room in which to go hunting for "something fresh." Even the keys jazz is played in are fairly limited. I don't think Pres ever recorded in any key with more than one sharp in its signature.

They say Lester Young stayed high a lot. If this contributed to his premature death, it's too bad, because the changes that are clearly evident in the subjective aspects of his personal style *would have found expression* in the compositional elements. Maybe, given another twenty years, Lester— like Verdi—would have come up with his own version of "all the world's a joke, and man is a born clown." God, what music *that* would have been. But then, Verdi was not an American Negro living in the atomic age.

I never knew Lester Young personally, but his work has provided me and still does provide me with great musical experiences. This little piece is dedicated to his memory and to my friends Jack Laird, Jim Salko, and Jack Schaeffer, good musicians in whose company and with whose help I came to understand something of the significance of Lester Young. And who know all too well that Pres won't be coming through town again.

Notes

1. André Hodeir, *Jazz: Its Evolution and Essence,* trans. David Noakes (New York: Grove Press, 1956), 111, puts it this way: "Jazz is an art in which conception cannot be divorced from means of expression and the way in which creative thought is given form."

2. Since a jazz solo is music conceived without pencil and paper, the gap between even the most carefully notated solo and the solo as sound is greater than in "art music." But those who maintain that "real jazz cannot be written" should be reminded that the "real Chopin" or the "real Schubert" is not what appears on the printed page.

On the other hand, transcribers of folk music who try by extensive use of diacritical marks to put everything down on the paper are wasting their time, especially when the performance is easily available on recordings. Anyone who wants to reproduce the music in performance will refer to the recordings. The main value of transcriptions really is that they facilitate reference.

3. One wonders whether Lester's references to Trumbauer and Freeman were not at least partially motivated by a desire to separate himself "positively" from any connection with Coleman Hawkins—as if that were necessary.

Here is one of the few places in Lester's recorded solos where I seem to hear a fragment that Bud Freeman might have made during the time he worked for Tommy Dorsey [1936–38]. This is the eleventh measure in Pres's solo (counting the four-measure modulatory break—see ex. 9) on Count Basie's record of "Easy Does It" (March 19, 1939). The upward-moving syncopation sounds "Freemanesque," doesn't it?

4. According to Lee Konitz, "I was on tour with Charlie once and I was warming up in the dressing room—I happened to be playing one of Lester's choruses—and Bird came noodling into the room and said, 'Hey, you ever heard this one?' and he played *Shoe Shine Swing* about twice as fast as the record. He knew all that. I believe he's probably whistling it up in heaven right now." Dave Brubeck and Lee Konitz, "A Conversation with Two Jazz Musicians," *Northwest Review* 1, no. 3 (Spring 1958): 48. This solo—"Shoe Shine Boy," mm. 23–24 of Lester's second chorus—

turns out to be the source of the first phrase of "Ornithology":

5. Gunther Schuller, "Sonny Rollins and the Challenge of Thematic Improvisation," *Jazz Review* 1, no. 1 (November 1958): 6–11, 21.

6. In general, Lester made rather sparing use of note values smaller than eighths. Curiously a good 75 percent of the small notes that he did use involve two pitches, F and G above middle C (concert pitch), no matter what key the solo is in [as in ex. 13]. On the horn these in turn involve the ring finger of the left hand—theoretically one of the slower-moving digits.

7. This question must be held in abeyance until the last records are available. Apparently the latest records currently available date from about 1956.

8. Brewster Ghiselin, *The Creative Process* (New York: New American Library of World Literature, 1958), 18.

Lawrence Gushee

Lester Young's "Shoe Shine Boy"

Lawrence Gushee, who also wrote numerous pieces for *Jazz Review* in the late 1950s as Larry Gushee, is a distinguished expert on medieval music theory at the University of Illinois, and much of his publishing is in that area. In the jazz community he is known as one of its foremost scholars, an expert at archival research as well as musical analysis and theoretical matters. Gushee's studies on the first generations of jazz players in and around New Orleans have yielded a spate of ground-breaking articles. In *Storyville* 98 (December 1981–January 1982): 56–59, he announced his discovery of Jelly Roll Morton's birthdate, which turned out to be in 1890, five years later than previously believed. And in the journal *American Music* 3 (1985): 389–412, he reconstructed Morton's professional travels before he began recording in 1923, an amazing feat of research that involved the use of many obscure periodicals of the day. The *Black Music Research Journal*, which is published once a year at Columbia College in Chicago, has presented Gushee's research on the Creole Band and other matters. Gushee's early jazz studies will eventually coalesce into a book. In the meantime we may enjoy this stimulating and far-reaching article.

Gushee's chapter is really an intensive look at the process of improvisation itself, using Young as an example. It was originally delivered as a talk at the convention of the International Musicological Society when it met in Berkeley, California, in 1977, so it was intended for an audience of music professors, primarily working outside the jazz field.

Originally published in International Musicological Society, *Report of the Twelfth Congress, Berkeley, 1977*, ed. Daniel Heartz and Bonnie Wade (Kassel: Barenreiter, 1981), 151–69. Copyright © 1981 by Lawrence Gushee. Reprinted by permission.

The talk was written for a symposium about how music is transmitted orally, and it was surrounded by reports about the ways that Christian chant was passed on. Gushee's talk illustrated the advantage of studying the transmission of musical ideas in jazz, where one has actual recordings that show how ideas develop from one take to the next. The reader should also note that, because of the unusual focus of his presentation, Gushee did not make reference to Young's other recordings. Ideally, Gushee has said, studies of jazz should relate each recording to the whole of that artist's music, and entire performances should be transcribed, not just the saxophone solos, in order to show how everybody interacts with each other.

Gushee would like to thank Mark Tucker, who took the time to edit three of the transcriptions for this reprinting, and Robert Witmer, who contributed some observations.—Ed.

This essay was originally entitled "What Kind of Oral Tradition Is Jazz?" and developed from the convergence of two interests of mine, jazz and medieval plainchant, for the latter of which recent work by Leo Treitler had opened new vistas of understanding. My consideration of a small sample of Lester Young's music was embedded in what now seems to me, and seemed at the time to the chairman of the study group, a rather artificial setting that purported to test the validity or applicability of the terms "oral composition" and "oral transmission"—as they had been construed by Albert Lord[1] in his work with Yugoslav epic singer-poets—to the music called jazz.

This attempt seemed worthwhile, since it is immediately obvious that much of the musical expression and construction in the jazz idiom and style is "oral," in being carried on without the aid of musical notation. Furthermore, we have or can have a great deal of detailed evidence of various sorts for the cultural context and specific musical procedures of jazz, as contrasted with, say, Eskimo song or medieval plainchant.

Treitler, however, did not encourage my desire to discuss his patent dependence on Lord. In the course of the session, it became clear to me why this was so, when he presented his historical-cultural models for musical transmission in which concrete circumstances of transmission and socially defined function and value were made fundamental. From these models, as well as from some of the other papers, it emerged—

although perhaps neither explicitly nor with the assent of all panelists—that *written* and *oral* per se were rather crude, if not misleading terms, each covering a variety of specific cultural or historical circumstances, and not very useful for a taxonomy of music, an analysis of poetic or "creative process," or an explanation of musical change.

My discussion of Lester Young's "Shoe Shine Boy" seems in retrospect to recommend a versatility in analysis, not simply as an exercise in the exhaustion of possibilities, but in recognition that in music—perhaps especially with functionally differentiated or stratified ensembles (as in jazz bands)—different kinds of relationships operate over different time spans. It may be that within one and the same kind of music, performers differ greatly in the emphasis or control of one kind of relationship, and in the way their memory functions at the various levels. And finally, I discover that my subject is chiefly oral composition, although the proximity in time of the two performances examined can be considered to involve a kind of transmission.

Some points to keep in mind in reading my remarks:

1. *Jazz* is used to denote style and practice of what is usually called the Swing Era, roughly the 1930s.
2. By the mid-1930s most professional jazz players could and did read music. Many had an acquaintance with harmony; some had studied standard instrumental études and methods (e.g., for trumpeters, Arban and Herbert L. Clarke).
3. Commercial recordings are made under special conditions, some of which run counter to oral compositional procedures.
4. The timing cycle that guides, stimulates, and limits jazz solo playing is tangibly audible in the rhythm section.

Lester Young, nicknamed "Prez," as for "the President," was born in Mississippi in 1909 and died fifty years later in New York City. He came to national prominence with Count Basie's orchestra, in which he played tenor saxophone between 1936 and 1940, and as accompanist to Billie Holiday in recordings of 1937 and 1938. Any history of jazz will name him as one of the two style leaders of saxophone playing between 1935 and 1945, along with his in some respects opposite number, Coleman Hawkins.

Young was first recorded commercially on [November] 9, 1936, in Chicago, with five other members of the Basie band, which was breaking in for national exposure at the Grand Terrace Ballroom on the South Side. Four tunes were recorded, "Shoe Shine Boy," "Lady Be Good,"

"Evenin'," and "Boogie Woogie," the last two with vocal by Jimmy Rushing. They were released on the Vocalion label a few months later under the name "Jones-Smith Incorporated," supposedly because the Basie band was under exclusive recording contract with Decca Records. The four performances have been reissued a number of times, and the first two named were well known to players and serious listeners during the fifties and sixties.

It was not until four years ago or so that another take of "Shoe Shine Boy" came to light; it has since been reissued three times, twice in Europe and once in the United States. Two other performances of "Shoe Shine Boy" involving the same musicians along with the rest of Basie's band were recorded from this period, both from January 1937. One is called "Roseland Shuffle," released by Decca; the other "Shoe Shine Swing," recorded from a radio broadcast originating in the Hotel William Penn, Pittsburgh. [The latter is from February 1937.—Ed.]

These four performances of "Shoe Shine Boy" all feature Lester Young and are the texts for this discussion. Transcriptions of most of Young's solo playing therein are included (see ex. 1).[2] The various versions will be lettered A–D according to the following key:

Version A

Chicago, October 8, 1936 [actually November 9]
Jones-Smith Incorporated (Carl Smith, trumpet; Lester Young, tenor
    sax; Count Basie, piano; Walter Page, string bass; Jo Jones, drums)
    mx C. 1657-1   *Shoe Shine Boy*   Vocalion 3441/Col CG
                                                33502 (USA)
                                                CBS 65384 (Europe)
                                                Tax (Sweden)

Version B

    mx C. 1657-2   *Shoe Shine Boy*   unissued take, reissues as
                                                above

Version C

Pittsburgh, February 8, 1937 [actually, the exact day in February is uncertain—Ed.]
Count Basie and His Orchestra (Joe Keyes, Carl Smith, Buck Clayton,
    trumpet; Dan Minor, George Hunt, trombone; Caughey Roberts,

alto sax; Jack Washington, alto sax, baritone; Herschel Evans, Lester
Young, tenor sax; Count Basie, piano; Walter Page, string bass;
Claude Williams, guitar; Jo Jones, drums)
(LP issue of recording made from a radio broadcast)

Shoe Shine Swing   Jazz Archives 16

Version D

New York, January 21, 1937
Count Basie and His Orchestra (personnel as above)

   mx 61545-A   *Roseland Shuffle*   Decca 1141/MCA 4050
                      (other issues as
                      The Count & Lester)

Specific locations within the versions are identified by the measure numbers of example 1, along with the letter designating the version, for
example, B.14–15. Occasionally, eight-measure segments of the AABA
song form will be called "A section" or "B section."

Preliminary Note on Jazz Analysis

There is no commonly accepted coherent method of jazz analysis. The
most thorough and consistent applications of analysis to jazz to date are
those of Thomas Owens dealing with the playing of Charlie Parker and of
Gunther Schuller dealing with the playing of Afro-Americans during the
1920s. These represent, in my opinion, two distinct approaches, which I
designate "formulaic" and "motivic," respectively. Two other approaches,
called here "schematic" and "semiotic," are encountered, along with
eclectic mixtures. My understanding of the characteristic features of the
four approaches or types are summarized in table 1. Whether these types
of analysis correspond to types of creation or perception is a question with
no general answer. In the present instance I believe they do.

Attested Effects of "Shoe Shine Boy," Version A

The Jones-Smith Incorporated recordings, along with those by the Basie
orchestra of 1937–38, have been much praised over the years as superb
examples of a "classic" small-band swing style. Critics have perceived a

EXAMPLE 1

EXAMPLE 1 (*continued*)

EXAMPLE 1 (*continued*)

EXAMPLE 1 (*continued*)

EXAMPLE 1 (*continued*)

EXAMPLE 1 (*continued*)

EXAMPLE 1 (*continued*)

EXAMPLE 1 (*continued*)

rarely achieved balance or equilibrium in the performance as a whole. But it is Lester Young's two solo choruses that have been heard as particularly coherent, flowing, and memorable.

Without pretending to have conducted an opinion poll, I am certain that this judgment applies to the sixty-four measures taken as a whole, rather than to each thirty-two measure chorus taken separately. This may be tested by reversing the order of the two choruses, either by manipulation of a tape or in the imagination. I recommend that this be done before one becomes too well acquainted with the actual order of events.

Although the welding of two choruses into a whole may seem a modest achievement by today's standards, it was not at all usual in 1936, with few players being given that much time on an approximately three-minute recording. Perhaps the thought is father of the deed; the drummer, Connie Kay, who worked with Lester Young off and on for a half-dozen years reported: "He [Lester Young] had a funny, codelike way of talking . . . a chorus was one long and two choruses two longs. . . ."[3]

Table 1

Type of Analysis	Methods Objectives/Content	Assumptions	Boundaries
MOTIVIC Tirro[a] Schuller[b]	Demonstration of organic relations, development, climactic (tension-release) structure. Logically connected ideas.	Criteria of logic. Aesthetic merit of the work.	The work itself
FORMULAIC Owens[c]	Labeling of phrases according to the lexicon. Appropriate choice of compatible formulas, with relaxed logical requirements.	Learning and performance by rote or imitation.	The collective style
SCHEMATIC Dauer[d] Hodeir[e]	Generation of specific expression by transformation of fundamental structures (including a tune or chord progression as well as other patterns).	Separable levels of mental activity.	The process of forming
SEMIOTIC (A great deal of the popular literature of jazz)	Meaning as given by the system of signs. Decoding of mythic structure.	The apparatus of general semiotics; or sociopolitical theory.	The culture

[a]Frank Tirro, "Constructive Elements in Jazz Improvisation," *Journal of the American Musicological Society* (1974): 285–305.

[b]Gunther Schuller, *Early Jazz: Its Roots and Musical Development* (New York: Oxford University Press, 1968); idem, "Sonny Rollins and the Challenge of Thematic Improvisation," *Jazz Review* 1 (November 1958): 6–11, 21.

[c]Thomas Owens, "Charlie Parker: Techniques of Improvisation," 2 vols. (Ph.D. diss., University of California, Los Angeles, 1974).

[d]Alfons M. Dauer, "Improvisation: Zur Technik der spontanen Gestaltung in Jazz," *Jazzforschung/Jazz Research* 1 (1969): 113–32.

[e]André Hodeir, *Jazz: Its Evolution and Essence*, trans. David Noakes (New York: Grove Press, 1956).

The Collective Structure of Jazz Performance

The discourse of "classic jazz" is carried out in four- and eight-measure phrases, choruses, and three-minute recordings, features that it shares with the U.S. popular song of the period. In jazz these units of structure are not "deep," whether internal (in each player and fully explicable by him) or external (in the activity of the rhythm section). The listener's (or participant's) knowledge of such things is perhaps more tacit, with, in any event, strong reinforcement from dancing or knowing the words of a tune. In addition the rhythm section is part of the performance, and its behavior is articulated at various levels (pulse, harmonic rhythm, hierarchical punctuation of the larger units). Within this highly predictable binary structure, there is much opportunity for briefly playing "against" the prevailing pulse, but not to the extent of muddling the major points of arrival or departure.

The jazz rhythm section is also noisy and resonant, with percussive time-keeping counteracted by cymbal shimmer, indistinct decay of the string bass, and the timbral liaison provided by guitar. Not only does such noise and resonance make for continuity, they may also be understood as "energizing" or giving a kind of meaning to single pitches that may be played by soloists (a concept more usually encountered in discussions of African musics).

These features combine to produce a merciful and supportive environment for the jazz soloist. It is difficult to become completely lost: at the rapid tempo of a "Shoe Shine Boy," there are points of reference passing by every four seconds or so. Errors are made, however, and in places that suggest the importance of eight-measure units in terms of memory encoding. In an AABA structure a performer may forget the second A section (or play the bridge too soon, however you wish). Another related error is to play the wrong bridge, or to forget the correct one.

In this already strongly connected environment, a soloist may play "ideas" of quite incoherent character—as judged by the norms of written composition—in successive four-measure units or, sometimes, especially in the bridge, in successive two-measure units. They can be taken as surface detail floating on the rhythm section: thus Schuller's dictum that "the average improvisation is mostly a stringing together of unrelated ideas." Often such decisions as to incoherence do not take into account such features as timbral continuity or a characteristic personal timing with respect to the rhythm section. The piece is already so strongly connected in its rhythmic order that a time-span of four measures may be perceived as linked to a preceding one merely by virtue of a note-group, or even a single pitch, played in the equivalent metrical position. Pitch-centered or motivic analysis will often not take this sufficiently into account. Also, such connections, clearly as they may be *heard* in performance, lose much of their force when *viewed* in a transcription.

Dramatization of the Collective Structure

In any popular song as well as in the harmonization that a jazz performance may follow, there are major and minor points of repetition and arrival in the timing cycle. Immediate repetition is relatively weak, but one that comes after significantly contrasting material at the same durational level is strong. The approach to measure 25 of a thirty-two-measure chorus (repetition after contrast) is more portentous than to measure 9 (repetition). While such weighting factors may be given their full expression in the performance of a popular song (or, even more, in an art song) and in the behavior of a jazz rhythm section, the situation is different for the jazz soloist. This is because practically all jazz solo performance avoids literal or close to literal repetition of four- and eight-measure units. If encountered, such repetition is immediately labeled as "composition." If the strategic or weighty places of the timing cycle are to be recognized in the solo, some means other than literal repetition must be found.

There is another kind of weight in the solo enterprise. To play a solo is to step out of, emerge from the band, eventually to return. During whatever period of time that is given by prearrangement to the soloist, or that he can lay claim to, his goal is to demonstrate "chops" (technique), "soul" (expressivity), and "ideas" (originality, and to some degree, logic). While these need not be used separately to mark off one part of a solo from another, or used in the service of a rhetoric corresponding to the social and formal articulations of a solo, I believe that they may be, and *are* in the performances of "Shoe Shine Boy" by Lester Young.

Formulas and Formulaic System

The distinction between formulas—more or less literal motive or phrase repetitions—and formulaic system—a more generalized structural outline embracing many specific formulas—would seem to be more obvious to the student of music than to the student of literature. Music claims transformation and varied repetition as a fundamental forming process. Whether we can isolate levels of organization in music so neatly as in language (see Nowacki) is to me questionable. In any event, my ensuing discussion of formulas in these performances will deal with melody, then phrase and harmonic structure as reflected in melody. But according to my table above, these last two topics can be seen as instances of schematic, not formulaic, analysis.

From attentive listening, but particularly from the paradigmatic transcription of versions A and B, certain phrases emerge as closely similar or identical. The one labeled γ (in ex. 2, as others in this section) has a strongly accented F-sharp, approached from below and left by eighth notes descending to the G below, then continued in a variety of ways, depending on the closeness of the cadence. With reference to the tune, the position of this peak tone is beat 3 of the first measure of the second half of the A section, and this is where we hear it in the performances, for the most part. But if it comes late, as in A.45 (due to the extension of the first four-measure phrase), there is no time for the rest of the chain to follow. Here Lester Young plays instead the second frequently recurring formula (labeled δ), a descending Am7/D9 arpeggio, usually in the third measure of a four-measure section. The form δ' found in A.3–4, 11–12, and 36 is physically the same kind of gesture but functions differently. Rather than a penultimate element of an eight-measure section, it is heard as transitional between the first and second four-measure sections.

No less frequent but far more variable in its appearances—and thus falling into the domain of a superformula—is the initial phrase α, which I take to have the basic form (D,) E, D-sharp, D in whole notes, also describable as a playing around with the fifth and sixth scale degrees or with the fourth and little fingers of the right hand. It is a lengthy process, nearly filling a four-measure section.

Three other initial phrases can be grouped together as β, characterized by note repetition and, in two instances, oscillation across the octave break of the instrument. They share with α a considerable length and a static melodic and harmonic character.

Perhaps we should also make a group for a number of often quite short (two or three beats) cadential phrases. The most common of these are permutations of the tonic triad, usually not ending on the tonic. I am inclined to add the half-dozen five- or six-note punctuating phrases (ε) using the descent E, E-flat, D, which a motivically inclined analyst might wish to describe as variants of α. From the formulaic point of view, as I understand it, this would be illusory, given the difference in time-span and function.

On the basis of Lester Young's general style, one would also wish to label as formulas or characteristic gestures the three or four instances of a "rip" upwards to the palm keys (A.9 and 10; B.45).

The C and D versions do not, for the most part, employ these formulas. Indeed, if I am correct in ascribing a functional or quasi-syntactic role to them, it would be nonsense to use them in a dialogue performance. It is striking, however, that the α formula is heard in a functionally ambiguous position in C.37 and D.61. Otherwise, in those performances we hear several occurrences of blues clichés, ζ, which,

EXAMPLE 2

EXAMPLE 2 (*continued*)

δ

Descending Am7/D arpeggio followed by G harmony

A.3

B.5

short suffix

A.11

A.30

A.35

C.39

A.46

C.47

cf. D.47

? A.59

B.12

A.62

C.70

C.79

Also cf. instances from bridge, mm. 23–24

EXAMPLE 2 (*continued*)

EXAMPLE 2 (*continued*)

although not formulaic in this very limited sample of Lester Young's playing, are often used by him.

There is one major instance in which a formula that on first listening is easily assignable to one class must be cross-referenced to another. B.33–36, involving the repetition of the pitch E, thus a static element prolonging tonic harmony, as A.25–28 and A.41–44, is in fact dynamic, as shown by the successive lowering of pitch in my transcription. This is achieved not by lipping down but by the successive closing of tone-holes below the one that remains open to produce e''. To me at any rate, this makes a link to formula-group α. This level of hearing is in part permitted by the possibility of running the magnetic tape at half or quarter speed, but it is

something that saxophone players might well notice during a performance. Whether the unalerted layman would notice it—thus making it
part of his perceived structure—is another question.

I doubt that such microscopic listening is required to study all jazz
performance from the formulaic point of view. In the present instance,
however, I believe it is, particularly because it relates to the boundary
problem. For example, in A.5–8 we hear a well-formed phrase (a quotation from Louis Armstrong?) that might be parsed γ + infix + cadence
and that completes the cadence on the first beat of measure 8. In B.13–15
the phrase ends early, leaving an awkward gap that might be called an
elision of the clear degree-progression of A. Close listening to the recording seems to show an uncertainty of fingering at the critical point in
version B, beat 3 of measure 14.

A related instance is A.4, in which I initially conceived the b' as the
end of formula δ. This led me to consider the additional d'' and b' of A.12
as a kind of additional flourish or as little "transitional" or residual tones.
The discrepancy sent me back to the tape, and relistening showed that d''
and b' had been played there as well.

The things I have described so far constitute in my opinion a formulaic economy that we may see as the result of a considerable degree of
digital memory as well as of an interest in working out in various manners
certain degree-progressions (e.g., E, D-sharp, D) or prolongations of tonic
harmony. I do not think we need to think of Lester Young as reaching
more or less unconsciously, and under the pressure of time, into his bag of
well-learned tricks. The one formula that might appear to function to
give Young time to think of what to do next (δ) also serves as a formal
element in an overall repetition scheme, and its less frequent use in
version B does not seem to entail any poverty of ideas. It seems clear that,
as with Lord's singer-poet-instrumentalists, the order of events may be
different in successive performances, but I think this is the case only
within certain limits given by the general structure of the AABA song
form: for example, initial material or formulas can appear in measures 1,
9, or 25, but not in measures 5, 13, or 29.

Phrasing and "Changes"

Much solo jazz performance of the twenties and thirties can easily be
regarded as melodic paraphrase. Even when this is not the case, one hears
a solo quite frequently as following the phrasing of the melody. Obviously

this cannot be simply a matter of binary construction, which would hardly be enough to differentiate one tune from another, but must involve preservation of other features of the tune in a solo, such as the actual duration of phrases or the number of tones in them. There is some possibility for self-deception, however, when a listener knows the tune very well himself and "hears" it along with a performance. But I have no doubt that it is part of the perception for the jazz musician as listener.

Version A has been described in print as a relatively "straight" performance. I accept this judgment but only with respect to the eight- and four-measure articulations of the tune, and not with respect to the tune itself. The eight-measure units are very strongly marked terminally, as a rule by long silences, statements of tonic harmony, or both. The four-measure divisions are also articulated, but rather subtly, for instance, by changes in direction or indefinite ("ghost") pitches, as in A and B.12. The shorter spans of one or two measures, analytically separable in the tune, do not generally appear to be observed, and a player would be unwise or unlikely to attempt to do so at this rapid a tempo. Also, melodic congruences at this level are not reflected in Lester Young's performance. Anyone acquainted with jazz would be startled indeed to hear A.2 = A.4, etc.

If one regards the tune as consisting of four measures of one sort, followed by two markedly different two-measure phrases, then surely version A can be considered to be constructed in the same manner. Version B seems to be a different affair.

Of course, one salient feature of "Shoe Shine Boy" appears in all performances, namely, the bridge or channel, with its contrastive character and sequential harmony. All versions reflect these features of the model with strongly similar renditions of the "underlying" chord progression. But it seems pretty clear that the playing of the bridge is something of a routine, with a fixed drum part accentuating Lester Young's phrases.

Here is where we might hope to test Lord's "enjambement criterion," that is, oral composition avoids such contradiction of construction in parallel verses.[4] I find it a tricky matter, inasmuch as the pickup or anacrusis is generally prevalent. But I think it would be fair to say that the expected seams or joints are not disguised or blurred as a matter of course (as becomes true in later jazz). That makes all the more dramatic the places where we hear musical enjambement: at the end of the bridge (all versions, 23–25, B.55–56; between choruses, B.32–33). At least the first of these has obviously been worked out, but it is interesting to observe how the different forms of measure 24—involving a different position on the instrument—entail differences in measure 25 and subsequent ones.

Jazz performance is sometimes explained as based on harmonic progression. This is often meant in some fairly strict sense, that is, jazz uses the pitches of the "vertical" harmonies as the primary constituents of "horizontal" phrases. An extreme example would be a solo consisting only of the arpeggiation of the changes. Approaches to such an extreme do exist but are not generally admired, unless in some instances as tours de force. Generally the changes are not considered so much as a schematic feature greatly facilitating improvisation but as a measure by which one may determine a player's originality, for example, Bix Beiderbecke playing accented ninths and thirteenths, Charlie Parker playing on the tertial extensions upwards of seventh chords, and the like. It is my opinion that the changes are most important for the act of performance—as opposed to that of analysis—in their ability to orient a player in the thirty-two-measure time cycle. Be that as it may, analysts of jazz are sometimes rather incautious in their assumptions about what the changes are, especially in deriving them from sheet music or a lead sheet or fake book rather than from the rhythm section as actually recorded. In "Shoe Shine Boy," for example, it is clear from listening to the various performances that the augmented V_7 is much favored by Count Basie and his sidemen as well. Thus, a feature that might be considered a deviation from the sheet music harmony is normal with respect to the changes actually used.

All in all, the changes of "Shoe Shine Boy" are, with the exception, once again, of the bridges, not prominently expressed in the melodies Lester Young actually plays. For instance, the E_7 of measure 1, etc., is neglected, the single exception being one of the most ear-catching measures of version B, measure 41, in which we note the suppression of the tonic chord in favor of an entire measure expressing E_7 horizontally. It should be said that to reflect harmonies changing twice a second might well have seemed ludicrous to musician and listener alike in 1936. Although I certainly do not hear Lester Young's performance as contradictory to the changes, neither do I hear it as in some sense following them. This is partly because V_7 is only present in considerably softened form. Am_7 with normal or flat fifth, and the active F-sharp is preempted as major seventh to the tonic. I would characterize the harmonic system underlying these solos in rather vague terms—or rather, vague from the standpoint of functional analysis but concrete with reference to the instrument: one ascending gesture, a tonic major seventh arpeggio with possible extensions by a diatonic third, up or down; and its counterpoise, a descending chain of thirds outlining the supertonic minor seventh, but with extensions up or down also possible.

Motives

Perhaps my questions so far might be considered as addressed to the how and the what of these performances. Be that as it may, I take the subsequent remarks to ask or answer, in part, why.

Should we relabel as "motives" the phrases or bundles of features I have designated formulas or expressions of an underlying scheme, the thrust of analysis shifts from the oral to the composed, from the performance as one possible arrangement among many to the performance as a unique creation, from the variations of a basic form to the repetitions or transformations of a motive that make form. I don't believe such a shift to be profitable.

There are some features of version A that would recommend the shift and the relabeling, namely, the recurrences, both pleasing and surprising, of the initial rhythmic-melodic motive of measure 1 in measure 15, and of measures 25ff. in measure 37. The aesthetic effect depends on brevity and recognizability, placing condensations of the motives in a functionally different position.

The major objections, to my mind, to using this effect as a springboard to a general motivic, compositional analysis are, first, that the many other instances of formulaic variation do not have the same dramatic effect and are not easily audible as repetitions; second, that in version B the two most easily encoded, potentially motivic gestures (B.1: "descending scale"; B.41–42: "running the changes")—which are furthermore placed at strong points of the time cycle—are not reused.

There is no reason, though, to rule out intentional motivic work from the oral poetic of jazz, especially at slower tempos or in the longer time cycles of more recent jazz. It is simply that in this style, at such a tempo, the time cycle's demands for change of any sort take precedence. In illustration of this constraint, I could mention the rather frequent judgment one makes that a pattern is ended too soon: the listener has the leisure to reflect that a process could have been continued to good effect. But the player, like Lord's epic singer, is always thinking ahead and has perhaps already forgotten what he's playing while still doing it.

This line of speculation arises from the comparison of versions A and B. I believe that the former will be both heard and seen to be better balanced, more thrifty, and more conjunct. But it may also be said that version A is more obvious, particularly from the schematic point of view. A.1–8 is a case in point. B.1–8 is more subtle; its balance is not so easy to represent in numbers or pitches, as the silences are part of a parallel rhythmic structure. It is parataxic or coordinate rather than hierarchical.

Our first-level criteria of economy are also somewhat simpleminded or overliteral. It is immediately clear that A.33–35 is very like A.1–3 with respect to degree-progression. But B.33–36 (mentioned above), which might at first be judged to be an easy cliché, serving to heighten intensity and unconnected with the formulaic or motivic vocabulary of version B, can be heard as a form of the pervasive slowly descending degree-progression.

If our model for Lester Young's performances is that of oral composition, the actual order of performance matters little. The comparative "straightness" of version A and the adventurousness of B may be understood either as a decision in the context of a recording session to take fewer chances or a desire to play something a bit more challenging. But if the model is that of reflective composition, working toward a more socially comprehensible sequence of ideas, then B–A appears to be the necessary order.

What does historical investigation tell us? First, the recent United States Columbia reissue of these recordings is the first to give matrix numbers for the two takes. If these numbers reflect the order of recording and not some other bookkeeping or manufacturing procedure, then the order must be A–B. This does not agree with the recollection of John Hammond, the organizer of the session, who says that version B was the first take and was marred by a messed-up run by Basie.

Careful listening supports the superiority of version A overall: in B the very end is messy, Jo Jones and Walter Page are uncertain in their breaks, and Tatti Smith breaks the flow of the concluding exchanges between the players. I am loath to believe that skilled players would do less well in such matters in successive performances. Unfortunately the only "run" that Basie plays less than perfectly is the whole-tone scale of version A, close to the end of his opening solo. Thus, external evidence is ambiguous, and internal evidence coercive only to the extent one accepts the principle stated two sentences above.

It may be that we must carefully distinguish immediately successive performances from those separated by an interval of time sufficient to diminish muscular memory. Also, conventionalization may be more prominent in the different circumstances.

The question of recording order is not without interest, but perhaps only a scenic tour that diverts us from asking whether behind the adventurous and variable detail of the two versions there lies an overall shape—particularly one comprehensible or perceptible by the ordinary listener (a category that may include many musicians). I've already suggested above that there may be a kind of rhetorical plan, serving not only to give "meaning" to these performances but to forge two choruses together. In fact, the plan I suggest could not practically unfold within the confines of one chorus.

1. The first move is a move out of the band or in juxtaposition to another soloist or both. It must catch the attention, and in Lester Young's case—who at this point in his career was not satisfied with rhetorical gestures alone—must be an intelligible musical idea. It will generally fill the first four measures.

The initial idea should not be too complicated. The place for tricky stuff, that is, cute ideas or technical display, is later—but how much later? The obvious point in a two-chorus solo is at the beginning of the second chorus, although one might start after the first bridge. In any event,

2. Demonstration of mastery, "chops," technique identifiable with respect to the instrument, normal harmony, or rhythmic construction. In Lester Young's case this often involves polymetric or otherwise unbalanced phrasing rather than rapid playing.

A.33–34 is a particularly flamboyant saxophone gesture, hardly reproducible on another instrument. B.33–34, though not difficult, is a bit of cleverness depending on the construction of the instrument. A.41–44 is difficult because of leaping across the octave break, as well as being a greater upsetting of the meter than anything else so far heard; at the same position, B is not so technically difficult but, due to its special harmonic character and rapid quasi-sequence, gives a sense of artistic pressure. In both A and B the climax—if one be granted at all—is located here, five-eighths of the way along the sixty-four measures. (Friends of the golden section take note.)

3. Return to the band, "wrapping it up," an expressive peak reached by using common property, a riff, or a well-known lick.

The only possible place for this, within the sixty-four measure time frame, is in the last eight measures, particularly since the bridge is stereotyped. In any event, those sections of versions A and B are heard as closely related by pitch, duration, and accent pattern. More important, they strike the ear as more naive and formulaic (in the communal frame) than anything else in these solos.

If the subjectivity of this last judgment be found disturbing, I suggest that the difference between these closing phrases and others can be stated without reference to a social infrastructure, and can be tested by consulting the equivalent of native speakers. (I can only offer myself as an immigrant.)

This three-part plan is not very complicated by itself but is somewhat at odds with two choruses; three choruses would be ideal but are rare in records of this time, except in blues, a very different undertaking. There is no reason why it should be complicated; after all, it only determines the course of musical events in a general way, and over relatively long durations. Perhaps it is in this respect not unlike the general thematic plan of an epic poet, or the sequence of movements in a concerto. Nor would I insist that Lester Young follows it always, for in playing two chorus solos he sometimes made each chorus in very much the same way (e.g., Count Basie's "Twelfth Street Rag," Decca). Nor does it preclude yet other plans, such as the singleminded dramatic "ride-out" of mounting intensity, much favored by trumpeters at this time.

Whether my characterization of these moves be found apt or not, I believe there is a *necessary* order in these performances that does not emerge from formula or schematic analysis, although not necessarily at every level (two, four, or eight measure) of temporal organization. One tool of verification is the commutation test at the various levels. I have done this in a rough-and-ready way (the making of unnoticeable splices is time consuming) in real time and in my imagination, but knowing so well how the solos really go, I am hardly an ideal subject, particularly since my preference usually goes to the "true" order. This is not always the case, however: where my ear absolutely rejects exchange of the first and second eight-measure phrases of B, it will accept interchange of A.9–16 with B.9–16, even at the cost of the parallelism of B.4 and 15.

To recapitulate: I believe that one may perceive in A and B four different processes at work. In each of these processes or levels, there are features that are collective or social and ones that are idiosyncratic. Some are more easily encoded—therefore memorable—or more easily imitated than others. They are all in some sense under the control of a performer at this level of mastery, but another player learning this piece, or Lester Young's style from this piece, can hardly be expected to (nor would he have been, in fact, expected to) remember or learn these bundles of features in the same way.[5]

I construe these processes according to the scheme of table 1 in the following way:

1. *Semiotic*. Lester Young, like many players, thought of a solo as "telling a story." This story transcends the repetitive, hierarchical structure of the tune and its harmonization, and depends on the use of typologically different material.[6]
2. *Schematic*. He also affirmed the pop song structure of "Shoe Shine Boy" in differentiating measure four from measure eight cadences (*ouvert* and *clos,* if you will), in observing the conventional character of the channel or bridge, and so on. In a few cases, that structure is deliberately upset.
3. *Formulaic*. As a saxophone player Young had his bag of propensities and tricks—call them conscious style or automatisms—such as false fingerings, rips upward to the palm keys, dramatic bombs in the extreme low register, chains of thirds. Beyond that, of course, he might use favorite motives having nothing to do with the saxophone per se.
4. *Motivic*. Young knew this tune as such—witness the prominent F-sharp—and found a degree-progression filling a four-measure segment that he used in various positions and shapes in versions A, B, and C. It may well not be specific to this tune.

In versions C and D, a dialogue performance between piano and tenor saxophone, these levels cannot work together or separately in the same way to produce a memorable aesthetic effect. For example, if a story is to be told, it must be a different kind of story altogether.

I think it important to note that the other two performers with solos on "Shoe Shine Boy" A and B, Count Basie and Carl Smith, pay little attention to the first and fourth processes detailed above. This does no injury to their work as good jazz or to their contribution to the excellent ensemble. It may, however, account for lesser "memorability," something I take to be easily perceptible. One can remember their brief two- and four-measure phrases, but not necessarily in correct order, and sometimes transposing phrases from one version to the other.

It will perhaps seem a small accomplishment if all I have done in these pages is to reaffirm the necessity of a sense of overall structure or an image of the whole work, if that work is to be valued and remembered in detail by those who come after. (Without saying, to be sure, that this is a guarantee of survival.) More than that, I hope to have shown that oral composition, at least in the distinctly mixed oral-written tradition called jazz, in some of its expressions, proceeds along several tracks at once. I suppose that I have tried to show that in addition to the communal, highly conventional organizing schemata of jazz playing, there are others that we must invoke or imagine in order to account for the extraordinary profundity or coherence of some jazz playing, wherever and whenever we may find it.

Note to the Transcriptions

The transcriptions sound a major ninth lower than written; they make more sense to me—as a player of the instrument—in this form and eliminate the many ledger lines that would have to be used. I have left them in the form in which they were presented to the panel, including a great many faint diacritical marks indicating phrasing, articulation, and accent. There is no need to review here the usual array of problems encountered in the transcription of highly individualistic performances, especially those that glory in playing *against* a consistent pulse. I think they will be found sufficiently reflective of the performance as it is considered here, although not for other conceivable discussions. Lester Young, it may be pointed out, suffers less in transcription than other saxophonists of the time, particularly his section mate, Herschel Evans.

The following special signs are used:

- ∿ strong vibrato
- ↓× "ghost" tone, almost inaudible
- (♩) a more definite, yet still indistinct pitch
- ⌐♩ scooped pitch, usually beginning on the beat
- ⌐♩ short "rip" upwards
- ↘♩ short fingered glissando before the beat
- ↓ ↓↓ flattening or progressive flattening of pitch
- (↤↦) pitch or phrase earlier (or later) than notated

Many rhythmic subtleties of considerable importance to the "swing" style are audible at slow tape speed. For instance, the very opening (A.1), which I represent ♪♩ ♪♩ , is actually better represented ♩♪♪♩ . Pairs of eighth notes are usually performed as triplets, although now and then they may be very close to equal, or very unequal.

I have not been entirely consistent in my indications of phrasing or articulation, partly because the transcriptions were made at different times and are intended to be suggestive of the overall shape rather than completely descriptive. All triplets are legato, and most eighth notes also, even when not under a slur.

Notes

1. Albert Lord, *The Singer of Tales* (Cambridge: Harvard University Press, 1960).

2. Peter Winkler has kindly granted me permission to use the transcription of version D prepared by him in conjunction with a paper read by him at the annual meeting of the American Musicological Society, Washington, D.C., 1976.

3. Cited in Whitney Balliett, *Improvising: Sixteen Jazz Musicians and Their Art* (New York: Oxford University Press, 1977), 188.

4. Lord, *Singer of Tales*, 57–58.

5. According to Lee Konitz, Charlie Parker learned Young's performance of this piece (undoubtedly version A): "Bird came noodling into the room and said, 'Hey, you ever heard this one?' and he played *Shoe Shine Swing* about twice as fast as the record." See Louis Gottlieb, "Why So Sad, Pres?" *Jazz: A Quarterly of American Music*, no. 3 (Summer 1959): 190 [and above].

6. Richard M. Sudhalter and Philip R. Evans, *Bix, Man & Legend* (New Rochelle, N.Y.: Arlington House, 1974), 192, report the following exchange between Wingy Manone and Louis Armstrong: "Hey, Pops, how do you play so many choruses the way you do?" . . . "Well, I tell you . . . the first chorus I plays the melody. The second chorus I plays the melody round the melody, and the third chorus I routines." Although one must doubt that this is a verbatim transcript of the conversation, it is descriptive of one of Armstrong's ways of dealing with multichorus solos.

Don Heckman

Pres and Hawk:
Saxophone Fountainheads

In the 1960s musician and composer Don Heckman wrote a series of
articles for *Down Beat* that were the most analytical works ever presented
by that magazine. Heckman's pieces on Ornette Coleman, Charlie Parker,
and others offered several transcribed solos in each article, carefully
chosen to illustrate various aspects of the artist's style. The present article
contrasts Young with his nemesis, Coleman Hawkins. Hawkins (1904–71)
was only five years older than Young, but it is important to remember that
Hawkins recorded at an early age, in 1921, whereas Young began recording at an unusually late age, in 1936. So although the difference in age
was fairly slight, the difference in their impact through recordings was
fifteen years!

Since Young grew up in the era that Hawkins dominated, he was
always asked about his opinion of Hawkins. Some wanted to know if he
consciously rejected Hawkins as a stance of defiance. Some looked for
similarities between the two (which exist but are not easy to find). Young
had bitter experiences with musicians and audiences rejecting him for not
playing in the Hawkins mold, and we have heard his own side of this
debate.

Heckman misses the opportunity to make a side-by-side comparison, taking fragments from Hawkins and laying them next to Young. For
example, both recorded a number of solos based on "I Got Rhythm"
chords, and these would make worthwhile comparisons. Instead, Heckman talks about each musician in turn. But along the way he sheds much
light on the works of both men.—Ed.

Originally published in *Down Beat,* January 3, 1963, 20–22. Copyright © 1963 by Maher Publications.
Reprinted by permission.

Rarely has an art form been blessed with a period as energetically creative as the late 1920s and 1930s were for jazz. Louis Armstrong, Jelly Roll Morton, Duke Ellington, Fletcher Henderson—the list is profuse with figures who made lasting contributions.

In the persons of tenor saxophonists Coleman Hawkins and Lester Young, this period produced the two fountainheads of contemporary jazz saxophone playing. Both were melodists of a sort rarely fashionable since the advent of bop. In their own unique ways, they created melodic improvisations that were spiritually oriented toward beauty and feeling. The great variance in the results they achieved was due to fundamental differences in their musical environments.

Hawkins predated Young as an active participant in the jazz scene. As a member of the Fletcher Henderson orchestra for ten years (1923–33), he was intimately involved with what was probably the most famous jazz ensemble of the time. Henderson's orchestra typified the eastern approach.

The Henderson, Duke Ellington, and Charlie Johnson orchestras all played for a variety of musical events before audiences that frequently were all white. Although they were considered (with the exception of Ellington at the Cotton Club) to be primarily dance bands, the type of dance music they played was considerably more diverse than that of bands further west. The Henderson group might be expected on any given night to play popular hits, tangos, Irish waltzes, and original jazz tunes. The music was usually written in complex arrangements, and the bands were carefully rehearsed. With some groups, in fact, well-drilled performances became more important than either improvisation or solos. Fortunately, this never happened with Henderson, who realized the importance of good soloists when Louis Armstrong joined the band in 1924. It was only logical that Hawkins's artistic growth would have been affected by such a musical environment.

Hawkins has had an amazingly long productive life, ranging from the mid-1920s to the present. Throughout his lengthy tenure as patriarch of the saxophone, he has shown great sympathy and understanding for the new movements that have come into jazz. His seniority was apparent from the beginning, and even his first solo with Henderson, a clownlike, slap-tongue effort, presaged important things to come. By the early 1930s he was a well-established leader on his instrument, and his influence was felt by nearly all the new saxophonists.

Young came to prominence in a completely different milieu. The Count Basie band was the pinnacle of Kansas City and southwestern jazz. Its music was blues-oriented, filled with riffing backgrounds and frequently based on spontaneous head arrangements. The soloists had more opportunity to stretch out than did the soloists in the more heavily orchestrated New York bands. Few of the Basie arrangements were very complicated; good intonation and well-drilled performances were not nearly as important as was the creation of a rolling, surging rhythmic swing. Kansas City jazz was dancing jazz, and the beat was the most important element. The revolutionary work of the Basie rhythm section made the Basie band something special. Their ability to generate a free-flowing, almost-alive pulse undoubtedly helped Young develop a rangy horizontal (i.e., melodic) playing style.

It is interesting to note that the rhythmic articulations of the original Basie band, when playing as a full ensemble, are not dissimilar to those in Young's solos. It is rather startling, in fact, to hear other soloists, like tenorist Herschel Evans or trumpeter Buck Clayton, emerge from the loose, driving swing of the ensemble with herky-jerky patterns of dotted eighth and sixteenth notes. In the purest sense Young *was* the Basie band. More than anyone else, even Basie, he extended it, invigorated it, and symbolized it.

It has often been said, and I think accurately, that Young was never the same after he left Basie. This has been attributed to the Basie rhythm section, to the rolling carpet of rhythm that it laid under him, provoking him to stretch his lines out beyond the usual cadential patterns. The reverse is less obvious, but as true: the Basie band never was quite the same after Young left. Of course, it was always a good band, even during the difficult postwar period, and it was an excellent band at times in the mid-1950s; but one was always aware of the shadow of Lester Young. Even during their frequent good moments, the post-Young Basie bands could only simulate the moments of sheer artistry in recordings such as "Lady Be Good," "Lester Leaps In," "Clap Hands, Here Comes Charlie," "Broadway," and so on.

Young became an important influence with breathtaking suddenness. A new batch of young tenor men in his likeness seemed to emerge overnight: Dexter Gordon, Gene Ammons, Allen Eager, Stan Getz, Wardell Gray—all tried to sound like Young. His work was cannibalized right down to the bone marrow. Yet all this was happening years after he had thoroughly developed his style of playing. One can sympathize with his feelings when he returned from the army, in early 1946, and heard accurate renditions of his late 1930s playing drifting out of every jazz club on New York's Fifty-second Street.

It is unfortunate that, although he was aware of what was taking place, he was unable to develop his own immensely gifted imagination further. While he struggled to find a more acceptable expression, his music was mimicked so accurately by so many other players that what once were startlingly original ideas now sounded as familiar as nursery rhymes.

When he joined the Basie band in the mid-1930s, Young was condemned for having a tone that supposedly sounded like an alto's. In retrospect it seems amazing that anyone could have suggested that Young change his tone. Listening to his recordings with Basie will ever be an electrifying experience. The fresh and totally unexpected newness of his choruses sounds as surprising as would the sudden appearance of a Charlie Parker solo in the middle of a Jelly Roll Morton Red Hot Peppers record.

His tone is not at all like an alto's, and it exploits the natural full-bodied sound of the instrument. What sounds at first like a pronounced tonal difference is more a matter of vibrato (Hawkins uses a heavy vibrato; Young used almost none). There also is an absence of a growl tone—a technique Hawkins used frequently—in Young's playing. But most important in explaining the impact of Young's solos is his amazingly contemporary rhythmic feeling.

Compared with Young, Hawkins sounds almost baroque. His music is filled with ornamentations and decorations, all dedicated to the continuous expansion of a soaring imagination. Appoggiaturas, suspensions, and slurs shift and turn the planes of sound in the same way that arches, spires, and flying buttresses produce complicated patterns of light and shade in a Cologne cathedral.

Young, on the other hand, like Frank Lloyd Wright, builds solos that rise up from the earth, that are a part of it and yet not a part of it, structurally emerging from, yet blending with, the soil. He is not a complicated player in the way that Hawkins is. He uses riffs as Van Gogh used color and has no compunctions about reusing materials. His solos are not structured in formal terms but rather reflect his feelings of the moment; certain pet phrases are always under his fingers, and he is not loath to use them, no matter how frequently he has used them before. The important

EXAMPLE 1. "Broadway" (Lester Young). By De Silva-Henderson-Brown, published by Harms, Inc.

thing is that, more than any other improviser since Louis Armstrong, Young plays licks that are genuinely original, making him one of the founders of the vast fund of material that is the common property of all jazz improvisers.

This is the real basis of Young's immortality. When he plays material that is not particularly original, he intuitively makes the small but significant alterations that completely change its character. Usually this takes the form of rhythmic displacement. Notice, for example, his line on the release of "Broadway" [CBS], beginning at bar 17 (see ex. 1). Most players would have played this line one beat later; Young, realizing that the ensemble is accenting the second and fourth beats, displaces the line so that its accents contrast the ensemble, resulting in a rhythmic opposition of stunning complexity.

Young's chorus also included some repeated material, yet one is never especially aware of repetitiousness. Bars 7 and 15, for example, are almost identical, and they fall at the same point in the phrase. The same thing is true of bars 12 and 28. And the three bars ending the first sixteen are almost identical to the three bars at the chorus's ending. It is a testimony to the freshness of Young's material that these facts are apparent only in an analysis of the solo and never in the listening.

In the first four bars of his solo on Basie's "Pound Cake" [CBS] (see ex. 2), Young plays a characteristic phrase based on the tonic and third that is complemented perfectly by the Basie rhythm section. Young used this phrase (or modifications of it) to begin a number of solos (listen to his chorus on "Lester Leaps In") in ideal expression of the blues principle of understated simplicity. Notice also how he takes a quarter-note phrase in bar 9 and expands it into an eighth-note phrase in the next bar, spicing the interest by using a descending chromatic chord change.

The ornamentation in the first two bars of the second chorus are about as close as Young ever gets to this sort of thing, and even here the icing is sparse. He stretches his lines out in this chorus, playing right through the C7 chord in bar 17. He overlaps this chord with a declamatory blues statement in bar 18 that is really the peak of the whole solo, then plays one of his bouncy phrases (bars 22–23) to end the chorus.

It is surprising that the heated arguments in the 1930s and early 1940s on the relative merits of Young and Hawkins were not even more violent. Young's playing was surely as revolutionary for the time as Parker's was later—in some respects even more so, since Young was not part of a highly publicized movement as was Parker and explored his paths in solitude.

Hawkins, on the other hand, was idolized by both his musical contemporaries and his audience. Almost single-handedly he raised the saxophone from filling out chords and producing occasional comedy effects to an important position as a solo instrument.

Hawkins's solos are at the polar extreme to Young's. One of his most influential choruses was played on "One Hour" [RCA], made in 1929 with the Mound City Blue Blowers (a group that included Chicagoans Gene Krupa, Eddie Condon, Red McKenzie, and Pee Wee Russell). Although not as widely known to the public, this chorus was, in some respects, more important than "Body and Soul" because it represents Hawkins's early exploration of this style. By the time he recorded "Body and Soul" in 1939, this technique had been highly polished and well thought out. Hawkins's "One Hour" solo is shown in example 3. [Heckman's transcription is in A major, but the recording is in A-flat.—Ed.]

EXAMPLE 2. "Pound Cake" (Lester Young). By Edison-Basie, published by Bregman, Vocco & Cohn, Inc.

EXAMPLE 3. "One Hour" (Coleman Hawkins). "If I Could Be with You (One Hour)," by Johnson-Creamer, published by Remick Music Corp.

The solo falls into regular two-bar patterns, directly opposite to Young's practice of ignoring two-, four-, and eight-bar phrase patterns. Hawkins does little to change the customary sequence; this was not one of his areas of primary interest. Since his playing is basically architectonic and harmonic, it depends upon a regular pattern of recurring chords. Notice how he plays an increasingly complex variation of his original paraphrase. Bars 3 and 4 are similar [to bars 1 and 2], but they are given more ornate decoration. In bars 5 and 6 Hawkins makes the phrase more complex by playing a double-time pattern. The balance of the solo contrasts warm legato passages with bursts of sixteenth notes.

"When Lights Are Low" [RCA; 1939] represents Hawkins at a period of peak influence. The dotted eighth- and sixteenth-note pattern is fairly constant throughout the solo. While there is little real melodic interest, the chorus has a tremendous driving pulse. The dotted eighths are an important factor in this, especially at the point where Hawkins enters the release (bar 17). Two particular stylistic devices are worth noting: the outline of chords (bars 6, 11, and 20) with bar 11 especially interesting for its inclusion of a flatted fifth—a very common Hawkins practice—and the use of diatonic, almost exercise-book type runs (bars 5, 13, 18, etc). [The original publication mistakenly included a Chu Berry solo here instead of the Hawkins. Since the Chu Berry transcription is not relevant to the discussion, it has been omitted.—Ed.]

The polarity so apparent in the work of Hawkins and Young extends to their careers as well. Hawkins has had one of the longest and most successful careers in the history of jazz. Although Hawkins's influence waned somewhat in the 1940s and early 1950s, saxophonists like Benny Golson, Sonny Rollins, and John Coltrane demonstrate evidence of the effect he has had on their playing. Just as important is the fact that Hawkins continues to be a vital contributor to jazz. Several recent recordings suggest that the importance of youthfulness to jazz has been grossly exaggerated.

Lester Young's story is more complicated. He burst upon the scene, a fully matured, brilliantly original improviser at the time of his first recording session, a small-band Basie date released under the name "Jones-Smith Incorporated." In fact his solo on "Shoe Shine Boy" made at that date ([November] 1936) is considered by some critics to be one of his very best. This is a rare accomplishment in any art form. But Young's truly productive period ended with his induction into the army in 1944. Although there is some critical opinion to the contrary, his playing after the war seems unusually listless and soft. With Basie his playing was relaxed and subtle; there was no lack of drive or rhythmic intensity. In the postwar recordings Young's notes frequently are played under or well behind the beat. His tone, instead of being warm and personal, simply becomes flabby. There are, of course, exceptions, but they are few. The energy that ignited his work of the 1930s was short-lived. Even after it failed him, his playing accomplishments from that period were sufficient to help generate the bop movement.

The influence of Hawkins and Young upon the new generation of jazzmen has been less obvious. But it is there. Eric Dolphy's fascinating structures owe much to Hawkins's ballad explorations. And the searing, probing melodic lines of Ornette Coleman and John Coltrane are directly descended from the rhythmically liberated solos of Young. As time progresses, further effects of their influence will become clarified. Even in the midst of a new jazz revolution, Coleman Hawkins and Lester Young continue to be the two major sources of inspiration for all saxophonists.

Bernard Cash

Trumbauer, Parker, and Young

Having looked at the Hawkins route, which Young rejected, we now present an amalgam of two chapters from an insightful master's thesis by Bernard Cash that, on the one hand, takes a look back at Young's origins in the music of Frank Trumbauer and his circle and that, on the other hand, takes a look forward at Young's influence on Charlie Parker.

Cash was a multitalented musician and educator. Primarily a bassist, he studied with Peter Ind, who, as a true disciple of the late Lennie Tristano, immersed Cash in the music of Lester Young and Bach. In fact, Ind and Cash recorded an album of Bach for two basses (*Contra Bach*— Wave 20). Cash also appeared as an additional bassist with Ind's jazz groups in concert and on records. In addition he was a good saxophonist and pianist, as I know well from having jammed with him at his house on Boxing Day in 1985. (In England, Boxing Day is the first weekday after Christmas—the name, by the way, has to do with boxes from gifts, not the sport of boxing!) My wife and I were treated to the hospitality of Cash's wife and family, as we shared a fine meal with them capped off with Yorkshire pudding—in Yorkshire.

Cash's involvement with Young's music intensified over the years. Three years after writing his thesis he premiered an hour-long jazz opera about Young to a text by playwright Alan Plater. This unique project was documented for BBC television in a program by John Jeremy, known for such superb jazz films as *Born to Swing*. This program has been shown on the Bravo cable channel in America.

Extracted from Bernard Cash, "An Analysis of the Improvisation Technique of Lester Willis Young, 1936–1942" (Master's thesis, University of Hull, 1982). Published by permission of Mrs. Vera Cash.

No other author has so carefully studied Trumbauer's music to determine just what Young did learn from the C-melody saxophonist. Nor has anyone else taken the care to detail the similarities and differences between Parker's and Young's music, even though all agree there is a connection. After all, Parker said he was "crazy about Lester." And, even though he denied that he wanted to copy Young—which is understandable enough for a musician with his own mind—Parker attracted attention when he first came to New York because, as Kenny Clarke recalls, he played like Young, although on the alto rather than the tenor saxophone. Cash presents his findings in clear terms and with ample musical illustrations.

Tragically, Bernard Cash died suddenly in Berlin in October 1988. It is a testament to his talent that he was on tour at the time with the Royal Philharmonic Orchestra, with which he played double bass. The publication of these chapters marks the first time that the general public has had a chance to see the fruits of his academic pursuits. Its publication here is dedicated to his memory.—Ed.

Lester Young claimed that the musician who had most influenced him in his early playing days was the white saxophonist Frank Trumbauer, who played and recorded with bands under his own name, as well as with Bix Beiderbecke and Paul Whiteman, during the late 1920s. Significantly, Trumbauer played the now virtually obsolete C-melody saxophone, which had a much lighter sound than the tenor saxophone. He used far less vibrato than was customary in the 1920s, and in that respect there is every reason to suppose that his sound did influence Lester Young, who also used very little vibrato. Trumbauer's playing also had a clarity of execution—more in the European tradition than in that of the early jazz saxophonists, whose execution was often crude and sloppy—an undoubted influence on Young whose own playing was also graced by clarity of execution.

A comparison of Trumbauer's solo on "Way Down Yonder in New Orleans," recorded in New York on May 13, 1927, with Lester Young's solo on the same tune recorded more than ten years later on September 27, 1938 [alternate take], is most revealing (see ex. 1). The improvising methods of the two players are in most ways disparate. The overall melodic shape of Young's solo, as is the case with all his solos, is evenly up

EXAMPLE 1. "Way Down Yonder in New Orleans" (Trumbauer and Young)

EXAMPLE 1 (*continued*)

and down, whereas Trumbauer's melodic line is characterized by frequent jumps in both directions.

Equally apparent is the lack of rhythmic subtlety in Trumbauer's solo. Every other bar of the first eight bars, for example, finishes on a half note, and the whole solo is made up of a succession of two-bar phrases. In contrast Young's solo is made up of longer phrases of varying lengths that also start on different beats of the bar. The first phrase, for example, lasts for three bars and one beat, and the second phrase, of equal length, starts on the third beat of bar 5.

Too much should not be read into the similarity of the first bar of each solo, because the original melody starts in similar manner. Nevertheless this does not preclude the possibility of direct influence, since Young is known to have carried Trumbauer's records around with him.

Trumbauer's solo relies more heavily on syncopation than Young's solo (see, for example, bars 3, 9, 10, and 26), as one would expect in jazz of the 1920s. The apparent syncopation in bars 3 and 6 of Young's solo is beat anticipation rather than genuine syncopation. Undoubtedly the angularity of Trumbauer's melodic style stems from the influence of his more famous associate Bix Beiderbecke. This is particularly true of bars 5–6, 9–10, and 19.

The most revealing aspect of the differing improvisational approaches appears when each solo is compared with the original melody. Young's solo is not melody dominated; phrase lengths differ completely as does the whole melodic line. In contrast Trumbauer's solo is clearly derived from the original; phrase lengths and choice of notes are very similar. Herein lies a qualitative difference between the simply good jazz musician and the great improviser; the latter has the ability to create completely fresh musical lines, whereas the former often provides a mere decoration of the composer's original melody. Nevertheless, this is a good solo by Trumbauer. It has great vitality, and the close derivation from the original tune is less noticeable on listening than in the transcription.

Harmonically the two solos have much more in common than they do melodically or rhythmically. In bar 2 of Trumbauer's solo, he plays only the ninth and thirteenth (F and C) of the underlying E♭7 chord, quite daring for the period. These notes also occur in Young's line in the same bar, the ninth not so prominently. Trumbauer's use of the major seventh in bars 4 and 28 [G over an A-flat chord] would seem uncommonly bold for the period were it not for the fact that it is a prominent feature of the original melody in bars 4 and 15, which gives the credit to Creamer and Layton. Young also uses the major seventh at the beginning of his second phrase starting in bar 5, but this stems from the expansion of the motive in the second half of bar 2.

Trumbauer features the "blue" third in bars 3 and 15, already in 1927 a standard harmonic procedure in jazz. More interesting is his repeated use of the augmented fifth over dominant seventh harmony in bars 7, 10, and 26. Young uses the same device in bar 20 of his solo, and his predilection for its use over dominant harmony in several of the solos may be evidence of direct influence from Trumbauer.

It might well be argued that the appeal of the augmented fifth of the dominant seventh chord relates to its position also as the flattened, "blue" third of the tonic chord, thereby creating an even more unified melodic concept. Trumbauer's use of it here is always immediately before the statement of the tonic chord. Young gives it greater emphasis by placing it on the first beat of bar 20.

While Trumbauer's playing is certainly advanced for the period— one has only to compare it with typical clarinet solos of the time to see how much so—Young's solo contains a greater degree of harmonic complexity, created by an upward extension of the seventh chords. (See, for example, the Fs in bar 2, the B-flat in bar 14, and the F-sharp in bar 24, all of which are ninths.) More advanced are the F-flats and G-flat over an $E\flat 7$ chord in bar 10, resulting in flattened ninths and a flattened tenth. Thirteenths also appear frequently, for example, the Cs in bar 7, the F in bar 13, the Gs in bars 17 and 18, and the C in bar 26, all revealing a consistent use and designation that relates to the presence of sevenths in the underlying harmony.

In terms of performance practice there are both similarities and differences between the two solos. Both maintain a consistent emotional level from start to finish, especially Young's solo (this in marked contrast to Louis Armstrong, who often built his solos in emotional stages, that is, in successive climaxes that owed more to dynamics, range, and intensity of tone than to considerations of line and harmony). Trumbauer uses a consistently sharper articulation than Young; he also plays in a more staccato fashion, particularly in the second eight bars. In this respect his playing is very close to that of his colleague Bix Beiderbecke. In contrast Young generates a greater sense of flow enhanced by his use of longer phrases. Although his execution is clear, he uses the tongue less than Trumbauer, and in this solo his playing is more langourous (as is often the case on his solos with Billie Holiday) than on the extended solos. This might well be a reflection of Trumbauer's influence, for the latter sometimes escapes effeteness by only a small margin.

In bar 7 the F in brackets is a "ghosted" note that was much a part of Lester Young's performances. In this instance it is felt rather than heard and results from a characteristic of the saxophone that he exploited more than any other saxophonist before him, that is, that the notes will often apparently sound when the fingers depress a key despite no [or little] air being blown into the instrument. Whereas Trumbauer did not utilize this at all, it was a characteristic of Young's playing and influenced Charlie Parker, in whose solos the same phenomenon can often be heard.

While Trumbauer accents many notes, Young only occasionally does so, most often on the long notes on which he employs a characteristic expansion of tone, for example, the F-flat half note in bar 10 and the C half note in bar 26.

Lester Young exploits a two-octave range throughout his solo, from the high C in bar 21 to the low C in bar 28, whereas Trumbauer restricts himself between the F of bar 2 and the D-flat of bar 15.

Although Young's own statement regarding Trumbauer's influence deserves to be taken seriously, the present study shows that it must also be qualified. Trumbauer's tone and lightness of approach certainly had a direct influence; his harmonic ingenuity might well have, too. But his improvising technique was not only decidedly different but also less productive in a profound musical sense.

Lester Young's influence on Charlie Parker was of an entirely different order. Parker was the most influential jazz musician from the 1940s onwards. His work has been thoroughly documented in a dissertation by Thomas Owens, who refers to Young's influence on Parker in his early period but cites very little evidence.[1]

Owens divides Parker's music into two phases: the early period until 1944 and the mature years from 1944 onwards. This periodization, however, fails to recognize that Parker's playing generally declined after 1949. His work after that year is often marred by what could be described as self-parody. Of course, with a musician of Parker's stature, what for him is self-parody might well be beyond the aspirations of lesser musicians.

Through analysis of his own transcriptions of Parker's solos, Owens isolates some one hundred motives used throughout Parker's works as "building blocks." He also submits certain solos to Schenkerian analysis. Unfortunately neither of these techniques produces a genuine aesthetic by which Parker's work can be judged. And without such an aesthetic mere technicalities are not truly illuminating.

As reported by Ross Russell, Parker learned to play Lester Young's solos by heart: "The twelve Lester Young solos contained in the record collection became Charlie's case-book. The records were already well played, *Lady Be Good* so often that the grooves were beginning to break down from the pressure of the steel needle and heavy pick-up head. . . . Charlie learned each solo by heart. . . . Charlie broke down Lester's method."[2]

Parker himself refuted the idea of Young's influence: "I was crazy about Lester. He played so clean and beautiful. But I wasn't influenced by Lester. Our ideas ran on differently."[3] But comparison of various solos clearly indicates that, perhaps in spite of himself, Parker's absorption of Young's music led to direct influence.

Earl Hines, in whose big band Charlie Parker played in 1943, comments on Parker's ability to memorize: "Charlie Parker had a photographic mind. When we would rehearse a new arrangement, he would run his part down once, and when we were ready to play it the second time, he knew the whole thing from memory. Naturally I have respect for musicians of that calibre."[4] Hines's comment suggests that Parker's ability to memorize allowed him to repeat phrases once created, and it also offers some clue as to Parker's fondness for inserting musical quotes into his improvisations. I do not favor the suggestion put forward by Owens that Charlie Parker's work in a "taxi" dance hall in 1938 started him in the practice of quoting, since it was necessary to learn a great number of popular tunes. That would hardly include *Petrouchka.*

Parker recorded "Lady Be Good" for the Wichita, Kansas, radio station KFBI on November 30, 1940, with Jay McShann's band, about which Count Basie said: "I'm glad I got out of here (Kansas City) as fast as I did, because he was breathing down our backs so hard. We had to get out and move over and let this cat in—Jay McShann."[5]

The opening phrase of Parker's solo (see ex. 2) is a quote from Lester Young's "Lester Leaps In," although here the quote is in the key of G rather than the B-flat of the original:

The methodology is similar in that Parker's solo also starts with a short phrase that is expanded and then followed by a longer, flowing phrase, in this case bars 4–7. The opening of this phrase is decidedly "Lesterian." It occurs in "Shoe Shine Boy," where its influence on Charlie Parker's "Ornithology" has been noted. It also occurs in the minor key in Lester Young's "Dickie's Dream":

A similar phrase, in the major, occurs in bar 49 of "Lester Leaps In":

The ascending third (in eighth notes) on the third beat of bar 7 of Parker's solo is also found in bar 11 of Young's first chorus (see ex. 2).

There are many such melodic fragments shared by both solos. The melodic line from bar 5, beat 2, of Young's second chorus occurs in Parker's line in bar 23, where it also appears in Young's solo. The ascending minor third preceded by an A-sharp, the opening motive of Young's solo, is also found in bars 27 and 31 of Parker's solo. The opening, descending phrases of Charlie Parker's middle-eight are similar to the phrases opening Lester Young's second chorus middle-eight. And in bar 21 Parker's line is almost identical with Young's line in the same bar of his first chorus.

The rhythmic organization of Parker's line is not as subtle as that of Lester Young's in terms of freedom from the underlying four-bar structure, although his line has internal rhythmic interest brought about by accentuation. For example, there are accents on beats 3 and 4 of bar 9 and 1 and 3 of bar 10. This kind of accentuation is also a feature of Young's work and provides further evidence of his influence on Parker.

Parker also constructs some very long phrases, for example, the last phrase (bars 25–32), which starts with a quote from the popular song "Mean to Me" (a song that Young had recorded with Billie Holiday on January 25, 1937). His phrases consist much more of notes of equal time value than Young's phrases. From the midpoint of bar 28, for example, Parker's phrase is entirely in eighth notes for sixteen beats. His second phrase (bars 4–7) is also made up entirely of eighth notes, twelve beats in length.

Of course, Young's solo is one of maturity, whereas Parker's is not; he was only twenty years old when he recorded this solo. Interestingly enough both solos represent the first recorded work of each player [except possibly for an undated solo disc by Parker—Ed.].

In spite of his youth, there is in Parker's solo evidence of his mature style. In his second phrase, for example, the flow of eighth notes points to the future, as do the upward leap from the E-flat to the B-natural, the chromatic descending D-flat in bar 6, and the descent in thirds in bar 7. The downward leap to E-flat in bar 14, again a two eighth-note figure on the third beat of the bar, is typical.

EXAMPLE 2. "Lady Be Good" (Parker and Young)

EXAMPLE 2 (*continued*)

Harmonic comparisons present much of interest. The first four bars of Parker's solo are diatonic, but in bars 5 and 6 he employs the flat ninth, E-flat, leaping, as already mentioned, to the B-natural thirteenth on the first beat of bar 6. The flattened ninth features in the whole of Parker's work. Here it has a precedent in Young's solo where in bar 6 the E-flat alternates with the eleventh, G. Of course in Young's line the E-flat occurs as part of a sequentially descending pattern—E to G, E-flat to G, D to G—whereas its occurrence in Parker's line is more blatant. Its use is even more conspicuous over the dominant chord in bar 14, where the E-flat is left unresolved and is part of a phrase that also includes the eleventh and thirteenth, G and B.

The similarity of the middle eight bars has already been pointed out, and the harmonic implications of both are the same. In bar 28 the second half of the bar occurs over G-major harmony, producing an augmented eleventh and thirteenth. Although this is probably another instance where melodic considerations overrule harmonic ones, the C-sharp (D-flat), nevertheless, is the enharmonic flattened fifth of the tonic chord, and the use of the flattened fifth in building substitute harmonies—generally for the dominant and minor seventh—became the staple diet of bebop. In melodic terms such a sequence of intervals has been noted in Lester Young's "Dickie's Dream," where in bar 20 of the originally issued take it occurs as follows:

The C-sharp in bar 28, incidentally, is the one note in Parker's solo that does not occur over the same G-major harmony in Young's solo, but it does appear once more in Parker's solo, as a passing note in bar 29, again producing a chromatic fragment with upward leap of a major third, variations of which can also be found in the solos of Lester Young (using both major and minor thirds, ascending and descending), for example, in "Dickie's Dream" (bar 18), "Charlie's Dream" (bar 14), "Lester Leaps In" (bar 33), and "Honeysuckle Rose" (bars 42–43). (See exx. 3a–3d.)

a. Lester Young, "Dickie's Dream," bar 18

b. Lester Young, "Charlie's Dream," bar 14

c. Lester Young, "Lester Leaps In," bar 33

d. Lester Young, "Honeysuckle Rose," bars 42–43

EXAMPLE 3

Another facet of Lester Young's imprint on Charlie Parker can be discerned in Buddy Anderson's trumpet solo, which follows Parker's in much the same way that Carl Smith's solo follows Young's on the Jones-Smith Incorporated record. On that issue Young continued to play a very soft riff under Smith in very sympathetic and supportive fashion. On the McShann record Parker can be heard doing exactly the same thing behind Anderson.

Notes

1. Thomas Owens, "Charlie Parker: Techniques of Improvisation," 2 vols. (Ph.D. diss., University of California, Los Angeles, 1974), 1:37.

2. Ross Russell, *Bird Lives! The High Life and Hard Times of Charlie (Yardbird) Parker* (New York: Quartet Books, 1972), 90–91.

3. Michael Levin and John S. Wilson, "No Bop Roots in Jazz: Parker," *Down Beat,* September 9, 1949, 12; quoted in Nat Shapiro and Nat Hentoff, eds., *Hear Me Talkin' to Ya* (New York: Rinehart and Co., 1955), 343.

4. Quoted in Shapiro and Hentoff, eds., *Hear Me Talkin' to Ya,* 340.

5. From the film *The Last of the Blue Devils,* quoted in *The World of Count Basie,* ed. Stanley Dance (New York: Charles Scribner's Sons, 1980), xvi.

Whitney Balliett

The President

Balliett basically dislikes Young's later work, and he begins this article with a typically (for him) eloquent evocation of Young's early style. But in his review of the *Jazz Giants '56* album and the accompanying quartet with Teddy Wilson (still available on Verve), he does find some moments of magic as "Young goes tantalizingly to work." His almost begrudging admission of value in this recording paves the way for the next group of articles, which wholeheartedly embrace Young's late efforts.—Ed.

The *Jazz Giants '56* and *Pres and Teddy: The Lester Young-Teddy Wilson Quartet* (Verve) are among the last records Lester Young made before his death, in March 1959, at the age of forty-nine. They are, by and large, reminders that toward the end of his life Young had slipped into the melancholy position of no longer being able to outstrip his multitude of imitators. But, in a way, this doesn't matter, for none of Young's admirers, among them such men as Stan Getz, Paul Quinichette, Zoot Sims, Jimmy Giuffre, and Lee Konitz, has ever mastered the basic quality of his style— a perfect balance between tension and relaxation. Instead, they have either emphasized the heated side of his playing, sometimes to the point of caricature (Quinichette), or thinned out his seemingly bland aspects (Getz, Giuffre, Konitz) into a colorless drawl. (These last three students of

Originally published in the *New Yorker* and reprinted in *Dinosaurs in the Morning* (New York: J. B. Lipincott, 1962), 33–37. Copyright © 1962 by Whitney Balliett. Reprinted by permission.

Young led tenor and alto saxophonists like Bob Cooper, Bud Shank, Lennie Niehaus, and Jack Montrose to become the chassis for the cool West Coast school, which refined itself out of existence a year or two ago.) Accordingly, Young's imitators, who ironically began appearing in the mid-forties, when Young was beginning to falter, have done a good deal of unintentional harm by producing countless inferior images of his work that have distorted the uncanny abilities he had at the height of his career.

Young, a stooped, soft-spoken, sleepy-looking man with a static, caved-in face, who affected porkpie hats and somber, droopy coats, which gave him a monkish appearance, was his own best obfuscation. He frequently spoke a language that referred to his employers as Pres and to his associates as Lady, and that used such expressions as "Have another helping," which meant, when addressed to a soloist, "Take another chorus." And in Count Basie's band he developed the distracting habit of veering his instrument to one side at a forty-five-degree angle, as if he were about to paddle a canoe. These irregularities were carried directly into his playing, which was unfailingly oblique. This stemmed in part from his tone. It had a dry, sandy sound, which fell between an alto and a tenor saxophone, and which recalled his early models—Bud Freeman, who has the same sort of hoarse, whitish tone, and Frankie Trumbauer. (On the clarinet, which, unfortunately, Young played infrequently, his tone—a limber, slightly metallic one that resembled Pee Wee Russell's with the kinks straightened out—was inimitably suited to the instrument.) Added to this was the singular way he attacked his notes. He gave the impression of almost trying to avoid them, even when playing directly on the beat, by slurring them, sliding just below or over them, or by pressing them together into unhurried, nearly motionless patterns. Indeed, Young's solos often resembled a collection of evasive, melodic hums that had the quality of a soundproofed room. But underneath this outwardly lazy, one-side-of-the-mouth approach, which most of his imitators mistakenly seized upon as the basis of his style, was an absolute mastery of broken-field rhythm and phrasing—the ability to emphasize the beat simply by eluding it—that is the secret of hot playing.

This apparent coolness has resulted in the axiom that Young and Coleman Hawkins are the totally divergent leaders of the cool and hot methods of playing their instrument. But both men have been, despite their surface differences, always after the identical thing—a controlled lyricism. Hawkins, with his vibrato and dark, rubicund tone, has pursued this lyricism by taking apart the chords of a tune, eliminating certain notes, adding others, and rearranging the residue into elaborate patterns pinned directly to the beat. Young, on the other hand, poked at the melody itself, in an easy, one-finger manner, until he had reshaped it into a starker design that appeared, in spite of its rhythmic liberties, to skid along parallel to the beat, as a revised and improved shadow of the original tune. Young, in fact, was among the first to demonstrate that the short, logical, on-the-beat phrases that for most of the thirties were tightly locked to the thirty-two-bar chorus could be broken into independent, juxtaposed patterns of various rhythms and lengths. A master of economy, he never fell into the excesses of the bop school, which derived in part from him and which, after a time, engaged in a battle of rhetoric by seeing how many irrelevant notes could be uttered in the space of a chorus.

In the first chorus of a slow number, Young would seem to state the melody in a straightforward way until one discovered that he was almost imperceptibly altering it by bending certain notes down, replacing others with silence, or holding on to still others for a beat or two longer than indicated. Then, the melody softened up, he would, without raising his volume or increasing his intensity, ease into superbly mixed, gradually more complex phrases occasionally fashioned out of short riffs—repeated several times with slight variations and neatly adorned by a brief vibrato—or out of long, almost level many-noted statements. These last might begin with an exuberant legato phrase, which was abruptly gathered into up-or-downstairs leaps as daring as some of the passages of Charlie Parker but that never called attention to themselves because of the peculiar flattening effect of his tone and attack. Young's intensity showed through more clearly at faster tempos. (It also broke out unforgettably in the slow blues, which he converted into swollen legato structures that rose and fell like slow, heavy breathing.) His vibrato dried up and his legato phrases were either halved or prolonged in half-time rhythms, as if he were pouring oil on the beat in an effort to still it. In fact, all of his understated, contrasted phrases—smooth, populated runs, bass honks, single notes spattered around the beat, slow-spinning sounds that lasted for perhaps a measure and a half—were forced backhandedly toward intensifying the rhythm. Some of Young's most enduring solos occurred on such Basie records as "Taxi War Dance," "Doggin' Around," and "Clap Hands, Here Comes Charlie." No matter how often they are heard, they remain classic improvisations; not a note, tone, or accent could be changed without destroying them.

Unfortunately, the reverse is often true of the aforementioned LPs. Joining Young on *Jazz Giants '56* for the five selections—a blues and four standards—are Roy Eldridge, Vic Dickenson, Teddy Wilson, Freddie Green, Gene Ramey, and Jo Jones. Young's style here first appeared in the mid-forties and is a less wieldy version of his earlier work. It recalls Herschel Evans, who, at the time of his death in 1939, was Young's sparring mate in the Basie band. Young's tone is thicker and even husky, and the vibrato is more pronounced; he uses fewer notes, and his variations sometimes have a blunt air. He goes tantalizingly to work, though, on a slow rendition of "I Didn't Know What Time It Was." Just before the close of the first sixteen bars, he evokes his old unpredictability and inserts a fast, complex phrase—seemingly executed in slow motion—and then sets off on a series of explorations during the following chorus and a half, in which, through subtle fluctuations and the repetition of simple clusters of notes, he seems to be rubbing the paint off the melody. On much of *Pres and Teddy,* he reverts to the groping, slightly sour playing that characterized most of his final work, but, regardless of how diminished Young sounds, the shape and manner are unmistakable a mile away.

Barry Ulanov

Lester's Blues

We move now to the later work of Young. Few writers during Young's lifetime had the perspicacity to see that he was not getting his full due as an artist. Barry Ulanov was an exception. In his *Down Beat* column he lamented the lack of interest in Young's work of that year, 1955. As he told me on June 8, 1989, in a telephone interview: "I was always knocked out by Pres, even when he was not at his best. . . . His style had become more reflective, more philosophical."

Ulanov made his mark in the 1940s and 1950s with a highly literate style of writing about jazz and a special understanding of the new music of Charlie Parker and Lennie Tristano. In fact he is more than literate—he holds a Ph.D. in comparative literature and was for many years a professor at Barnard College of Columbia University in New York City, where he taught courses in literature, history, theology, and the arts. Ulanov also wrote one of the best histories of jazz in 1952 (*A History of Jazz in America* [New York: Viking Press; repr. New York: Da Capo Press, 1972]) and an important early book on Ellington (*Duke Ellington* [New York: Creative Age Press, 1946; London: Musicians Press Limited, 1947; repr. New York, Da Capo Press, 1975]).

As an early associate of John Hammond, Ulanov had the privilege of attending some of the recording sessions Hammond produced, including, as he mentions in this article, the "Lester Leaps In" session. He recalled in our telephone conversation that "this was a session that swung from start to finish. And it still swings—you don't have to go back in time to appreciate it. I remember being struck by Lester's economy of notes, and his long melodic lines. Each line had a shape and a goal." Since Ulanov knew Young's work intimately from the early days, his appreciation of the later work carries special weight.—Ed.

It was most fitting that the recent memorial concert for Charlie Parker [April 2, 1955] should have opened with Lester Young's tribute. It was right for so many reasons. Right, because the line from Lester to Charlie is as direct as it is distinguished. Right, because these two musicians more than any other two made modern jazz what it is. Right, because their incomparable contributions to our music stand side by side for all of us to hear and admire and applaud.

Sure, it was sad hearing Lester right after Bird, listening to him play "I Can't Get Started" a few minutes after all of us in Carnegie Hall had listened to Bird's "Now Is the Time" on the PA system.

But it was heartwarming, too. The sounds went so well together, one set of long lines after another, one striking personality after another, one persuasive modernist after another.

And it reminded some of us that there were still giants in our midst and that jazz was not entirely for the history books and the nostalgic anecdotes. Here was a master of his horn whose place was assured alongside Louis Armstrong and Bix Beiderbecke and Duke Ellington and Charlie Christian, one of the men who made our music, still blowing, blowing beautifully.

I was reminded, listening to Pres that night, of another occasion when he had played beautifully. It was back around a half year ago at Birdland late one night.

The club wasn't packed, but there were enough persons present to generate an atmosphere and fill in the open spaces and keep the sound from clattering hollowly back and forth across the room. When Pee Wee announced "the great Lester Young," there was a polite scattering of applause, just enough to rise over the banging of the bottles and the glasses and the shifting of the chairs and the undulating conversation at the tables and behind the ropes and around the bar.

Then Lester picked up his tenor and slung it up near his shoulder in that remarkable way of his that suggests nothing so much as a man possessed of superhuman strength in his wrists, somebody who can do maybe 100 or 150 chin-ups and is proud of it and wants to tell the world.

What he told the Birdland world that night had nothing to do with physical strength, however; it was a gentler story, one far more subtle than athletic and of touching musical quality throughout.

It was the blues. More choruses of the blues than I could count or possibly remember if I had counted them. It was a fairly simple blues, really, as Lester's have a way of being, but not babyish, not just a series of riffs repeated endlessly and monotonously. It was the blues made moving, made melodic and tied together, chorus after chorus, to make one long statement of surpassing beauty that said as much as anything else that there is still much to be done with the blues, that there is still warmth and rhythmic vitality and singing melody left in the steady alternation of tonic and subdominant and dominant.

What did the half-filled nightclub do? Did it hear and admire and applaud? It didn't seem to me that many could have heard—the conversations went on right through Lester's blues, and the glasses and bottles continued to clink, and the chairs danced as nervously as ever to the restlessness of an audience that didn't know when it was privileged or how much joy was there for the asking.

Lester was alive and kicking, but how many realized it? How many do realize it, outside Birdland back some months? How many at Carnegie at Bird's requiem concert recognized the size of the man who opened the affair?

I ask these questions now and in this space not only because of the Carnegie appearance Lester Young made and the reminder of the Birdland evening it afforded but also because of a new album of old music that has just come my way.

It's a twelve-inch Epic collection of Count Basie sides made in 1936, 1939, and 1940, all featuring Lester. It's called after Pres's most famous record performance, "Lester Leaps In," which it includes along with the wonderful "Dickie's Dream" made at the same date (September 5, 1939), which I had the pleasure of attending.

There are also the fetching Jones-Smith sides of 1936, which first brought Lester's sound and ideas to my attention and to that of many others. And there are such masterpieces—Basie's and Young's—as "Twelfth Street Rag" and "Taxi War Dance" and "Rock-a-Bye Basie."

If you don't know these sides or only have a faint impression of their quality, make sure you get to listen to this little library of great jazz. There aren't going to be many records issued this year—even with the colossal quantity of jazz that pops up in grooves nowadays—that will rank with this one.

But don't stop with vintage Pres; pay attention, please, to what he's playing today, on records and in person. Listen to that fine Norgran twelve-incher called *The President,* which includes Lester's "Confessin'," for me at least *the* side of 1954 [now on Verve—Ed.].

We shouldn't take musicians like Lester Young for granted. Hear him and the few others of like stature and appreciate what you hear and let them know it. Young is one of the very few jazzmen playing today who is really entitled to that overworked adjective of the entertainment business, "immortal." But remember, this immortal, like all the others, is very much a mortal.

Erik Wiedemann

Lester Young: The Postwar Years

Erik Wiedemann makes the case that Young's early works may have had
the greatest influence, but that his middle works—especially from 1945 to
1950—were his greatest artistic accomplishments. In this article he explains why. Wiedemann is a highly respected critic in his native Denmark,
but because of language barriers his work is not well known to the main-
stream of jazz scholars. I omitted a few paragraphs reviewing Young's
biography and edited the translation for idiomatic expression, with Wiedemann's permission.—Ed.

For further reading. Those who read French will be interested in another overview
of Young's work, a lengthy one by Demetre Ioakimidis published in *Jazz Hot* 143
(May 1959): 6–11. Ioakimidis surveys Young's entire career and offers some
positive comments on his later work.

How many people Lester influenced, how many lives!

—Lee Konitz

In 1945 the following entry appeared in *Tribune,* a Danish jazz magazine
of the time: "In an army camp in Alabama where Lester Young was doing

his military service, he was apprehended with some of those ill-fated marijuana cigarettes on him. The result: one year in prison and a dishonorable discharge from the army. The latter doesn't worry Young all that much, and his military service might easily have lasted more than a year."

No one at that time could have envisaged how fateful Lester Young's controversy with the U.S. military would prove to be. People later realized that the fifteen months he spent away from jazz marked the decisive watershed in his life and musical career. . . . In recent years there has been a noticeable tendency to depreciate Lester Young's playing in the postwar years, compared with his playing before or during the war.

Certainly not much was left of the lively, skittish vitality that could be heard in his Basie solos when he returned to jazz at the end of 1945. But his music had gained a new dimension, a more resonant soundboard, without having lost any of its artistic authority. Admittedly his playing during the 1950s gradually became increasingly preoccupied and weak— as his visits here in 1952, 1953, and 1956 confirm—but the years immediately after the war have to be considered his most important period artistically, the period that gave us his most monumental solos.

Slower tempos and ballads were now his specialty. This was not a side of his playing heard on the Basie records, although it was in evidence in a number of recordings with Billie Holiday and Teddy Wilson. And there is no doubt that this form of jazz playing coincided with a basic characteristic of his temperament: his phlegmatic nature. Lester Young was a passionate devotee of slowness—no wonder he was most at home when playing slow numbers.

You can get a clear impression of this new facet of his style by comparing his "These Foolish Things" from April 1944 with that of December 1945, the latter version saturated with a painful experience of life and a feeling of loneliness unknown in jazz and whose like is only seen in Parker. Complete emancipation from the theme is another new, refreshing characteristic, one that attests to the increased strength of Young's musical creativity.

Among other recordings worthy of mention from these years are the three ballads "She's Funny That Way" from 1946, "On the Sunny Side of the Street," and "Confessin'" from 1947, and the slow "No Eyes Blues" from 1947, which continues and completes ideas found in "Salute to Fats" and "Four O'Clock Drag" from 1944 and "Back to the Land" probably from 1946.

The many recordings made for Norman Granz from 1950 onwards vary considerably in quality, but in several numbers Young demonstrates that he is still the master, for example, in "I Can't Get Started" from 1952. His playing is also immortalized in a number of recordings of Jazz at the Philharmonic concerts between 1946 and 1955. Quite clearly the atmosphere at these concerts was normally not to his liking and made for an unfortunate setting for his music. Even so, there are some ballad solos worth remembering, for example, "I Can't Get Started" from 1946, in which he is followed by Charlie Parker but not outshone by him, and especially "Embraceable You" from 1949.

It is customary to single out the LP *Jazz Giants '56* as one of his best from the later years, but his solos here do not differ in any significant way from the rest of his production from this period, and they lack both the concentration of Roy Eldridge and the elegance of Teddy Wilson found on the same record.

And maybe Young doesn't feel completely at home among these contemporary swing musicians. He once turned down a suggestion to record with other former Basie musicians so as to recapture the music of that time on record: "I can't do that. I don't play like that any more. I play different and I live different. . . . You change, you move on." But *Jazz Giants '56* is precisely that, an attempt to recapture a lost era.

If you look at the musicians he chose for his own groups, you find predominantly younger men, not swing musicians—for example, the piano players Dodo Marmarosa, Joe Albany, Junior Mance, and John Lewis and drummers such as Chico Hamilton, Roy Haynes, and Connie Kay.

Lester Young liked to play with modernists, though not with the more fanatical among them, and it felt natural for him to do so, as opposed to Coleman Hawkins, who with younger musicians was like a bull in a china shop. At this point it is interesting to note that Young himself stressed that he "plays *swing* tenor. . . . My music is swing music." To my knowledge Hawkins has never made a similar claim.

On a couple of occasions Lester Young revealed which of his recordings satisfied him the most. They were all recorded between 1936 and 1939: Basie's "Shoe Shine Swing," "One O'Clock Jump," "Every Tub," "Swinging the Blues," "Taxi War Dance," "Clap Hands, Here Comes Charlie" ("a spark of my heart"), and "Lester Leaps In" and Billie Holiday's "Sailboat in the Moonlight" and "Back in Your Own Backyard."

Is this because people always remember their first triumphs? Or was Young too modest to name his own recordings? Or didn't he find any real highlights in his later production? Perhaps it is true that the artist is often the last person to know what is the most essential in his own work.

No matter what the truth really is, and no matter how much of merit you can find in Lester Young's playing before 1945, it is still legitimate to assert that one cannot fully understand the range of Young's art until one hears his postwar solos.

Young's historical importance, however, lies elsewhere. In this respect it is the Basie period—and this alone—that deserves mention.

A music as personal as Young's in the postwar years cannot directly inspire other musicians—at best it can only be imitated, as Paul Quinichette has done. Young's own comment after a tenor duet with Quinichette is illuminating: "I don't know whether to play like myself or like Lady Q, 'cos he's playing just like I play."

There is nothing really remarkable about the fact that Lester Young's influence can first be felt on a broad front a decade or so after he had become known himself. This was also the case with Armstrong and Parker. But Young's position in this development, midway between these two stylistic innovators, meant that his influence was less than theirs. Even though the Lester Young of the 1930s was ahead of his time, musical developments had already passed him by when he was at the peak of his influence in the 1940s. Parker had taken a decisive step further.

The young tenor saxophone players who grew up with the Lester Young of the Basie period as their idol soon found themselves distracted by a younger and more advanced style of playing and faced with something of a dilemma: they either had to approach the new concept—with the risk of falling between two stools—or they had to reject it—with the risk of falling behind the modern trends.

Among the older group of Lester Young's followers (born between 1921 and 1925), the three black tenor saxophone players Wardell Gray, Dexter Gordon, and Gene Ammons chose the first solution, which accounts for the mixture of influences in their music. This is perhaps most evident in the playing of the most gifted of them, Wardell Gray, who, certainly as late as 1950, was Lester Young's own favorite among younger tenor saxophone players.

A slightly younger group of Lester Young disciples (all born between 1925 and 1927) include the white tenor saxophone players who, to a large extent, came to characterize cool jazz: "the brothers" Stan Getz, Herbie Steward, and Zoot Sims and such "half-brothers" as Al Cohn, Allen Eager, and Brew Moore. Lester Young is, of course, the spiritual father of cool jazz, and his influence is especially tangible as regards these tenor sax players. The higher, lighter sound and partiality for the upper register of the instrument (also found in the playing of the alto sax player

Lee Konitz and the baritone sax player Gerry Mulligan) obviously spring from Young's "alto tone." [Young does not in fact favor the upper register but seems to because his sound is relatively light, even in the bottom of the range.—Ed.] Getz and Steward, however, have successfully included elements of Parker's phrasing into their playing, and Sims found his own solution in a light staccato style of playing that might be the result of the influence of Miles Davis.

Eager ("if you're talking about the gray boys, then Allen Eager can play," Young once said), Moore, and Cohn kept closer to Young's style of playing, but the first two soon disappeared from view, and Cohn's playing was characterized by something of Young's relaxed style but nothing of his élan—the same weakness found in Jimmy Giuffre, who has tried to keep Young's clarinet style alive. (Young: "He sure plays me, especially in the low tones.") All four musicians can be seen to have chosen the second solution to the above-mentioned dilemma—with the predicted result.

Comparing the Lester Young school with the Coleman Hawkins school means comparing Wardell Gray, Stan Getz, and Zoot Sims with Chu Berry, Ben Webster, and Herschel Evans. With all due respect to the first-named, you have to conclude that Hawkins's influence on tenor sax playing has been more fertile than Young's. It has also been a dominant force much longer, from the early 1930s to the late 1940s, whereas Young's lasted from the late 1940s to about 1955, when Sonny Rollins came into the picture.

From a different, perhaps more essential perspective, Young's importance for jazz has nevertheless been greater than Hawkins's. His historical role consists of more than just having exercised an instrumental influence and created a school within tenor sax playing. What makes him the most important jazz soloist of the era after Armstrong and before Parker is something that goes far beyond the instrument itself and concerns the fundamental character of jazz playing.

Lester Young was the first great soloist to show that jazz didn't have to be boiling hot to be jazz. Other musicians had been on a similar track previously, but the sober style of Teddy Wilson is combined with a certain lack of temperament, and the undramatic nature of Benny Carter's playing often has a touch of sentimentality. None of this is true of Lester Young's playing, which is far too realistic to be overloaded with feeling and far too virile to border on colorless elegance.

Twenty years before cool jazz he made coolness a real quality of jazz and thereby carried out a revolutionary expansion of the register of jazz. Just how much he came to mean for Parker on that account is difficult to say, but there seems to be a link between the two Kansas City musicians that should scarcely be neglected.

Parker himself has narrated that as a young man he heard Young in Kansas City—this was about 1935–36, when Parker was fifteen or sixteen years old. He has also related how enthusiastic he was about Young's playing but has stressed that he was not influenced by Young and that their ideas went in different directions. It is not possible to speculate further about this period, since the earliest recorded Parker solos are from the spring of 1941. [Parker's 1940 recordings were not available when this was written.—Ed.]

At that time, Kenny Clarke says, musicians began to get interested in Parker, "because he played like Pres on the alto sax." If you listen to his solos from the Jay McShann period today—with our present familiarity with Parker's playing—it seems incontestable that there is a lot more Parker than Young; but it may have seemed otherwise at the time, and a detailed investigation would doubtlessly demonstrate a Lester Young influence on some of Parker's slow and medium tempo solos—as well as a Parker influence on some of Young's solos from the late 1940s onwards. At any rate it is reasonable to claim that Young, with his reaction against vibrato and the special rhythmic relaxedness he introduced, more than anyone else prepared the way for Parker and for the new rhythmic intensity that he brought to jazz.

Much more evident and direct is the link between Young and Miles Davis, especially when you consider that for both of them—as opposed to Parker—it is the length of tones and their placement rather than their accentuation that creates the rhythmic life of the phrases. You might almost speak of a rhythm of quantity, introduced by Lester Young and further developed by Davis more than anyone else. Were we not struck by a feeling of kinship that transcended all stylistic differences when we heard the two musicians play together at a concert here in 1956?

This perspective must carry more weight in placing Lester Young in the history of jazz than the obvious tangible influences that can be studied with the playing of the tenor saxophone—just as Young's own example, and the fact that a Miles Davis was able to develop it further, says more about the value of the concept of jazz Lester Young introduced than certain of the more lukewarm products of cool jazz.

When one considers the development of jazz between Armstrong and Parker, Lester Young's name springs first to mind. That is no mean achievement. But Lester Young also paid a price for being "The President." Isolation and loneliness were his lot, as they were Charlie Parker's and most other innovators'.

POSTSCRIPT—On rereading my article thirty years later, I should like to add a few comments. I feel that my rather categorical statements regarding the importance of Young's controversy with the military and the artistic superiority of his postwar work should certainly be modified somewhat. It should also be stressed that I am referring to Dexter Gordon's early work (1955 and earlier) and that I did not, in 1959, know Charlie Parker's "Lady Be Good" solo with Jay McShann ([November] 1940), which does show a definite Young influence. However, the importance of Frank Trumbauer and Bix Beiderbecke as precursors and inspirators of Young ought to have been stressed already in 1959, as well as the use of linear, scalar improvisation as another important link between Young and Miles Davis.

Graham Colombé

Time and the Tenor:
Lester Young in the Fifties

In Part One we encountered Colombé as the compiler of words about
Young. Here he speaks for himself as he discusses the last decade of
Young's career. He praises Young's later work for its emotional openness
and maturity, and while he understands that this emotional depth may be
difficult for some listeners to accept, he makes the case that that is the
listener's problem and not Young's. He surveys virtually all of Young's
studio recordings for Norman Granz with a clearheaded approach, neither claiming that all are great nor dismissing them out of hand. Colombé
has slightly revised the article for this reprinting.—Ed.

It has been a common attitude to see Lester Young's career as a steady
artistic decline after the departure from Basie's band, so I must make it
clear at once that I do not accept this view. The evident decline in the early
forties was followed by a struggle to pull himself together after his army
service and come to terms with bop; there was then a settling down about
1948 and 1949 into an unstrained, totally personal style that was related
to the earlier one but had its own identity and merit. A similar view was
expressed but with insufficient detail and evidence by Burnett James in
his *Essays on Jazz* [(London: Sidgwick & Jackson, 1961)], and the case for
decline was put with rather more specific comments by Benny Green in a

Originally published in *Into Jazz*, April 1974, 32–35. Copyright © 1974 by Graham Colombé. Reprinted, with
slight revisions, by permission.

chapter in *The Reluctant Art* [(New York: Horizon Press, 1963; repr. Plain-view, N.Y.: Books for Libraries Press, 1975)], to which I shall refer later.

While considering Lester's music in the fifties, I shall deal only with studio sessions under his own name, except in 1957, when these give too one-sided a picture. In 1950 Lester signed a new recording contract with Norman Granz, whose company produced (again excepting 1957) at least one album a year for the rest of Lester's life. The first date (March 1950) was not a complete success because of the presence of Buddy Rich, but it does make clear certain aspects of Lester's style. On the medium fast "Up 'n' Adam," it's obvious that Rich's heavy, inflexible drumming doesn't suit Young at all, although he struggles against it and manages to produce some soaring, floating phrases that glide above the heavy ground rhythm. More relaxed work from the rhythm section (including Hank Jones and Ray Brown) improves the other four performances, and two of them are exemplary of a number of later recordings. "Too Marvelous for Words," at an easygoing medium tempo, has the theme played in a stealthy, subdued manner in the lower register but changes to a more forceful mood in the upper register for the second chorus. This very effective practice dramatizes Lester's solemn, almost respectful attitude to the tunes he played and their words, and then his feeling of freedom as he takes over with his own stream of melody. "Polka Dots and Moonbeams" shows the nature of Lester's ballad playing for the rest of the decade and also makes clear why certain listeners have been unable to come to terms with his later music. On this track Lester drops his guard and plays not just with an emotional depth equaled by only a few but with an extreme frankness rare even in jazz. His solo here has beauty, tenderness, and sadness, but these can all be found elsewhere. What is unique here is Lester's expression of his vulnerability. His approach to this song is an admission that life can be painful and dreams can be shattered, and the only solace for what has happened is here and now in the beauty of music. This mature tragic awareness is what distinguishes Lester in the fifties from Lester in the thirties, and with the advantage of hindsight it's easy to understand how the magical, buoyant optimism of the early years could not last, given the man Lester was and the society he lived in. His later music is therefore sometimes disturbing and confusing, but it does tell a certain emotional truth about what the United States did to Lester Young. Many people like listening to jazz as a simple, refreshing, uplifting experience, and I can understand why this music may not appeal to them; Benny Green, in his essay on Billie Holiday, showed he was prepared to go further than that into the music, so it's with reluctance that I accuse

him of a superficial response when he compares Lester's "bland virtu-
osity" of the thirties with the later "weary sentiment." To me it seems that
neither phrase does justice to the strength and depth of Lester's music.

Mr. Green rightly draws attention to the saxophonist's uncertainty
in the lower reaches of his horn, and this is an inescapable characteristic of
his later work. But I don't see why listeners who can accept the fluffs on
some of Armstrong's and Davis's classic recordings should not accept this
fault also. The comparison is not made lightly, because I think there are
tracks in the fifties that are classic performances in the Young canon.
"Count Every Star" from Lester's next session is an excellent track that
allows a number of observations about Lester's style. The rhythmic approach may at first suggest the advent of diminished technique, or a lack
of alertness, but, since certain very lively phrases make it clear that was not
the case, we must accept, as we do with Monk, that Lester has chosen to
play this way, and we must try to acclimatize ourselves to it. We can
discover then that, although Lester may now lag even further behind the
beat than before, his music still swings, again like Monk, in a very personal
way. Apart from the fast "Neenah" this session (July 1950), with John
Lewis, Joe Shulman, and Bill Clark, has four medium to slow tracks where
Clark's drums are barely audible, producing a sound that foreshadows the
later Jimmy Giuffre Trio and underlines the beauty of Lester's tone. This
has certainly changed, but the husky vibrato is hardly "grossly sensual," as
Benny Green calls it. Lester, in fact, displays a delicate control over his
tone, and the subtle variations he employs are usually appropriate to his
phrases, which often form a pattern of sudden contrasts. Legato, mourn-
ful figures, drawn out over the rhythm, are followed abruptly by exhilarating, rising patterns, fingered with extreme rapidity.

The next two sessions (January 16, 1951, and March 8, 1951) were
made with the rhythm section Lester was using at Birdland—John Lewis,
Gene Ramey, and Jo Jones. Lewis's personal, elegant simplicity blends
well with the tenor and encourages the gentler side of Lester, so that in
spite of the lift that Jo Jones gives the rhythm section, Lester does not
fully reveal the drive of which he was still capable, preferring to float
along in a blithe, sometimes almost gay, mood that shows that his melancholy was not yet pervasive. Nevertheless two of the best tracks are the
slow "Undercover Girl Blues" and the even slower "Slow Motion Blues"
(prophetically titled because his playing actually acquired a feeling of slow
motion a few years later). Lester was a great blues player, and in the fifties
his playing of slow blues, as with the ballads, took on a deeper involvement. The surprising achievement of his blues playing is to retain the

blues feeling yet to convey, usually by employing the ninth and thirteenth extensions of the chords, a sublime lyricism at the same time. Bechet is the only other person who comes to mind as managing this blend, though of course in a more forceful manner. The lyricism is also there naturally in numbers like "A Foggy Day" and "Let's Fall in Love," which Lester rescued from oblivion, and it is particularly striking, as Lester moves from the tune to his improvisation, that there is, so to speak, no loss of melody. His own inventions are frequently as memorable as the tune.

The following year Lester attended a lengthy session with Oscar Peterson, Barney Kessel, Ray Brown, and J. C. Heard [November 28, 1952]. It began with four extended tracks, and the busy, prodding drive of this group at first had the effect of inhibiting Lester and restricting his phrasing to small intervals and simple patterns. By the time the third track—a fast "Tea for Two"—was recorded, he had adjusted to the situation, and he plays two solos that, though less inventive than those with Lewis, exceed them in drive and momentum and demonstrate Lester's continuing technical ability. Among the shorter tracks recorded later, "I Can't Get Started" and "These Foolish Things" are very moving performances in the mood of "Polka Dots and Moonbeams," and the melodic quality of the improvising is again impressive. By the time "On the Sunny Side of the Street" was played, Lester was at home enough to indulge himself. The theme statement starts straightforwardly but suddenly jumps to a definitely post-Parker, double-time phrase before reverting to a decorated version of the tune, descending to a throbbing low note, after an unexpected pause, and returning deviously to the tonic to complete the first sixteen bars; the middle eight begins with a simple, declamatory, Armstrong-like phrase and develops in this way until another double-time run leads back to a masterly paraphrase of the tune in the last eight bars. The sheer variety of phrasing available to Lester at this time is quite astonishing.

This variety is underlined on the next two sessions, by Lester's regular band (December 11, 1953, and December 10, 1954), where he has Jesse Drakes on trumpet as frontline partner, and the square, rigid, limited nature of the trumpet's phrasing emphasizes the opposite qualities in the saxophone lines. When Connie Kay told me that Drakes was in the band as straw boss as well as trumpeter, the musical incompatibility was at last explained. He is an anonymous "modernist," technically competent enough but lacking Lester's warmth and melodic invention. In fact Lester's involvement makes Drakes sound cynical, and I wish Charles Fox, who wrote in a recent *New Statesman* that Lester himself was "often

cynical-sounding" at this time, would listen to these records and recon-
sider. From the 1953 session two interesting tracks are a fast "Jumpin' at
the Woodside" and an even faster "Lady Be Good," which are actually the
last examples of Lester in command at up-tempo. He is in command in
that he produces satisfactory solos without struggling, but he is not capable, at this tempo, of invention to match what he can do when he has more
time. The session a year later included an Ellington tune, "It Don't Mean
a Thing," and "Rose Room," another melody associated with the Duke,
and it's intriguing to wonder what music might have resulted if Lester had
ever joined the Ellington band, particularly as the sound of Paul Gonsalves's off-mike playing of "Happy Reunion" at the Rainbow in 1973 was
the nearest thing I've heard to Lester's thin, husky, passionate tone on
much of his later ballad playing. This sound and passion are evident on
two beautiful ballads from this date, "I'm in the Mood for Love" and
"Come Rain or Come Shine," where the tone seems slightly thinner than
before but the feeling more intense.

For the next session (December 1, 1955), Granz decided to choose
the players himself, and he obviously hoped to stimulate Lester by a
reunion with Harry Edison, supported by a rhythm team of Peterson,
Ellis, Brown, and Rich. Naturally enough the first number was a fast "One
O'Clock Jump," and Peterson develops a very swinging groove in his
opening choruses. When the tenor comes in, it's at once obvious that
something is wrong. The tempo is too fast for Lester, and he's in trouble,
neither brain nor fingers can cope. In fact this is the first really weak solo
in the Young discography, and it was due to his lack of concern for his
health having finally caught up with him. Very soon after this date he
went voluntarily to the hospital for treatment and rest. Nevertheless on
the slow tracks that followed "One O'Clock Jump," he played valid, moving solos with an entirely new atmosphere, and I cannot refrain from
quoting W. B. Yeats in an attempt to explain it:

> *An aged man is but a paltry thing,*
> *A tattered coat upon a stick, unless*
> *Soul clap its hands and sing, and*
> *louder sing*
> *For every tatter in its mortal dress.*

What Lester somehow conveys now is an impression of a man in totally
exceptional circumstances, perhaps even a man who knows he has not
long to live because he is not going to make much effort to stay alive. For
the rest of his life there is a haunting quality in his music that can
transcend technical failings and reach straight inside the right listener.

Charlie Parker's first "Loverman" had the same quality. On this 1955 record Lester floats in slow motion over the rhythm, some of his runs relating to Coltrane's "sheet of sound," in that it's hard to pin down their relation to the beat though it's undeniably there. His tone, now wispier than before, becomes even more distinctive, and his gentle lines are sometimes interrupted by louder, piercing phrases of an almost heart-rending quality. However, the logical sequel to this record did not occur for another year and a half, and the two sessions that took place less than two months later present a Lester transformed.

Granz's second attempt to stimulate him with fresh companions must have succeeded beyond his wildest dreams. After some weeks in the hospital, Lester came out refreshed and ready to play, and the three men who I think encouraged him most on the *Jazz Giants '56* date (January 12, 1956) were Roy Eldridge, Teddy Wilson, and Jo Jones. Well though Edison had played six weeks before, Eldridge had the edge over him in his ability to rise to an occasion, or even initiate one, and this was an occasion everyone rose to. As the music is fortunately available on Verve, I need not emphasize the excellence of the solos by Eldridge, Wilson, Jones, and Vic Dickenson or the invaluable rhythm work of Freddie Green and Gene Ramey. What is important here is to understand Lester Young's contribution. Most striking at first is his tone, which has changed yet again. In fact the tone he plays with here and on the following day has an identity of its own, which clearly separates it from both earlier and later recordings. His sound is broader and warmer, as if, after confronting a vision of his own end, Lester was able, through the support of people who mattered to him both as musicians and as friends, to find again in music, if only tempo-rarily, the hopes of personal fulfillment it had offered him at the beginning of his career. His solos are simpler than those of a few years before, but more confident; it seems he has blended an earlier style with the Armstrong-inspired mode that had preceded it, though retaining an occasional, almost shyly inserted, double-time figure derived from the language of bop. The obliqueness of earlier times has all but vanished, and Lester has extended the impression of total openness that emanates from "Polka Dots and Moonbeams" to his medium tempo solos (perhaps not the fast "Gigantic Blues"), so that this session, though not represent-ing him at his artistic peak, is unique in showing him competing suc-cessfully in terms of unconfined, rhapsodic passion (terms that he had replaced in the thirties with his own dry, contained economy) with Bechet, Armstrong, and Hawkins (and of course with Eldridge, who was actually there).

The next day Lester recorded a further seven titles (also on Verve), with Wilson, Ramey, and Jones. These retained the mood of the previous day, but with an occasional lessening of intensity and a hint of awareness that this was only a temporary recovery. "Pres Returns," the medium-tempo blues that was the first number recorded, is one of Lester's best recordings (with excellent drums from Jones), and it points the way to his final phase, where feeling and sound were to become so touching that they could make concern for technique and imagination seem almost irrelevant.

The following year Lester recorded with Harry Edison again, and it was as if the 1956 session had never existed. This date (July 31, 1957) is the weakest available on record from Lester's entire career. Apart from Lester's tenuous grip on himself, it sounds at times as if the octave key on his saxophone is not working properly. The first track recorded, a blues called "St. Tropez," features Lester on a new metal clarinet, and the tone he obtains is very reminiscent of the Kansas City Six session. Unfortunately he seems to be having technical problems on this instrument, too; in three separate solos he plays a total of sixteen choruses, of which a few are coherent but several are disastrous, with harsh squeaks and places where he blows but no note comes out. Nevertheless on other tracks where he plays tenor ("Flic" in the Jepsen discography is really "Waldorf Blues" and the sleeve details on American Verve MGV 8298 are inaccurate), Lester manifests the ability mentioned before to communicate in spite of technical difficulties. Toward the end of "Sunday" he suddenly produces, after a number of slow, slurred, legato phrases, an abrupt, leaping figure that astonishes with its sudden suggestion of hidden life and agility. This session must have represented a particularly bad day for Lester, because at a Los Angeles concert with JATP three months later, he produced some nimble phrases in the up-tempo "Merry Go Round" and a finely controlled "Polka Dots and Moonbeams" in the ballad medley. The famous "Sound of Jazz" television program in December of the same year showed on the recording made at the rehearsal a tantalizing snatch of Lester playing an obbligato to Billie Holiday on "Fine and Mellow." This fragment gives a breathtaking insight into the new rapport that could have developed between Lester and Billie, and the mystery of why Granz did not record them together in the fifties, when he had them both under contract, is something somebody should ask him about.

Early next year (February 7, 1958) there was another date with Edison that produced a medium "Flic" ("Waldorf Blues" in Jepsen) and a slow "You're Getting to Be a Habit with Me" to complete the album begun a year before. Lester is in better health, and his tone is a little rounder and slightly less husky. The haunting quality mentioned earlier dominates, and his spare, legato phrases spread like oil over the waves of the rhythm giving a feeling of timeless tranquility. The next day Hank Jones replaced Lou Stein, and, more important, Roy Eldridge was added to the group. The album recorded that day was called *Laughin' to Keep from Cryin'* and has on the cover a quite exceptional photograph of Roy leaning toward Lester, whose face is creased in laughter presumably at what Roy is telling him. Without detracting from Edison's playing, which is by his own standards excellent, I would say that only Buck Clayton could have equaled the sensitivity with which Roy matches Lester's fragile probing here, and he would not quite have distilled the emotional intensity that Roy and Lester bring to the music. I find this is a very good session, but I realize that others may not agree as willingly as they would over the 1956 recordings. There is no other music in jazz to relate to this final style of Lester's, and the emotional response of the listener can be, as it is in my case, so powerful that it's impossible for me to imagine how the music comes across to those who hear it more objectively. Lester plays clarinet again on two tracks, happily with more success than on "St. Tropez," and the sound of the thirties is uncannily recaptured. Although certain phrases that the richness of the tenor would have supported come over as rather too simple, his playing on the opening chorus of "They Can't Take That Away from Me" is so tremendously affecting that Edison's solo, which follows, sounds cold and shallow in comparison (though actually it's not), and it is not until Roy's muted entry that Lester's mood is regained. On the other three tracks Lester is back on tenor, and the solo that finishes the long blues called "Romping" is a triumph in making simple phrases moving and meaningful.

Lester's last studio session was in Paris [March 2, 1959] less than a fortnight before his death. Although his tone is slightly thinner, he is a little more lively than he was the previous year. (An intriguing aspect of these later recordings is that Lester's sound is never quite the same in any two years, and one comes to distinguish the different vintages). The rhythm section is dominated by the magnificent drumming of Kenny Clarke, who fills the gaps in Lester's lines with intelligence and swing. Lester plays a dozen of his favorite tunes, and the resulting album provides a clear summation of his final style and a convincing demonstration of how his musical spirit survived the physical wasting away. His tone may be tattered here, but "soul claps its hands and sings." Whether in the intense melancholy of "I Can't Get Started" or the surging swing of the final "Tea for Two," Lester's music still had beauty right up to the end of his life.

In conclusion I would suggest that Lester's later music has been considered suspect because rigid concepts of sex roles make some people expect men to play jazz with "virility." Lester was an opponent, consciously or otherwise, of "machismo." Surely his personal and musical communion with Billie Holiday was a result of his willingness to accept aspects of himself that many men would consider feminine. In his last ten years he had the courage and the honesty to express those aspects in music, and for that, as for his earlier pioneering achievements, he deserves our profound gratitude.

H. A. Woodfin

Reconsiderations

Woodfin states outright that "Young's finest works were made after he left Basie and that they extend from 'Afternoon of a Basie-ite' in 1943 to 'This Year's Kisses' in 1956." He defends his position convincingly by studying two recordings of "These Foolish Things," the powerful version for Aladdin from 1945 and the very different, highly lyrical one from 1952. Woodfin is not alone, of course, in thinking that Young got better—trumpeter Buck Clayton says as much in the film about Young, *Song of the Spirit,* and on page 119 of his book *Buck Clayton's Jazz World* (New York: Oxford University Press, 1986).—Ed.

For further reading. Gary Giddins's review of the volumes of "live" Young from 1956 put out by Pablo (produced by Young's former producer Norman Granz) makes the point that his late works had their own distinctive beauty, independent of the early works and not meant to be compared with them. The review, "Lester Young Grows Deeper," is reprinted in Giddins's book *Rhythm-A-Ning* (New York: Oxford University Press, 1985).

The career of the late Lester Young is rather oddly chronicled in jazz criticism and history. While he is nearly unanimously credited as being one of the seminal creators in the history of the art, nevertheless his greatest works are seldom commented upon. Sometimes one has the

Reprinted from *Jazz Review,* July 1959, 30–31.

impression that the greatest weight is given to the works produced in conjunction with Basie, such as "The World Is Mad" and "Taxi War Dance." Certainly, performances such as these are well deserving of the honors granted them, but they are not creations of Lester Young. Rather their greatness lies precisely in their totality, which is made up not alone of Young's contributions, as interesting as they are, but of those of Basie and the band with the other soloists such as Wells, Clayton, and Edison as well.

A thesis worth considering is that Young's finest works were made after he left Basie and that they extend from "Afternoon of a Basie-ite" in 1943 to "This Year's Kisses" in 1956. Now, this is somewhat of a heterodox opinion. The by now usual approach is summed up in the following citation from Raymond Horricks's *Count Basie and His Orchestra* [(London: Victor Gollancz, 1957; repr. Westport, Conn.: Negro Universities Press, 1971), 107]:

> Running from the mid-1940's to the present day, there is the evidence of a decline in spirit; his playing style, once so radical and full of fresh ideas, has become more of a routine, and the majority of his record dates seem to be treated with the "just another job" attitude. In this last phase of his career Lester has been financially successful while replaying the various phrases and devices which were once so revolutionary; frequently he has given to sensationalist audiences exactly what they wish to hear (namely, honking noises and other vulgar mannerisms). As a result he has become the victim of an increasing ennui, the tiredness of his appearance overflowing and spreading its way into the once so inventive mind. Nowadays Lester is seldom jogged out of his state of lethargy.

I submit that such a judgment as the above is quite false and that a simple examination of Young's recorded work from the mid-forties on will amply verify my contention. As evidence, I propose that we consider two of Young's purest masterpieces, his two versions of "These Foolish Things," one dating from the mid-forties, the other from the early fifties.

Only three factors are constant in both improvisations. First, they are both examples of the free variation approach that Gunther Schuller has described as "in the strictest sense no variation at all, since it does not proceed from the basis of varying a given thematic material but simply reflects a player's ruminations on an *unvarying* (Schuller's italics) chord progression." Secondly, both exhibit the phenomenal rhythmic flexibility of Young at his best, which is most apparent in his up-tempo works but which is equally present in slower tempos as well. This flexibility makes the constant 4/4 rhythm act as a place to which Young can return from time to time, only to begin a fresh rhythmic flight, as well as a stable element from which his own rhythmic ideas rebound. Indeed, in up-tempo works this freedom almost draws the attention away from his great melodic gifts. Thirdly, these works are in an AABABA form, each lasting forty-eight bars [one chorus and a half].

From the opening bars of the first version, we are aware Young has begun to construct a melodic study of great originality. Constantly floating in and around the beat, Young continues a steadily developing rumination (to use Schuller's term) until in the last bars of the first bridge he briefly states a fragment of the original melody, only to abandon it almost immediately to surge on to the last eight bars of the first chorus and from there to the half chorus following. There are no further citations of the original.

Considering this work in the line of Young's development, certain things are striking. His sonority became slightly heavier and thicker, although he still continued to eschew the use of a vibrato, thus maintaining an airiness of sound made possible by this lack of vibrato combined with the rhythmic interplay of Young's rhythm with the rhythm section. This provided a strange contrast taken together with the heavier sonority Young began to utilize. Yet it must be emphasized that the essential greatness of the work lies not in these elements alone but only taken in conjunction with the melodic beauty of Young's line.

As mentioned above, there is a similarity in formal outline between the two versions, and it is very probable that Young had the earlier version well in mind when he produced the second. Young begins the second version with a brief quotation of the original, to which he does not return. Once more the most striking feature of the work is the melodic development, which is surely equal to the first version in beauty, and which in the last eight bars of the first chorus rises to a peak that is clearly superior to anything in the first version and that, to my knowledge, is not surpassed by anything else in Young's recorded work.

But again it is not just the melodic elements in isolation that make the greatness of this performance. We find still that the rhythmic contrast between Young and the rhythm section is of great importance, plus the beauty of his sonority. And a word must be said of this factor. Young's sound has in this record, and in others of the same period, become even thicker and heavier, and there is a slightly more perceptible use of vibrato. Indeed, in some works of this period, although for brief moments only, Young almost sounds like Ben Webster. Yet there is still the fundamental airiness of sound that is a constant characteristic of Young's work.

Nor should it be thought that these works are untypical of Young's production in the latter part of his career. One could cite such equally effective recordings as the splendid "Slow Motion Blues" and "Stardust" [also Verve]. It is most unfair to ignore such fine items as these simply for the lack of spadework on the part of critics who are content to accept critical errors and clichés without investigation.

Dan Morgenstern

Prez in Europe

We look to Dan Morgenstern for a sensitive, fair-minded account of jazz, and we're not surprised that he is one of the most passionate defenders of late Young. The album *Prez in Europe* is unfortunately out of print as of this writing, but it still turns up occasionally in used record shops. It contains some of the best evidence in support of Morgenstern's case—live recordings made during Young's tour of Europe late in 1956. Young was like most other jazz musicians in that he opened up at live sessions, trying things he would never try in the studio, and at greater length. On these superb performances he solos for as long as five minutes at a time, his longest recorded solos. They also bear surprising stylistic resemblances to his work of the 1930s.

Morgenstern's notes stand well on their own. His poetic musings about Young's style use the moments on this LP as a focal point but go beyond that to introduce us to many magical moments from the 1950s. He provides a soulful ending for this book.—Ed.

There was only one Pres. To say he was unique is an understatement; he was miraculous. And since everything he played contained his unique pres-ence, nothing he has left us is less than precious.

Don't let them tell you how Pres (some people spell it with a z) couldn't play any more in his later years. Sure, there were times when the strength required to fill the horn just wasn't in him, and then it was painful to intrude. But he usually managed to make the instrument do his bidding, and the power of his imagination was not ever impaired.

The Lester of 1956 is not the Lester of 1936, but should we want him to be? It is the fate of the artist, as unfair as it is unavoidable, to always be measured against himself; he may be faulted for changing too much as well as for not changing enough.

In Lester's case, we know nothing (except scattered, dimly remembered impressions of musicians who heard him then) of his earlier style or styles, before he finally got to record at twenty-seven (relatively late as great jazz figures go). It could surely have been as different from 1936 as that in turn from 1956.

Lester as the world first heard him, leaping out from "Lady Be Good" and "Shoe Shine Swing," was so pure, so perfect that he became a measure not only for himself but for all of the music. The perfection of his work with Count Basie, with Billie Holiday—with anyone—during the late thirties and early forties is such that it stands on heights inhabited by only a very few other genuine miracle makers.

Yet that perfection is the work of the same man who made the music on the record you now behold. He never was less than Lester Young, or other than Lester Young. And that was never less than enough.

This is some of the best late Lester Young you'll hear.

The year 1956 had begun auspiciously with the recording—for Norman Granz, who never lost faith in his greatness—of an album, *Jazz Giants '56*, which contained things that made even the naysayers take notice. On the following day he did a quartet date that, among other gems, produced a blues named "Pres Returns." The title had reference to a recent bout with illness—general debilitation rather than any specific ailment—from which he had emerged refreshed.

The jazz scribes have painted a so unmitigatedly gloomy picture of Lester's years after his traumatic experiences in the United States Army— that is to say, from late 1945 until his death on March 15, 1959—that one is tempted to overemphasize the positive aspects for the sake of just balance. The only unbiased witness is his music of those years, and while it sometimes speaks of pain and suffering impaired by the abuse to which he subjected his body, it often speaks with such power and conviction, humor and love—even joy—that it is quite impossible to accept the gloom-and-doom reporters' picture.

Their vision is impaired by certain prejudices—not racial but social

and cultural—against his unorthodox behavior that kept them from understanding and appreciating Lester in his later stages. For instance, his
drinking and smoking. (Jazz writers, by and large, reflect an astonishingly
dense and puritanical attitude toward marijuana—at least, officially—
that isn't very different from the average Rotarian's.) Or his eccentric
demeanor and speech, which gave rise to all manner of doubts about his
sexual orientation (he was a man) and sanity (he was saner than most of
us, to the end). Did these petty, mean-spirited attitudes, refracted in far
too much of what was and is written and said about him, cause him to
withdraw even further into himself? We can only guess.

We—I—do know, however, that when we heard and saw Pres during those years, it was more often than not an exhilarating experience. It
is not at all true that he had lost his audience to bop by the late forties;
packed houses at the Royal Roost and Birdland then and later would
cheer him. He was loved well. It is not true, either, that he was ill at ease
and discomfited with Jazz at the Philharmonic because so-called honkers
were pitted against him. Listen to "Lester Leaps In" or "The Opener" and
see if Flip Phillips bothered him. That he wasn't an extrovert didn't mean
he couldn't play bold, outgoing music. And don't tell me that these
examples (from late 1949) are too early to prove the point: check out
"Lester Gambols" from late 1953, or "The Slow Blues" and "Merry Go
Round" from late 1957. [All these are on Verve.—Ed.]

Aside from these JATP things, Lester made a long series of studio
albums for Norman Granz, from 1950 to the end, which contain many
musical marvels. Sure, he was slowly, tragically destroying himself. But—
and this is a large but—he remained a powerfully communicating artist.
He was, despite the hurts and abuses, still a loving, giving man and artist,
still capable of and willing to communicate beauty, hope, even strength.
There is a touching sense of resignation in very late Lester. He was tired
of fighting ugliness, stupidity, insensitivity with the only weapons he had:
beauty, wit, total awareness. And there was frequently physical pain as
well, fought off with pharmaceuticals that then in turn aggravated it. And
yet the message, even in resignation, remained a positive one.

The figure painted by the writers—a pitiful, degenerating man—is
denied by the lack of self-pity in his music. Maybe Lester was laughing to
keep from crying, as the title of one of his last albums has it, but his was
the laughter of the gods. The last time I saw and heard Pres, in his final
months, he softly admonished his faltering pianist: "Never give up. Don't
ever give up!" It wasn't Lester who failed us.

The circumstances under which the music on this record was recorded are little known. In the fall of 1956, Lester went to Europe with a so-called Birdland package tour; apparently, he decided to remain there after its conclusion, working as a single or with pickup groups.

The bulk of what is presented here for the first time on record was taped in Frankfurt, Germany, in October—the exact date has been lost. [Frank Büchmann-Møller has recently found that the exact date was November 9, 1956.—Ed.] Apparently, the locale is a club for American servicemen. This is indicated by the occasionally audible audience response—"work, work"—and the sporadic whistling and sing-along are distinctly un-Germanic in ambience. Another clue is the presence of drummer Lex Humphries, who was then serving in a jazz-studded army band that also included, at one time or another, Cedar Walton, Leo Wright, Eddie Harris, and Don Ellis—as well as, more than likely, Al King. The Swedish pianist Lasse Werner is hampered by a poor instrument.

The recording device and setup are primitive, but no matter. In recent years a tremendous amount of privately, noncommercially recorded material, on-the-spot and off-the-air, has come into release (often, unfortunately, under auspices that make no effort to compensate the musicians). When I began to collect jazz more than thirty years ago, there was no tape and the existence of such abundant material unknown, at least to novices. Now, our whole picture of the music of the past is changing. Music from broadcasts, jam sessions, private music making, nightclub sets, concerts is shedding much light on what was hitherto known largely through studio recordings—and what light! Some of the greatest music is also some of the worst recorded, but if recording quality were the ultimate criterion, Caruso would long have been eclipsed.

No, there's enough here of the sound of Pres—and what a sound; far from pale—to carry the message. If there isn't always a lot of the other instruments (drums excepted), no matter. Pres is it, and he was in fine spirits. Rather weak support notwithstanding, he stretches out, makes himself comfortable as only he could (Lester was the ultimate in relaxation, another innocent source of resentment from uptight folks), and spins his enchanting tales. He observes, he understands, he laughs—sometimes mockingly, never maliciously—he dances, he sings, he floats.

Lester was a dancer, a dreamer, a master of time and its secrets. Foremost among them: equilibrium. He never stumbles on the tightrope of swing, of tension and relaxation held in perfect yin-yang balance. He is a juggler, a high-wire artist without a net, a diver, a gambler, a gamboler.

The discoveries, the clear profundities of late Lester have been little understood. Some of his exquisite languor, no doubt, was the result of the need for conservation of energy. But what he made of this necessity! He was indeed a mother of invention, Pres was.

The last two selections, obviously played before a large audience, possibly outdoors, are of more obscure genesis than the Frankfurt session. Discographical sources suggest a television show, perhaps in Europe, and a date of January 2, 1957. We know that Lester returned to the United States in December 1956, and as far as I can tell, there is no record of another trip to Europe so soon. I suggest an earlier date, perhaps a stop on the aforementioned Birdland tour. The rhythm section certainly is together. And Pres is in great form.

"Lester Leaps In"—what genius it took to make up a piece so simply containing the essence of the jazz spirit. The tempo (you can hear Pres beat it off) is a mite slower than customary, tailored to the limitations of the rhythm players. "No bombs, pres—just titty-boom," was Lester's standard instruction to boppishly inclined drummers. Humphries is at first more boom-chick than titty-boom, but he warms to his task. As does Pres himself. Dig the stop time. And the tonguing—what a master of that he was. And the humor and gaiety (only way Pres was gay) of the performance! Is this the music of a weak, faded, wasted man?

"These Foolish Things"—a favorite of his. He paints a picture, with that warm sound so falsely described as small or thin. It is the perfect sound to convey the inner meaning of the music. He ascends with perfect control into the uppermost musical register of the tenor for the final half chorus, picking it up at the bridge. And what a bridge! All great soloists on their favorite pieces quote themselves; here it's done to set up the cadenza.

"There'll Never Be Another You"—a worthy sequel to the 1952 version. He opens with five wondrous choruses, first doing justice to Harry Warren's fine tune. ("There's not a poorly chosen note in the melody. It's sinuous, graceful, gracious, sentimental, totally lacking in cliche."—Alec Wilder, *American Popular Song*.) He floats, suspended on air. Ingenious use is made of repetition in the fourth chorus; the ultimate in sophisticated simplicity was Lester—sooo concentrated. He had more ideas in thirty-two bars than some musicians manage to come upon in a lifetime. And note the return to the melody for the climax of the solo—a Louis touch, also in the singing of it. (You can always sing Pres.)

"Lester's European Blues"—a blue fantasy by a master bluesman, a man who made up a whole new thing on the blues. Into a wryly happy groove, having a little conversation with himself, trading phrase for phrase (and how many phrases did he imprint into the jazz language?). He starts to holler, gets very blue (with a quote from "Blue Lester" and another from "Shake, Rattle and Roll" that cues a sing-along). Then he davens, goes way down, and ends as he started out. A ten-minute trip through Lester's beautiful head.

"Lullaby of Birdland"—Shearing's inversion of "Love Me or Leave Me" transformed into Lestorian arcs of sound. Third chorus into it— "Hear me talkin'"—and a nice and typical ending. Drummer is with it here.

"Polka Dots and Moonbeams"—another fine standard, by Jimmy Van Heusen. Lester loved it. (Once, on an Art Ford TV show, a certain ballad was suggested. Said Pres: "I don't want to play 'Waterfront.' I want to play 'Polka Dots and Moonbeams,'" stressing the *moon*. He did. On that occasion he had brought a stray kitten to the studio in his saxophone case.) The main strain, Alec Wilder notes, "is made up mostly of a series of ascending and descending scale lines." Lester, utterly relaxed, gives us four bars of the melody, then glides into Lesterland. The coda is superb.

"Lester Leaps In"—faster this time, the support firmer. The fact that the drummer uses his foot makes the kit sound like a different instrument. This is all Pres, strong Pres—a mere fragment yet a whole. Pres could say it in four bars. Hell, he could say it in a note.

Long live gentle Lester, who loved life despite what it had done to him, and who never stopped reaching out, gifts in hand. To hell with those who call your strength weakness because you turned the pain inward, upon yourself rather than on others, and offer simplistic explanations for your singular fate. Perhaps they envy you your immortality.

Appendix 1

Miscellaneous Short Recordings of Young's Voice

Young's soft, high voice may be heard briefly on a number of recordings, a few of which have been issued to the public. On the Jubilee armed forces broadcast of spring 1946 (issued in 1989 on Jass CD 18, *Prez Conferences*), he exchanges a few rehearsed words with the host, including references to his recent stint in the army. On another broadcast ten years later, December 8, 1956, Young introduces two of the tunes. The broadcast is also on Jass CD 18. (This is from the same engagement with the Bill Potts trio that resulted in four LPs on the Pablo label.)

There is a bit of Young's voice from his appearance on the Art Ford television show of September 25, 1958. The visual portion of the show is lost, but the audio survives and is issued on the LP Enigma 301 under the name of Coleman Hawkins, who was also featured on the program. Young can be heard talking as he steps up to the microphone for his feature. After a little banter with the pianist, Willie the Lion Smith, he says, "Ivey divey! Like that! Go ahead, make me about eight, and I'll catch it" (i.e., "Give me an eight-bar introduction, and I'll join in"). Young can be heard scat singing while he counts it off. Later, Young takes the horn out of his mouth and says presumably to Sonny Greer, who has been playing the drums with brushes: "Little tinkty boom!" Then he scats for a second before he resumes playing the saxophone. "Tinkty boom" was his way of describing the sound of a drummer swinging on a cymbal. He is telling Greer, "Give me a little cymbal instead of brushes"—and Greer does.

There are a few unissued tidbits from Verve studios. Granz arranged to record Young playing clarinet on July 31, 1957. By all accounts the session was a failure, and the voices on the unissued master reel help to explain why. Young seems to be asking for some practice time in the studio—"I haven't played *nothin'*," "That's got to be fifteen years old"—and Granz just ignores him in the attempt to get some tracks recorded. Granz asks the rhythm section to start, and Young eventually joins in.

Finally, Young's novelty vocal on "It Takes Two to Tango" was recently issued for the first time on the CD of the 1952 session. On the master reel there is some interesting dialogue between the two takes:

YOUNG: Should I open up singing?

NORMAN GRANZ (producer): Just like you did before. (*To Oscar Peterson*) A little funky intro, Osc.

YOUNG: There's some ladies out here.

GRANZ: Huh?

YOUNG: You said some funky introduction—there's ladies out here.

GRANZ: (*Laughs.*)

Granz didn't understand that to a black man of Young's generation, "funky" meant filthy and low-down, even disgusting. It wasn't polite to talk that way in front of the women who were guests in the studio. To Granz, "funky" meant low-down in a good sense—bluesy, with feeling. This is a revealing moment of cultural clash.

Appendix 2

Where to Find Unusual Published Photographs of Lester Young

There are many photographs of Young in periodicals and in photo books on jazz, such as Frank Driggs's and Harris Lewine's *Black Beauty, White Heat: A Pictorial History of Classic Jazz, 1920–1950* (New York: William Morrow, 1982) or Orrin Keepnews's and Bill Grauer's *Pictorial History of Jazz: People and Places from New Orleans to the Sixties* (New York: Crown Publishers, 1955; 2d rev. ed. 1966; repr. New York: Bonanza Books, 1981). Here I want to mention three photo articles, with brief text, that are rarely noticed.

In its January 22, 1945, issue, *Life* magazine presented three pages of stills drawn from Gjon Mili's film *Jammin' the Blues*. Mili was a famous still photographer for *Life*, and the article shows how he posed and lighted his subjects in order to get the visual effects in the film, which won him an Academy Award. Only one of the shots includes Young.

In August 1949 *Ebony* published a fascinating photo essay entitled "How to Make a Pork Pie Hat." Young is shown in a series of four photographs taking a hat and folding in the top to give it the porkpie effect. There are four other photographs, including one of him with his cat, "Macaroni," and one of him playing a wooden recorder, which is identified as "a new reed instrument with a tone like a flute." (The recorder is actually at least five hundred years old.) The text also includes a few of Young's comments on fashion—for example, he preferred black because "you can do so much with it." As for his music, the article notes that "Young uses a no. 3 plastic reed on a no. 7 mouthpiece, very rare for tenor sax players. 'It's very hard on the chops,' [says Young]." Young used the plastic reed for at least a year around this time (it is mentioned also in the Leonard Feather interview, above) and possibly for much longer. Plastic reeds have the advantage over wooden cane of longevity, but the disadvantage of making it difficult to get the ideal sound quality. A number 7 is a very open mouthpiece—just how open depends on the manufacturer—which requires more air than a closed one, but for the effort one is repaid with a fuller sound and greater dynamic range. Combined with the number 3 plastic reed, which is more than medium hardness, this setup would be fairly hard to play, as Young says, although not unreasonably so.

Herb Snitzer's fine photographs from the Five Spot club in New York were featured in a *Metronome 1959* yearbook spread called "Pres Plays a Date." In about fifteen photos we follow Young from his arrival at the club to his banter between sets and finally to his packing up and going home on the subway. The accompanying text is by Bob Perlongo.

Index

Page numbers in italics indicate music examples

Adderley, Julian "Cannonball," 187
"Ad-Lib Blues," *210*
"Afternoon of a Basie-ite," 302
Albuquerque, 21, 51, 76, 79, 96
Algiers, La., 7, 8, 9, 10, 175
Allen, Henry "Red," Jr., 8, 27, 77, 199
Allen, Henry, Sr., 8, 10
Allen, Walter C., 25, 30n
Alvin Hotel, 80–81, 83, 97
Amarillo, Tex., 50
Ammons, Gene, 150, 257, 288
Anderson, Buddy, 276
Armstrong, Louis "Satchmo," 10, 13, 14, 37, 44, 68–71, 94, 107, 120, 166, 198–99, 200, 245, 254n, 256, 269, 288, 289, 295, 297
Atlanta, 12
Augusta, Ga., 135

"Back in Your Own Backyard," 146, 287
"Back to the Land," 185, 286
Bailey, Buster, 52
Ballott, Shelby, 9–10
Banks, Eric, 6
Barefield, Eddie, 6, 15, 25, 76, 207
Basie, Count (William), 25–31, 32–33, 41, 42, 51–56, 60, 65, 69, 71, 73, 76, 77, 78, 79, 92, 131, 134–35, 136, 138–39, 143, 144–45, 146, 155, 159, 161, 166, 168, 171, 174, 177, 180, 187–88, 190, 195, 198–201, 204, 205, 206, 223n, 226–28, 247, 249, 252, 257–60, 262–63, 271, 283, 286–88, 302
Beal, Eddie, 42
"Beautiful Eyes," 145
Bechet, Sidney, 295
Beiderbecke, Bix, 14, 15, 69, 76, 133, 162, 247, 269, 291
Bellevue Hospital Center, 58, 62
Beneke, Tex, 97
Benjamin, Ben, 188
Berg, Billy, 38, 41–42
Bernie, Ben, 14
Bernstein, Leonard, 113
Berry, Chu, 27, 40, 52, 54, 160, 289
Bigard, Barney, 42
Birdland All-Stars, 58, 80, 308–10
Birdland club, 6, 36, 65, 84–88, 90, 95, 96, 97, 108, 155, 282–83
Bismarck, N.D., 15
"Blitzkrieg Baby," 145
"Blow Top," *216*
Blue Devils, Thirteen Original, 25, 51, 76, 134, 143, 159
"Blue Lester," 309
Blue Note club (Chicago), 137
Blue Note club (Paris), 92, 188

315

"Blues for Helen," 200
"Blues in C Sharp Minor," 40
"Blues in the Dark," 200
"Blues 'n' Bells," 201
"Body and Soul," 172, 260
"Boogie Woogie," 29, 144, 227
Bop City (club), 78, 79, 150
Boston, 59
Bostonians. *See* Bronson, Art, and
    Bostonians
"Bouncing Ball, The" 35
"Broadway," 42, *259–60*
Bronson, Art, and Bostonians, 25, 51, 76,
    133, 138, 142–43, 159, 166, 178–79
Brooks, Dudley, 39
Brown, Ray, 110, 152–53, 293
Brussels, 45
Bryant, Marie, 42
Bryant, Willie, 41
Büchmann-Møller, Frank, 4
"Bugle Blues," 12
Bunn, Teddy, 41
Byas, Don, 107

Café Bohemia, 84
Café Society Downtown, 29, 39, 78, 145
California, 137
Callender, Red, 29, 38, 42, 205
Calloway, Cab, 27, 54
Campbell, Cydner "Paul," 36, 38, 42
Camp Gordon, Ga., 29, 57
Capri Club, 41–42
Carbondale, Ill., 13
Carlisle, Una Mae, 145, 205
Carnegie Hall, 63, 203, 206, 282–83
Carpenter, Charlie, 59–60, 95, 136, 145,
    155, 158, 160, 164
Carter, Benny, 27, 54, 289
Cash, Bernard, 208–10, 264–65
"Chain Gang," 99
"Charlie's Dream," 275
Cheatham, Jimmy, 48
Cherry Blossom club, 53
Chicago, 26, 27, 28, 55, 78, 79, 136, 137,
    144, 166
Chicago Defender, 32
Christian, Charlie, 30, 51, 146, 202n
Cincinnati, 143
"Clap Hands, Here Comes Charlie," 163,
    185, 206, *209*, *218*, 279, 287
"Clarinet Marmelade," 15

Clark, Bill, 294
Clarke, Kenny, 66, 265, 290, 299
Clayton, Buck, 26, 28, 48, 198, 207, 257,
    299, 301
Cloud, Luther, Dr., 86, 89–92
Cohn, Al, 66, 288–89
Coleman, Ornette, 255, 263
Cole, Nat "King," 16, 29, 41, 61, 97, 99,
    185, 202n, 205
Collins, John, 145
Collins, Shad, 145
Colombé, Graham, 3
Coltrane, John, 186–87, 262, 263, 297
Columbia University, 5
Columbus, Ga., 12
"Come Rain or Come Shine," 36, 296
Como, Perry, 63
Condon, Eddie, 137, 139
"Confessin'." *See* "I'm Confessin'"
Congress Hotel, 27
Coon-Sanders Nighthawks, 13
Cooper, Al, 59
Cooper, Bob, 66, 278
Copland, Aaron, 104
Cotton Club (Minneapolis), 159
Cotton Club (New York), 27, 52, 256
Count Basie and His Orchestra, 302
"Count Every Star," 294
Crosby, Bob, 156

Dali, Salvador, 93
Daniels, Doug (musician), 41
Daniels, Douglas H. (author), 4, 5
Daniels, Wilbur, 41
Davis, Miles, 61, 160, 289, 290–91
"D. B. Blues," 57, 91, 135
Debussy, Claude, 68, 69
Delaunay, Charles, 65
DeParis, Sidney, Sr., 12
Desdunes, Sidney, 10
Des Moines, 15
Desmond, Paul, 66, 104, 107, 111
Detroit, 139, 190
Devils Lake, N.D., 21
Dickenson, Vic, 132
"Dickie's Dream," 271–72, 275, 283
"Ding Dong," 201
Dixon, George, 30n
Dodge City, Kans., 23
"Doggin' Around," 199, 279
Dolphy, Eric, 263

Dorsey, Jimmy, 35, 75, 76, 154, 155, 158, 181
Dorsey, Tommy, 151, 223n
Down Beat, 26, 32, 41, 48, 66, 83, 97, 136, 148, 255, 281
Drakes, Jesse, 67, 78, 95, 160, 295
Dupré, Bryant, 11

Eager, Allen, 66, 146, 155, 288–89
"East of the Sun," 206
"Easy Does It," *217, 223n*
Ebony, 72, 131, 313–14
Edison, Harry "Sweets," 61, 65, 115, 195, 198, 207, 296, 297, 298–99
Eldridge, Roy, 55, 110, 112, 206, 287, 297, 299
Ellington, Duke, 28, 85, 150, 256, 281, 296; and "Jump for Joy" show, 39
Elliott, Jerry, 95
Ellis, Herb, 115
El Reno, Okla., 13
"Embraceable You," 287
England, 61
Europe, 161, 170, 204, 305–10. *See also* Brussels, England, Frankfurt, Paris, and Stockholm
Evans, Gil, 74, 80, 124, 183
Evans, Herschel, 28, 29, 33, 41, 51–53, 55–56, 68, 135, 143–44, 150, 160, 180, 190, 253, 257, 280, 289
"Evenin'," 29, 144, 227
"Every Tub," 163, 200, *217–18*, 287
"Evil Gal Blues," 140

Famous Door club, 120–21
Farmer, Art, 67
Feather, Leonard, 8, 140, 148
Fenton, Nick, 145
Fields, Kansas, 174, 176–78
"Fine and Mellow," 79, 298
Finkelstein, Sidney, 70
Fitzgerald, Ella, 5, 117, 204
Five Spot club, 83
"Flic," 298
"Foggy Day, A," 67, 295
Ford, Art, 310, 311
Fort McClellan, Ala., 29, 56
"Four Brothers," 66, 149, 157, 160
"Four O'Clock Drag," 286
Fox, Charles, 295–96

France, 65, 83
Frankfurt, 308–10
Freeman, Bud, 69–70, 151, 159, 181–82, 213, 223n, 278
Fruscella, Tony, 78
Fuller, Curtis, 84, 86, 88

Gaillard, Slim, 41, 65. *See also* "Slim and Slam"
Ganz, Rook, 25
Garner, Erroll, 87
Gelly, Dave, 208
Getz, Stan, 66, 92, 104, 107, 205, 257, 277, 288–89
"Gigantic Blues," 297
Gillespie, Dizzy, 42, 77, 94, 106, 170
Giuffre, Jimmy, 61, 66, 101, 162, 277, 289, 294
Gleason, Ralph, 35, 66, 119
Goldkette, Jean, 14
Golson, Benny, 262
Gonsalves, Paul, 150, 296
Gonzales, Louis, 38, 42
Goodman, Benny, 26, 27, 28, 34, 40, 43, 64, 162, 202n, 203
"Good Man Is Hard to Find, A," 162
Good Morning Blues, 32
Gordon, Dexter, 66, 257, 288, 291
Gordon, Max, 41
Gottlieb, Louis, 200, 211
Grand Terrace ballroom, 28, 55, 144, 166
Granz, Norman, 29–30, 36, 38, 42, 45, 58, 61, 67, 70, 73, 79, 101, 115, 117, 145, 158, 171, 183–84, 206, 292–300, 307, 311–12
Gray, Lizetta. *See* Young, Lizetta
Gray, Wardell, 46, 66, 146, 257, 288–89
Green, Benny, 292–94
Green, Freddie, 26, 162
Greenville, S.C., 12
Greer, Sonny, 311
Guarnieri, Johnny, 205
Guillod, Eric, 131
"Gully Low Blues," 200
Guy, Joe, 207

Hakim, Sadik (a.k.a. Argonne Dense Thornton), 93–94
Hamilton, Jesse "Ham," 11
Hammond, John, 3, 25, 51, 52, 249, 281

Hammond, La., 7, 8
Hampton, Lionel, 16, 38, 203
"Happy Reunion," 296
Hardman, Glenn, 205
Harlan, Ky., 12
Harlem club (Kansas City), 51
Harris, Bill, 150, 151
Harris, Pat, 136–37
Hart, Clyde, 43, 145
Hartford, Conn., 100
Hawkins, Coleman "Bean," 37, 49, 52, 55, 61, 68–70, 75–77, 79, 107, 131, 134–35, 141, 143–44, 150, 154, 160, 166–67, 170, 171–72, 181, 190–91, 198, 213, 223n, 255–63, 278–79, 287, 289, 311
Haymes, Dick, 141
Haynes, Roy, 95
"He's Funny That Way." *See* "She's Funny That Way"
"He's Got the Whole World in His Hand," 172
Hear Me Talkin' to Ya, 55–56, 66, 136
Henderson, Bobby, 54
Henderson, Fletcher, 13, 25, 27, 30–31n, 37, 52, 55, 76, 79, 136–37, 139, 141, 144, 160, 166–67, 190–91, 256
Henderson, Leora (wife of Fletcher), 37, 52, 76, 144, 160, 191
Hentoff, Nat, 47, 82, 84, 87, 88, 157
Herman, Woody, 66, 151, 157
Hibbler, Al, 163
Higginbotham, J. C., 27
Hill City, Kans., 23
Hines, Earl, 177, 271
Hines, Frank, 76
History of Jazz in America, A, 66
Hodeir, André, 49, 70, 222n
Hodes, Art, 131
Hodges, Johnny, 71, 191
Holiday, Billie, 26, 27, 29, 34, 36, 40, 43, 48, 54, 55–56, 63–64, 77, 78, 79, 132, 145, 146, 152, 163, 167, 185, 204–5, 269, 286, 287, 293, 300
Holley, Major, 152–53
"Honeysuckle Rose," 275–76
Horricks, Raymond, 302
Hotel d'Angleterre, 174
Hotel William Penn, 227
"How Come You Do Me Like You Do?" 12
"How High the Moon," 67
Howard, Bob, 41

Humphries, Lex, 308–10
Hunter, Mary Young (aunt), 6, 7

"I Ain't Got Nobody," 206
"I Can't Get Started," 36, 37, 282, 287, 295, 299
"I Cover the Waterfront," 86
"I Didn't Know What Time It Was," 87, 118, 280
"I Got Rhythm," 54, 86, 204, 255
"I Left My Baby," 200
"Imagination," 43
"I'm Confessin'," 284, 286
"I'm in the Mood for Love," 296
"In a Mellotone," 85
Indianapolis, 12
Ind, Peter, 264
"I Never Knew," 199, *214, 215, 216*
Institute of Jazz Studies, 4, 11, 16, 33, 82, 89, 125, 126
"I Only Have Eyes for You," 102
"I Remember Bird," 140
"It Don't Mean a Thing," 296
"It Takes Two to Tango," 312

Jackson, Edgar, 45
Jackson, Leroy, 95
Jackson, Mahalia, 172
Jackson, Milt, 61
Jacquet, Ill., 107, 205
James, Burnett, 292
James, Harry, 26
Jammin' the Blues (film), 29, 90, 206, 207, 313
JATP. *See* Jazz at the Philharmonic
Jazz: A People's Music, 70
Jazz at the Philharmonic, 30, 44–46, 57, 58, 60, 64, 65, 79, 92, 95, 99–118, 123, 152–53, 161, 170, 187, 204, 287, 298, 307
Jazz Giants '56 (LP), 93, 206, 277–80, 287, 297, 306
Jazz: Its Evolution and Essence, 70
Jazzletter, 99
Jazz Makers, The, 188
Jazz Record, 131
Jazz Review, 74, 197, 224
Jazz Times, 148
Jazz Tradition, The, 197
"Jeepers Creepers," 87

Jeremy, John, 264
"Jive at Five," 200, 211, 218–*19*
Johnson, Charlie, 256
Johnson, Clarence, 15
Johnson, Everett, 28
Johnson, Pete, 28
Jones, Hank, 293
Jones, Jo, 9, 26, 28, 29, 51, 55, 56, 60, 64,
    67, 69, 78, 93–98, 124, 125, 144, 159,
    249, 294, 298
Jones, Otto "Pete," 11
Jones, Ray, 14
Jones-Smith, Inc., 27, 41, 213, 227, 228,
    262, 276, 283. *See also* Jones, Jo
Jones, Thad, 124, 125
Jones, Willie, 83, 84–85, 87, 124–25
Josephson, Barney, 39
"Jump for Joy," 39
"Jumpin' at the Woodside," 296
"Jumpin' with Symphony Sid," 95, 201

Kansas City, 21, 27–28, 51–53, 60, 76, 79,
    92, 120, 133, 134–35, 138–39, 143,
    144, 145, 166, 190, 256, 290
Kansas City Six, 71, 141, 162, 206, 207, 298
Kay, Connie, 93, 95–97, 236, 295
Kenton, Stan, 150, 151
Kessel, Barney, 65
Kirby, John, 52
Kirk, Andy, 52, 53, 137, 139, 144, 150, 167,
    190
Konitz, Lee, 66, 196, 223n, 254n, 277, 285,
    289
Krupa, Gene, 99, 100
Kyser, Kay, 141

"Lady Be Good," 29, 68, 144, 204, 220–*21*,
    226, 271–76, 291, 296, 306
Lady Sings the Blues, 48, 54, 63–64
Lakeland, Fla., 12
Lawrence, Kans., 23
Lee, George, 52, 143
Lees, Gene, 99
Leloir, Jean-Pierre, 173–74
"Lester Gambols," 307
"Lester Leaps Again," 216–*17*
"Lester Leaps In," 27, 85–86, 163, 171–72,
    186, 200, 204, 206, 210, *214*, *215*, *220*,
    260, 271–*72*, 275–*76*, 281, 283, 287,
    307, 309–10

"Lester's European Blues," 206, 309–10
"Let's Fall in Love," 295
Levin, Mike, 155
Levy, Morris, 84
Lewis, Ed, 200
Lewis, John, 49, 64, 67, 71, 74, 76, 78, 93,
    96, 98, 161, 206, 294
Lewis, Ted, 13
Lexington, Ky., 12
Little Rock, Ark., 52, 139, 144
Log Cabin club, 64
London, 45–46. *See also* England
Lopez, Vincent, 13
Lord, Albert, 225
Los Angeles, 8, 16, 33, 38–39, 40, 41–42,
    57, 61, 80, 298. *See also* California
Los Angeles Times, 140
Love, Clarence, 76
"Love Me or Leave Me," 310
"Loverman," 297
Lucie, Lawrence, 30n
"Lullaby of Birdland," 310

McDonough, John, 30n, 47
McRae, Gordon, 150
McShann, Jay, 271, 290, 291
Mahones, Gildo, 67, 161
Mance, Junior, 95
"Mandy Is Two," 43
"Man I Love, The," 37, 77
Manone, Wingy, 254n
"Margie," 12
Marsh, Arno, 66
Marsh, Warne, 66
Mayan Theatre, 39
"Mean to Me," 85, 163, 272
Melody Maker, 45, 53, 91
Memphis, 10, 177
"Me, Myself, and I," 200
"Merry Go Round," 298, 307
Metronome, 6, 70, 83, 97, 154, 314
Mili, Gjon, 29, 90, 313
Mills Brothers, 103, 189
Mingus, Charles, 84
Minneapolis, Kans., 13
Minneapolis, Minn., 13–14, 21, 22, 25, 34,
    50–51, 52, 76, 135, 138–39, 143, 159,
    177
Minton's Playhouse, 67, 145
Mitchell, Whitey, 64–65
MJQ. *See* Modern Jazz Quartet

Mobile, Ala., 12
Modern Jazz Quartet, 93, 95, 161
Monk, Thelonious, 294
Monroe's Uptown House, 66
Montreal Forum, 115
Montrose, Jack, 278
Moore, Brew, 66, 104, 288–89
Morgenstern, Dan, 82–83
Morris, Marlowe, 67
Morrison, Allan, 72–73, 131
Morton, Benny, 30–31n
Morton, Jelly Roll, 224
Moten, Bennie, 27, 51, 52, 76, 143
Mound City Blue Blowers, 260
Mulligan, Gerry, 289
Murray, Albert, 32
Myers, Bumps, 29, 38–39, 41–42

Napoleon, Teddy, 100
Natalbany, La., 6, 17
"Neenah," 294
Nest Club, 76, 138
New Bedford, Mass., 60
New Orleans, 6–10, 14, 50, 69, 92, 130,
    136, 138, 142, 158, 175–77, 224
Newport Jazz Festival, 79, 188, 204, 206
New York City, 5, 27, 29, 47, 78, 80, 83, 145,
    166–67, 190–91
Nichols, Red, 14, 162
Nick's club, 145
Niehaus, Lennie, 278
"Nobody Knows," 200–201
"No Eyes Blues," 84, 94, 201, 286
"Now Is the Time." *See* "Now's the Time"
"Now's the Time," 282

Oakland, 120
Oklahoma City, 51, 79, 143
Oliver, Gurvis, 14
Oliver, Joe "King," 25, 51, 76, 129, 143,
    159, 166
"Ol' Man River," 219
"One Hour," 260–61, 262
"One O'Clock Jump," 143, 163, 200, 217,
    287, 296
"On the Sunny Side of the Street," 286, 295
"Opener, The," 307
Original Blue Devils. *See* Blue Devils
"Ornithology," *223n*, 271

Owens, Thomas, 228, 270–71

Page, "Hot Lips," 27, 28, 134
Page, Walter, 26, 28, 51, 134, 143, 144, 159,
    249. *See also* Blue Devils
"Pagin' the Devil," 200
Palatka, Fla., 12
Panama Club, 28
Paris, 45, 58, 65, 81, 91–92, 173–74, 181.
    See also France
Parker, Charlie "Bird," 5, 42, 61, 83, 84,
    90–91, 94, 95, 108, 120, 146, 155, 161,
    191, 206, 207, 209–10, 216, 223n, 228,
    247, 254n, 270–76, 281, 282–83, 288–
    91, 295, 297
"Parker's Mood," 83
Paseo club, 52, 144
Paulussen, Diethelm, 6
Pell, Dave, 66
"Pennies from Heaven," 84
Pensacola, Fla., 12
Pepper, Art, 104, 107
Perkins, Bill, 66
Perlongo, Robert A. (Bob), 6, 314
Peterson, Oscar, 46, 110, 115, 184, 296, 312
Pettis, Jack, 14
Philadelphia, 95, 165
Phillips, Clarence, 11
Phillips, Flip, 46, 307
Phillips, Leonard "Phil," 4, 6, 11–14
Phoenix, 21
Pierce, Nat, 84–85, 87
Pittsburgh, 227
Plantation club, 145
Plater, Alan, 264
"Polka Dots and Moonbeams," 36, 67, 293,
    295, 297, 298, 310
Porter, Jake, 41
Postif, François, 6, 74, 81, 173–74
"Pound Cake," *214*, 260–61
Powell, Bud, 61, 83, 87–88
Powell, Mel, 40, 205
Powell, Rudy, 56, 63
Powers Girl, The (film), 43
Pres and Teddy (LP), 277–80
President, The (LP), 284
"Pres Returns," 298, 306
Prez in Europe (LP), 206, 305–10
Price, Sammy, 200
Procope, Russell, 52

Pullman, Peter, 174

Quinichette, Paul, 6, 66, 155, 160, 277, 288

Race, Steve, 45
Radisson Hotel, 14
Ramey, Gene, 77, 94
Record Changer, 68
Renaud, Henri, 65
Reno club, 27–28, 53, 135, 138, 144
Rich, Buddy, 100, 106, 151, 293
"Riff Interlude," 215
Roanoke, Va., 12
Roberts, Caughey, 76
Robichaux, Joe, 10
"Rock-a-Bye Basie," 283
Rollins, Sonny, 49, 186–87, 262, 289
"Romping," 299
Rooney, Mickey, 16
"Roseland Shuffle." *See* "Shoe Shine Boy"
"Rose Room," 296
Rowles, Jimmy, 40–43, 74, 75, 78, 80
Royal, Marshall, 41
Rushing, Jimmy, 28, 56, 60, 63
Russell, Pee Wee, 77, 151, 278
Russell, Ross, 67–70, 207, 270–71
Rust, Brian, 25
Rutgers University, 4, 11, 16, 82–83, 125, 126

"Sailboat in the Moonlight, A," 146, 163, 205, 287
St. Albans, Queens, N.Y., 58, 89, 158
St. Joseph, Mo., 52, 144
St. Paul Hotel, 14
"St. Tropez," 298, 299
Salina, Kans., 13, 23, 51, 133, 138, 142, 159, 166, 178
"Salute to Fats," 286
San Antonio, 10
Schaap, Phil, 4–5, 30n, 39, 174
Schoenberg, Loren, 203
Schuller, Gunther, 198, 228, 302–3
Scott, Bobby, 3, 60–61, 64, 99, 115, 124, 126
Scott, Ronnie, 61; nightclub, 93
Sears, Al, 47, 78, 145
Seattle, 41

Shank, Bud, 278
Shaw, Artie, 151, 162, 207
Sheldon, Jack, 101–2
Sherman, Tex., 79
"She's Funny That Way," 200, 286
"Shoe Shine Boy," 29, 144, 163, 199, 216, 223n, 226–54, 229–36, 262, 271, 306
"Shoe Shine Swing." *See* "Shoe Shine Boy"
"Shouting Liza," 12
Shreveport, La., 8
Shulman, Joe, 78
Simon, Bill, 66
Sims, Zoot, 48, 66, 74, 80, 104, 107–8, 277, 288–89
Sinatra, Frank, 90, 112, 163
"Singin' the Blues," 15, 133, 162
"Six Cats and a Prince," 206
Slim and Slam, 41, 42
"Slow Blues, The," 307
"Slow Boat to China," 141
"Slow Motion Blues," 294, 304
Small's Paradise (club), 84
Smith, Bessie, 165, 169, 172
Smith, Buster, 27, 28, 143, 159–60
Smith, Carl "Tatti," 28, 144, 249, 252, 276
Smith, Stuff, 43
Smith, Willie (saxophonist), 109
Smith, Willie "the Lion," 311
Snidero, Jim, 196
Snitzer, Herb, 314
"Sometimes I'm Happy," 78
Song of the Spirit (film), x, 301
"Sound of Jazz, The" (TV show), 79, 298
South Side Ballroom, 14
Spanier, Muggsy, 151
Spencer Hotel, 15
Spirits of Rhythm, 41–42
Spokane, Wash., 40–41
Stacy, Jess, 40
Stafford, Jo, 112, 169
"Stardust," 304
Starr, Kay, 169
Stearns, Marshall, 82, 84, 87, 89
Steward, Herbie, 66, 288–89
Stewart, Slam, 41, 85. *See also* Slim and Slam
Stitt, Sonny, 150
Stockholm, 59
Strayhorn, Billy, 39
Strike Up the Band (film), 16
Sulieman, Idrees, 67

"Sunbonnet Blue, A," 40
"Sunday," 298
Sunset club, 28
"Swinging the Blues," 163, 204, *214*, 215, 287
Symphony Sid. *See* Torin, Sid
Syms, Sylvia, 74, 77

Tabou club, 65
Talbot, Jimmy, 19, 20
"Talk of the Town," 37
Tampa, Fla., 12
"Taste of Honey, A," 99
Tate, Buddy, 6, 74, 79–80, 124, 126
Tatum, Art, 41
"Taxi War Dance," 69, 146, *209*, 219, 220–21, 279, 283, 287, 302
"Tea for Two," 86, 207, 295, 300
Tenot, Frank, 61, 65–66, 67, 71
Theatre Owners Booking Association, 7, 12
"Them There Eyes," 200
"There'll Never Be Another You," 87, 309
"These Foolish Things," 36, 37, 108, 195, 201, 286, 295, 301–4, 309
"They Can't Take That Away from Me," 299
Thibodaux, La., 6, 7, 8
Thielemans, Toots, 189
"Things 'Bout Coming My Way," 200
"This Year's Kisses," 163, 302
Thompson, "Sir" Charles, 29, 64
"Tickle Toe," 146, 201
Time-Life Giants of Jazz, 47–48
"Time Out," 41
" 'Tis Autumn," 43
TOBA. *See* Theatre Owners Booking Association
"Too Marvelous for Words," 293
Topeka, Kans., 23
Torin, Sid ("Symphony Sid"), 84–87, 95
Townsend, Irving, 25
Treitler, Leo, 225
Tribune, 285
Tristano, Lennie, 264, 281
Trouville club, 42
Trumbauer, Frank, 14, 15, 34–35, 75, 76, 133, 154, 155, 158–59, 162, 181–82, 213, 265–70, 278, 291
Turner, Joe, 42
Turrentine, Clyde, 14

Tuskegee Institute, 6, 142
"Twelfth Street Rag," *218*, 251, 283
"Twelve Tone Blues," 140
Twine, Arthur, 38, 40, 41

Ulanov, Barry, 66, 70, 281–82
"Undercover Girl Blues," 294
"Up 'n' Adam," 85, 88, 293

Vaughan, Sarah, 137
Village Vanguard, 41, 145

Walder, Herman, 53
"Waldorf Blues," 298
Warren, Ark., 11
Warren, Earle, 205
Washington, Dinah, 140
Washington, Jack, 27
Watkins, Doug, 84–85, 87
Watson, Leo, 41–42
"Way Down Yonder in New Orleans," 12, 162, 171, 202, *209*, 265–70
Webster, Ben, 27, 40, 50–51, 53, 55, 79, 107, 150, 160, 289, 303
Wein, George, 59, 67
West, Hal, 145
West Virginia, 143
"When Lights Are Low," 262
"When You're Smiling," 202, *220*
White, Leroy, 25
Whiteman, Paul, 13, 35
Wichita, Kans., 271
Wilkerson, Ben, 14
Willard, Pat, 16
Williams, Arthur, 13
Williams, Cootie, 12
Williams, Martin, 197
Williams, Mary Lou, 53
"Willow Weep for Me," 77
Wilson, Dick, 53, 144
Wilson, Gerald, 39
Wilson, Teddy, 26, 27, 29, 34, 40–41, 145, 163, 286, 287, 289
Woodville, Miss., 6, 7, 8, 50, 102, 130, 158, 175
Werner, Lasse, 308–10
"World Is Mad, The," 302
Wright, Laurie, 25, 129

"Yes, Sir, That's My Baby," 12
"You Can Depend on Me," 202
"You Go to My Head," 132
Young, Austin "Boots" (cousin), 10, 19–20
Young, Irma (sister), 8, 10, 11, 12, 19, 20, 21, 50, 138, 142, 182
Young, Isaiah "Sport" (cousin), 10, 19–20
Young, Jacob (uncle), 6
Young, Lee (brother), 6, 8, 12, 16–24, 29, 33–43, 47, 50, 51, 61, 77, 97, 119, 135, 138, 142, 145, 205–6
Young, Lester, Jr., 58, 114, 158
Young, Lester Willis: clarinet playing, 71, 77, 108, 141, 162, 171, 184–85, 198, 200, 206–7, 278, 289, 298–99; date of first recording, xi, 28; drumming, 10–11, 18, 50, 132–33, 177–78; grandparents, 17; saxophone reeds, 141, 196, 313–14; speaking style, 42–43, 75, 94, 96, 98, 114–15, 149, 278; syphilis, 122–26
Young, Lizetta Johnson (mother), 7, 8, 9, 138, 175–76
Young, Martha (aunt), 6, 8
Young, Mary (aunt). *See* Hunter, Mary Young
Young, Mary (last wife), 58, 158
Young, Mary (second wife), 32, 48, 57
Young, Sara (stepmother), 8, 10, 13, 18–19, 33–34, 145
Young, William (uncle), 6
Young, Willis Handy "Billy" (father), 6–15, 17–24, 47, 50–51, 75–76, 78, 132–33, 137–38, 142, 145, 158–59, 176, 182–83
Young, Yvette, 58
"You're Getting to Be a Habit with Me," 298